A

With expert readings and forecasts, you can chart a course to romance, adventure, good health, or career opportunities while gaining valuable insight into yourself and others. Offering a daily outlook for 18 full months, this fascinating guide shows you:

- The important dates in your life
- What to expect from an astrological reading
- How the stars can help you stay healthy and fit
  And more!

Let this sound advice guide you through a year of heavenly possibilities—for today and for every day of 2012!

**SYDNEY OMARR'S® DAY-BY-DAY
ASTROLOGICAL GUIDE FOR**

ARIES—March 21–April 19
TAURUS—April 20–May 20
GEMINI—May 21–June 20
CANCER—June 21–July 22
LEO—July 23–August 22
VIRGO—August 23–September 22
LIBRA—September 23–October 22
SCORPIO—October 23–November 21
SAGITTARIUS—November 22–December 21
CAPRICORN—December 22–January 19
AQUARIUS—January 20–February 18
PISCES—February 19–March 20

IN 2012

SYDNEY OMARR'S®

DAY-BY-DAY ASTROLOGICAL GUIDE FOR

ARIES

MARCH 21–APRIL 19

2012

by Trish MacGregor
with Rob MacGregor

A SIGNET BOOK

SIGNET
Published by New American Library, a division of
Penguin Group (USA) Inc., 375 Hudson Street,
New York, New York 10014, USA
Penguin Group (Canada), 90 Eglinton Avenue East, Suite 700, Toronto,
Ontario M4P 2Y3, Canada (a division of Pearson Penguin Canada Inc.)
Penguin Books Ltd., 80 Strand, London WC2R 0RL, England
Penguin Ireland, 25 St. Stephen's Green, Dublin 2,
Ireland (a division of Penguin Books Ltd.)
Penguin Group (Australia), 250 Camberwell Road, Camberwell, Victoria 3124,
Australia (a division of Pearson Australia Group Pty. Ltd.)
Penguin Books India Pvt. Ltd., 11 Community Centre, Panchsheel Park,
New Delhi - 110 017, India
Penguin Group (NZ), 67 Apollo Drive, Rosedale, Auckland 0632,
New Zealand (a division of Pearson New Zealand Ltd.)
Penguin Books (South Africa) (Pty.) Ltd., 24 Sturdee Avenue,
Rosebank, Johannesburg 2196, South Africa

Penguin Books Ltd., Registered Offices:
80 Strand, London WC2R 0RL, England

First Printing, June 2011
10 9 8 7 6 5 4 3 2 1

First published by Signet, an imprint of New American Library,
a division of Penguin Group (USA) Inc.

CONTENTS

CHAPTER 1

Paradigm Shift

There's more hype about December 21, 2012, than there was about the Y2K scare at the turn of the century. Depending on which Web site or book you read, the world will end on that day, the poles will shift, the aliens will land. In fact, there's been so much hype that in March 2007 *USA Today* ran an article titled "Does Maya Calendar Predict 2012 Apocalypse?"

"Maya civilization, known for advanced writing, mathematics and astronomy, flourished for centuries in Mesoamerica, especially between A.D. 300 and 900. Its Long Count calendar, which was discontinued under Spanish colonization, tracks more than 5,000 years, then resets at year zero," wrote G. Jeffrey MacDonald in the *USA Today* article.

It resets on December 21, 2012. It's the day that marks the winter solstice in the northern hemisphere. It's also the day that the sun will be aligned with the center of the Milky Way galaxy for the first time in nearly 26,000 years or, to be exact, in 25,625 years, what the Mayans considered to be a single galactic day. They divided that galactic day into five cycles of 5,125 years, and on December 21, that fifth cycle ends. So, what's that mean for us?

According to Mayan Indian elder Apolinario Chile Pixtum, it definitely doesn't mean the end of the world. He, in fact, says the doomsday theories spring from

Western, not Mayan ideas. "I came back from England last year and man, they had me fed up with this stuff."

Jose Huchin, a Yucatan Mayan archaeologist, says that if he went into Maya-speaking communities and asked people what was going to occur in 2012, they wouldn't have any idea. "That the world is going to end? They wouldn't believe you," he says.

A likely possibility for 2012 is a shift in paradigms. If 2011 was the year of transitions, then 2012 can be viewed as the year when people begin to embrace new ways of thinking about themselves, the society in which they live, and the world. With the meltdown in the financial and housing markets in 2008–2009, the election of the first African-American president, the bailouts of banks, rising foreclosures and unemployment, and the broken health-care system, a shift in belief systems seems inevitable.

As Daniel Pinchbeck wrote in *2012: The Return of Quetzalcoatl*: "If we were to conclude, after careful consideration, that our modern world is based upon fundamentally flawed conceptions of time and mind, that on these fatal defects we had erected a flawed civilization ... then logic might indicate the necessity, as well as the inevitability, of change. Such a shift would not be 'the end of the world,' but the end of a world, and the opening of the next."

How You Can Adapt to the Paradigm Shift

Our lives are marked by transitions. We make the *transition* from adolescence to adulthood, from dependent to independent, from being single to being married, from youth to middle age to old age, from life to death. These transitions are often marked by rituals—diplomas, ceremonies—that recognize our rites of passage.

In astrology, we have similar transitions, but they are triggered by the movement of the outer planets—Jupiter, Saturn, Uranus, Neptune, and Pluto. These planets are the slowest moving, so they exert the most impact on our lives. The lineup in 2011 pushed us toward the paradigm shift that will occur in 2012.

So now you're asking, *How's it going to affect me?* That depends on the angles these slower-moving planets make to your sun sign—and on your attitudes and deepest beliefs. After all, the planets only depict possible patterns that may occur. *We're* the scriptwriters. We have free will, the ability to make choices. Astrology simply provides information that makes those choices easier. To be informed is to be empowered.

The planet to watch in 2012 is Neptune, which enters Pisces on February 3 and remains there until the end of March 2025. Neptune was in Pisces briefly in 2011—from April 5 to August 5—then turned retrograde and slipped back into Aquarius for a final time. Since it takes this planet fourteen years to transit a single sign, it won't be back to Aquarius for another 168 years!

Now let's take a closer look at what Neptune's transit may mean for each of us.

The Role of Neptune in 2012

Neptune is an elusive planet, so far away from the sun that it's one of two planets that can't be seen without a telescope. The temperature of its surface clouds is around -218 degrees Celsius. Its atmosphere is composed of hydrogen and helium, and its interior is mostly ice and rock.

When Voyager 2 flew past Neptune in 1989, it was discovered that Neptune had a dark area composed of gas that swirled violently with the force of a hurricane. They called it the Great Dark Spot and compared it to the Great Red Spot on Jupiter. In 1994, however, the Hubble telescope found that that spot had disappeared. So we know that Neptune, like Jupiter, has weather patterns.

To understand Neptune's influence in our lives and how it will impact us from 2012 to 2026, when it moves through Pisces, let's take a walk through a brief slice of history.

The planet was discovered in 1846—not because it was spotted through a telescope, but due to a disturbing characteristic in the orbit of Uranus. Astronomers suspected the erratic orbit was created by the gravitational pull of another planet. In a sense, then, the way in which Neptune was discovered is a metaphor for its elusive characteristics in astrology. It symbolizes imagination, spiritual and intuitive talents, psychic experiences, artistic inspiration. On the downside, it represents our illusions, our blind spots, and governs alcoholism, drug addiction, confusion, escapism of all kinds. Astrologer Steven Forrest calls Neptune "the planet of consciousness . . . the blank state."

Shortly after Neptune was discovered, the California gold rush began (illusions). The Romantic movement (inspiration) also started, a reaction against intellectualism, materialism, and the rigidity of social structures that protected the wealthy, the privileged. Then in 1848, just two years after Neptune's discovery, the Spiritualist movement was born in a small cottage in Hydesville, New York, where the Fox family lived.

John and Margaret Fox and two of their daughters, Margaret and Kate, had moved into the house in December 1847. The place was reputedly haunted and strange noises and rappings could be heard at night, which kept the family awake. On the night of March 31, about three nights after the family had moved into the house, young Kate heard the noises and responded by snapping her fingers and called out, "Mr. Splitfoot. Do as I do." She then clapped her hands several times.

The pattern of her clapping was instantly duplicated. Her sister then joined in and demanded that "Splitfoot" do what she did. Her four claps were immediately answered with four claps. Mrs. Fox asked the invisible guest to rap out the ages of all of her seven children, which it did, with a pause between each one to individualize them.

Mrs. Fox began to question the rapper. Was it a human being? There was no response. She then asked it to rap twice if it was a spirit. It rapped twice—and the spiritualist movement was born.

Twenty-nine years after Neptune's discovery, a medium named George Colby of Iowa was holding a séance at the home of a local resident, a fellow named Wadsworth. Nothing extraordinary had happened so far that night. Colby was already a successful medium, and he'd done the usual things that night—passed on messages from the dead to the living.

Then, suddenly, Colby received a message from his Indian guide, Seneca, instructing him to travel immediately to Eau Claire, Wisconsin, where he was to hook up with T. D. Giddings, a Spiritualist. Once he was in Wisconsin, Seneca said, further instructions would be given. Colby, being a product of a time when the Spiritualist movement was sweeping across the country, did the expected thing. The next morning he packed up and left for Wisconsin. He met up with Giddings, and at a séance shortly afterward Colby and Giddings were given instructions to leave Wisconsin and head to Florida.

Colby was only twenty-seven years old at the time, a single man ready for adventure. Giddings, however, had a family and took them along. Back then, steamboats and trains were the only route south, and this odd little entourage took both. They rode a train to Jacksonville, Florida, then traveled by steamboat down the St. John's River to a place called Blue Springs. This frontier town was supposedly in the general vicinity of their final destination.

Seneca had described the place they were going to settle as having hills and a chain of lakes. The only thing that lay beyond the borders of Blue Springs looked like dense, subtropical forest. But when Seneca made contact and told the two men to begin their trek into the woods and to follow his directions, they did so.

They made their way through dense growth and after several miles arrived at the spot where Seneca said the Spiritualist camp would be created. Everything—from the high bluffs to the lakes and the lay of the land—looked exactly as Seneca had described.

Colby built a house on the shores of Lake Colby, and Giddings and his family built a home nearby. Colby eventually obtained a government deed for seventy-four acres that adjoined the area where he and Giddings had settled. They were apparently the only people for miles around.

For eighteen years, Colby didn't do much of anything about establishing a Spiritualist community in the area. He adopted several orphans, however, and raised them. He also operated a dairy.

In 1893, a Spiritualist named Rowley showed up and decided to establish a Spiritualist center in either De-Leon Springs or Winter Park. He invited a number of prominent Spiritualists from the north to travel to Florida to check out the area. Two of these Spiritualists were women who were prominent in the Lily Dale Spiritualist camp in New York. They didn't particularly care for Rowley, but Colby won them over, and they decided to create a Spiritualist camp on his property.

In October 1894, twelve mediums signed the charter for the Southern Cassadaga Spiritualist Camp. According to the charter, the association was to be a nonprofit organization that would promote the Spiritualist beliefs in the soul's immortality, "the nearness of the Spirit World, the guardianship of Spirit friends, and the possibility of communion with them," as the charter reads.

Seneca, Colby's guide, apparently advised him to remain in the background during this time, so his name doesn't appear on the charter, and he didn't have much to do with the organization of the camp. However, in 1895, he deeded the association thirty-five acres of his land. The first meeting was held in late 1895 and lasted three days. A hundred people attended the event to meet and sit with the mediums who had been invited.

Within three years of that first meeting, eight cottages, a dancing pavilion, a lodging hall, and a library had been built on the association grounds. Wealthy mediums from the north were being enticed to move to Cassadaga on a more or less permanent basis. From the late 1800s to the early part of the twentieth century, not much is written about the town. The camp apparently flourished, however, because the Cassadaga Hotel was built in 1922 and so were most of the cottages that still stand today.

In the century plus since Cassadaga was established, the rest of central Florida has grown up around it. Just thirty minutes south of it on I-4 is a whole other kind of world—Disney World! But as soon as you turn off Interstate 4, memories of Dumbo and Epcot, Universal and MGM, give way to southern pine forests. A kind of presence infuses the still air. You can't help but feel that nothing is what it appears to be.

For years there wasn't even a sign for Cassadaga. It was almost as if the people who are supposed to find their way here did so in spite of the lack of directions. Even today Cassadaga is little more than a black dot on a map, a punctuation point in the vastness of the pine forest. Lake Helen is the nearest town.

But if you blink too fast, Lake Helen is already a memory. Just beyond the outer edge of the town, the road climbs and dips through a series of low hills and shallow valleys. The trees seem thicker and darker here, the Spanish moss sways in the breeze, and shapes eddy across the shadowed road. A hush lingers in the air. Stop your car, lower your windows, and you probably won't hear a sound.

About half a mile outside of Lake Helen, you'll see a sign announcing that you're now in Cassadaga. But it isn't until you come around the next sharp curve that you know you're there. A large two-story stucco building looms in front of you, the Cassadaga Hotel. Its Mediterranean architecture dates back to the 1920s, during the heyday of Spiritualism. Along the right side of the building stretches a wide porch filled with rocking chairs. At dusk some evenings, when the light plays tricks with perception, some of the empty chairs rock, creaking softly in the quiet.

Spirits enjoying the evening? One never knows for sure. But perhaps that's part of the lure and the mystique of Cassadaga.

Given the uncertainty of the times in which we live, it's not surprising that business in Cassadaga is flourishing. On any weekend, the hotel lot is jammed with cars, and everywhere you look, people are walking around in search of the right psychic. Both sides of the main street are lined with small buildings that have signs posted out front advertising the kind of reading available. Unlike the early days of Cassadaga, when it was mainly Spiritualists, today's psychic offerings are vast. You can find everything from astrologers, tarot readers, and Reiki healers. But the mediums are still the draw, the magnet. As one young woman explained to us during a recent trip, "Everything is changing so fast, life is moving at such a rapid clip, that people are turning more and more to spiritual and intuitive insights and guidance."

And that pretty much sums up a large part of what Neptune's transit through Pisces may bring for each of us.

Neptune in Pisces

We had a brief taste of Neptune in Pisces, the sign it rules, between April 3, 2011, and August 4, 2011. Then Neptune turned retrograde and slipped back into Aquarius. But on February 3, 2012, it enters Pisces again. For clues about how this transit may manifest itself for you, look back to those four months in 2011. What was going on in your life then? Did you feel more creative? Did you take up a new artistic hobby? Did your spiritual beliefs undergo some sort of transformation? Were you more intuitive? Were you called upon to give selflessly in some respect? Did you feel your life was confusing, your goals muddled? Did you indulge more frequently in alcohol and drugs?

All of these areas fall under the governance of Neptune. So now let's look specifically at each sign for possible shifts under Neptune's fourteen-year transit through Pisces.

Aries ♈

Cardinal, fire

You're the trailblazer of the zodiac, known for your fearlessness, impulsiveness, and well, yes, sometimes your recklessness. You enjoy anything that induces an adrenaline rush—from extreme sports to love affairs to high-wire creative projects. You think outside the box, aren't known as a team player, and would rather delegate than be delegated to. In love, your passions are often extreme, you can be jealous and possessive, but when you fall, you fall hard, with your entire heart.

You're like an action hero, always on the move, doing, figuring the angles. Even your strong intuition comes through action—mostly impulses and burning hunches on which you act quickly. Your spiritual beliefs probably aren't traditional, i.e., not associated with a particular religion or church. It's more likely that you've pieced together your own beliefs over the years and are still adding to them.

During Neptune's transit of Pisces and your solar twelfth house, your intuition and spirituality will deepen, the scope will broaden, and chances are it will all begin in the privacy of your interior world. Your dream life will be more vivid, and it should be easier to recall your dreams and work with them. You should have greater access to your own unconscious, so that it's easier to recall past lives and understand your own motives and psyche. In fact, the more you work consciously with your intuitive abilities and spiritual beliefs, the easier this paradigm shift will be for you.

Since the twelfth house represents institutions, it's possible that you may have more contact with hospitals, nursing homes, even prisons. You might be an employee or volunteer in one of these organizations. In some way, this experience enables you to reach for the greater good rather than for what is good only for you.

Taurus ♉

Fixed, earth

Your stubbornness, patience, and resoluteness are legendary. You complete whatever you start and often end up completing what other people start as well. In other words, due to your resilience and endurance, you often win where others fail. Where Aries trailblazes, you cultivate—relationships, a beautiful home, a family, a career, a garden. You enjoy being surrounded by beauty but aren't necessarily an extravagant spender.

Some signs need drama to thrive, but you're not one of them. You're a romantic who enjoys a harmonious relationship in which creativity can flourish. You tend to keep things to yourself—not so much secretive as circumspect. You speak when you have something meaningful to say.

Once Neptune enters Pisces, the tide will turn more in your direction. Pisces is a water sign that's compatible with your earth-sign sun, and you'll find that it deepens your innate curiosity about the deeper mysteries in life—telepathy, precognition, psychokinesis, synchronicity, what makes the universe tick, communication with the dead, UFOs, crop circles. You may join groups that support these interests and get involved with charitable organizations that support ideals in which you believe.

The eleventh house symbolizes groups, friends, our wishes, hopes and dreams, the people you hang with, goals, your life plan. So during Neptune's transit through Pisces, groups will be a major theme for you. You may join online groups that support your ideals, interests, and goals. There may be a psychic or intuitive component to these groups. Perhaps you end up in England, investigating crop circles. Or you might join a ghost-hunting group, a writer's group, a theater group. You might teach yoga for meditation to groups. You get the idea. One way or another, through group participation, online or off, you learn to reach for the greater good, the higher inspiration, the greater spiritual ideal.

Gemini ♊

Mutable, air

You're the communicator of the zodiac and can talk circles around anyone, anywhere, at any time, on virtually any subject. Your knowledge may not always be deep, but it's broad. When you don't know something, you research and ask questions incessantly, until your burning curiosity is sated.

Because you're ruled by Mercury, the planet of communication, you tend to use your rational, intellectual mind to explore your world. Your rational analysis of everything—from ideas to relationships—probably drives you nuts at times. But when this characteristic leads you into an exploration of psychic and spiritual realms, you're more grounded. With Neptune's transit through Pisces, you're going to have plenty of opportunities for this kind of exploration.

Neptune will be transiting the career section of your chart for fourteen years, suggesting that your professional life will be the focus of subtle but important change. In some way, psychic and spiritual exploration will become part of your professional endeavors. Opportunities will present themselves in these areas. Your creative ventures during this time will have a deeply psychic and spiritual texture to them. Your own intuition should deepen considerably, and as long as you act upon that inner knowledge, you won't be disappointed.

If you're not satisfied with your profession when this transit starts, then you may change career paths. Don't worry about how this will come about. You'll recognize the choices you should make and will have a strong inner sense about when to make them. During this transit, you'll learn to trust this inner sense and through your profession will learn to reach for inspired creativity and for what is best for the larger good, not just for what is good for you.

Cancer ♋

Cardinal, water

You need roots, a place to call home, and it doesn't matter if that place is a camper, a palace, or a state of mind. Home is your harbor, your refuge, your retreat.

As a cardinal water sign, your intuition and perceptions are finely honed. Just about everything for you is filtered through a subjective lens, through your emotions and intuition. You may not always be able to explain to others why you make certain decisions, but you don't have an overpowering need to explain yourself. You do what you do because it feels right to you.

You're affectionate, passionate, and even possessive at times. Emotionally, you act and react the same way that a crab moves—sideways. It's how you avoid confrontation and revealing who you really are, deep within. You're often moody and changeable, but once you trust someone, you trust forever.

With Neptune in fellow water sign Pisces, transiting your solar ninth house, you'll be enjoying a prolonged period of psychic and spiritual development that your Cancer nature will love. Workshops and seminars on intuitive development are a possibility—you take them or teach them! Travel to foreign countries is likely, but it won't be strictly for pleasure. You could be on a spiritual quest of some kind, visiting sacred sites in different countries in search of answers, information, illumination.

In romance and love, any relationship that develops under this transit may have a deeply spiritual component to it. The person could be someone you have been with in past lives and now you're together again for this psychic exploration.

Leo ♌

Fixed, fire

Life is your stage, Leo. Your flamboyance and flair for drama infuse you with great magnetic appeal toward which others gravitate. You seek to succeed in everything you do and undertake, want to make an impact in every situation and usually do. Your generosity and loyalty are legendary, but not without strings! You expect to be the sun around which others spin like planets. Nothing short of center stage suits you. Perhaps this is why so many Leos enter the dramatic and creative arts. It's an area where they excel.

Your leadership abilities, fun-loving nature, and genuine compassion are much appreciated by your friends and loved ones. You bring passion and commitment to everything you do, and it's these qualities that enable you to tackle challenges head on. In love and romance, you're passionate and loyal.

During Neptune's transit through Pisces and your solar eighth house, you may find the boundaries between you and others blurring. It's as if you're being asked to move off center stage for a while so that you can give freely of your time, money, energy, to others. The eighth house represents shared resources—usually with a spouse, but it can be anyone with whom you share expenses, time, energy, expertise. So it's possible that your spouse or partner's income may be muddled or confused during this transit.

Since the eighth house also represents inheritances, there could be some confusion concerning a will. But however this transit unfolds for you in terms of specific events, the point is to heighten your spiritual and intuitive awareness so that you reach first for the greater good.

Virgo ♍

Mutable, earth

You're the perfectionist of the zodiac, something you probably consider both a blessing and curse. Your attention to detail is extraordinary—think Tony Shalhoub in *Monk*. The man walks into a room, and in a single sweeping glance the details leap out at him—the pencil aligned with due north, the faintest smudge of lipstick on a coffee mug, the rug slightly askew. Thanks to this attention to detail, you're able to penetrate deeply into any topic you study, any research you conduct. You dig and dig until you have all the information you need.

Like Gemini, you're ruled by Mercury, so your mind is lightning quick and you communicate your ideas with great authority. Duty and responsibility are important to you, and your focus is on doing your job, whatever it is, efficiently and well. There's no harder worker than you, Virgo.

Neptune's transit through Pisces and your solar seventh house means it will be opposed to your sun for fourteen years. Oppositions are like an itch you can't scratch; you just learn to live with it. During this period, your greatest lessons and challenges will come through business and personal partnerships. You may be called upon to place a partner's interests and well-being before your own. The best way to navigate this opposition is to develop your intuition and learn to rely on your inner guidance.

There may be some confusion around partnerships too. But if you continually strive to associate with upbeat, spiritual individuals, to seek out those of like minds and interests, you should do just fine. Any relationships in which you get involved are likely to have deep past-life connections.

Libra ♎

Cardinal, air

You're the mediator, Libra, the one who sees both sides of an issue because you can step into the other guy's shoes, zip yourself up inside his skin, understand how and why he feels the way he does. You're all about finding harmony and balance, the very quality that often eludes you. But seek it you must, as if it's your prime directive. In love, you're a romantic who flourishes in a committed, enduring relationship. But regardless of how long the relationship lasts, you still need to be shown and told that you are loved.

You excel in any profession that requires a balanced intellect and sensitivities. Music and the arts suit you, but so does the law, teaching, research, investigation. During Neptune's transit through Pisces, your daily work will take a decided turn toward the spiritual and psychic. You may begin to take time each day to meditate, practice yoga, or engage in creative work that develops and enhances your intuition.

You may find that the individuals who enter your daily work life during this transit are people you have known in past lives, and you're coming together again for a specific purpose. Perhaps you're going to join forces for some large-scale project that makes a difference in the world. Or maybe you meet up again simply to support each other. One thing is for sure: it's going to be an intriguing fourteen years. The best way to navigate it, Libra, is to pay close attention to synchronicities. They're your guides.

Scorpio ♏

Fixed, water

Intensely passionate, secretive, and downright psychic, you're one of the most strong-willed signs in the zodiac and certainly one of the most misunderstood. Like your fellow water signs Cancer and Pisces, you live in a world of feeling and intuition, filtering all your experiences through a subjective lens. But you're also vastly different from your brethren water signs. You're basically fearless, with a great capacity for endurance that rivals Taurus, and you don't know the meaning of the word "indifference." You live pretty much in a black and white world, where things are either right or wrong, without nuance.

You're the consummate investigator. Easy answers never suit you, so you dig deeper and deeper, connecting the dots the rest of us miss. You have a rich inner life, glean a lot of information through nontraditional means, i.e., psychically, and never apologize for it.

During Neptune's transit of Pisces and your solar fifth house, you're in for a treat, Scorpio. Your considerable intuition will deepen even more. You'll be so in tune with your muse that your creativity simply flows out of you. Since the fifth house also symbolizes love and romance, you can expect some intense relationships that are madly passionate and perhaps rooted in past lives. If you have a child during this transit, he or she will be intensely creative in some way, with some special talent. It will be up to you to help the child develop and nurture that talent.

Because Neptune blurs the boundaries between us and others, it's possible that you'll be called upon to give of yourself in a selfless way—to a lover, a child, a creative project. If you resist the urge to get lost in escapism—drugs, alcohol, sex—then this transit should prove beneficial in your evolution as a human being.

Sagittarius ♐

Mutable, fire

You're blunt, witty, nomadic. You're the seeker of truth, express what you feel and believe, and don't care if anyone agrees with you. You're after the big picture, the broad canvas of any issue, belief, situation, relationship. Mundane details bore you. Intellectually, you're logical and rational, like Gemini, your polar opposite. But there are some important differences. Gemini is focused on the here and now; you've always got one eye on the future, on the larger family of humanity, the planet, the universe.

You love your freedom, the ability to just take off on a whim, with a pack and your ATM card, and chafe at any restrictions others try to put on you. Yet, in a relationship, you're passionate though rarely possessive; attentive to your partner and yet careful to maintain your freedom.

Once Neptune enters Pisces and your solar fourth house, you may find that your natural interest in mysticism, metaphysics, and things that go bump in the night takes on a whole new meaning. Suddenly, but subtly, your home and family life could become a hub of psychic activity and spiritual exploration. Your quest involves your family, your emotions toward them and vice versa, and you may discover layers of meaning in these relationships that you simply didn't see before.

There can be confusion during this transit too. If you move, there could be confusion about the neighborhood, the house, the contract. Depending on your age, one of your parents may need additional help and support or may move in with you. However this part of the equation unfolds, you may have to give more than you receive. But ultimately, your intuition becomes your compass, and through giving without expectation of compensation, you learn to extend yourself for the greater good.

Capricorn ♑

Cardinal, earth

Any boss worth her job knows that if you give a task to a Capricorn, it gets done with a shocking efficiency, dedication, and understanding of the nuances involved. But it's not just work at which you excel, Capricorn. This is how you conduct everything in your life—you appraise the situation, event, or relationship, figure out a strategy, then set things in motion that are intended to reach the goal, whatever it may be.

You're industrious, disciplined, structured, and have so much common sense it sometimes works against you! When you need intuition, right-brain thinking, your left brain, your rational mind, hurls up blocks and urges you to rely solely on logic. But that's going to change under Neptune's transit through Pisces and your solar third house, Capricorn.

The third house governs communication, and during Neptune's fourteen-year transit through Pisces, your conscious mind becomes more intuitive, psychic, right-brain. It will be easier for you to grasp the larger picture of your goals, daily life, and relationships with siblings, friends, neighbors. Whereas before you might have been intent on a particular course, now you'll be urged to explore other options, to take interesting detours into unexplored realms.

You'll learn to rely more and more frequently on your gut feelings, your hunches, your initial sense about people, situations. Your intimate partnerships will have a richness and depth you haven't experienced before. The spiritual and psychic connections you feel in these relationships will be based on your genuine beliefs and not on something you've learned to believe from parents, peers, friends. You'll be operating on a whole different level and will learn to trust these feelings first and foremost.

Aquarius ≈

Fixed, air

You value freedom and individuality above all else, and it's evident in the way you think, your belief system, your passions, and interests. Others may sometimes see you as eccentric, but in truth you're the visionary of the zodiac. You believe that whatever you can imagine, can become tangible.

You're a conundrum to the people who know you. You're a nonconformist who conforms when it suits you and a passionate advocate for your causes, but from an intellectual rather than an emotional basis. Once you commit in a relationship, you still demand your freedom and space, and this is true for all facets of your life. You work best in avant garde fields—film, electronics, the arts, television, broadcasting.

Neptune's transit through Pisces and your solar second house will impact your finances and your values. For instance, you may become more cognizant of how you spend your money. Do you, for instance, buy products from a company that promotes ideals that are contrary to your own? Do you use your power as a consumer to make statements about your ideals and beliefs? Are you generous toward charities and nonprofit organizations whose causes are in line with your ideals? Is your profession in line with them?

You may find that you begin to value different qualities in your romantic relationships. You may be looking for a deeper spiritual or psychic connection with a partner. You may decide that the area where you live no longer feels right for you. There are many possible ways this transit can unfold for you. But you will certainly discover that you now seek the greater good for the collective—family, friends, community, world.

Pisces)(

Mutable, water

Like Scorpio and Cancer, you live primarily through your emotions and intuition. You also have a fantastic imagination that takes you places denied to the rest of us. Your inner world is rich, textured, alive with arche-typal material, past-life memories, and connections to the collective unconscious. Your empathic nature makes you something of a psychic sponge, so it's important that you associate with positive, upbeat people.

With Neptune in your sign for the next fourteen years, there will be many subtle changes in your life. You may decide to change careers, to pursue a line of work that is more spiritual or psychic in nature. You may find your-self growing away from certain people in your life whose interests and beliefs aren't aligned with your own. It's possible, too, that you take up meditation, yoga, or other mind/body practices that enable you to stay grounded and attuned.

In romance and love, your needs and desires will shift. You'll want a partner whose ideals match your own and will need to feel a deep spiritual connection with anyone with whom you get involved. There can be confusion with this transit—Neptune often fogs the brain!—but as long as you resist escapism, you should do fine.

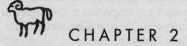

CHAPTER 2

Astrology 101

On the day you were born, what was the weather like? If you were born at night, had the moon already risen? Was it full or the shape of a Cheshire cat's grin? Was the delivery ward quiet or bustling with activity? Unless your mom or dad has a very good memory, you'll probably never know the full details. But there's one thing you can know for sure: on the day you were born, the sun was located in a particular zone of the zodiac, an imaginary 360-degree belt that circles the earth. The belt is divided into twelve 30-degree portions called signs.

If you were born between July 23 and August 22, then the sun was passing through the sign of Leo, so we say that your sun sign is Leo. Each of the twelve signs has distinct attributes and characteristics. Leos, for instance, love being the center of attention. They're warm, compassionate people with a flair for the dramatic. Virgos, born between August 23 and September 22, are perfectionists with discriminating intellects and a genius for details. Capricorns, born between December 22 and January 19, are the worker bees of the zodiac, serious-minded, ambitious, industrious.

How Signs Are Classified

The twelve signs are categorized according to element and quality or modality. The first category, element, reads like a basic science lesson—fire, earth, air, and water—and describes the general physical characteristics of the signs.

Fire signs—Aries, Leo, Sagittarius—are warm, dynamic individuals who are always passionate about what they do.

Earth signs—Taurus, Virgo, Capricorn—are the builders of the zodiac, practical and efficient, grounded in everything they do.

Air signs—Gemini, Libra, Aquarius—are people who live mostly in the world of ideas. They are terrific communicators.

Water signs—Cancer, Scorpio, Pisces—live through their emotions, imaginations, and intuitions.

The second category describes how each sign operates in the physical world, how adaptable it is to circumstances:

Cardinal signs—Aries, Cancer, Libra, Capricorn—are initiators. These people are active, impatient, restless. They're great at starting things, but unless a project or a relationship holds their attention, they lose interest and may not finish what they start.

Fixed signs—Taurus, Leo, Scorpio, Aquarius—are deliberate, controlled, resolute. These individuals tend to move more slowly than cardinal signs, are often stubborn, and resist change. They seek roots and stability and are always in the game for the long haul. They aren't quitters.

Mutable signs—Gemini, Virgo, Sagittarius, Pisces—are adaptable. These people are flexible, changeable, communicative. They don't get locked into rigid patterns or belief systems.

SUN SIGNS

Sign	Date	Element	Quality
Aries ♈	March 21–April 19	Fire	Cardinal
Taurus ♉	April 20–May 20	Earth	Fixed
Gemini ♊	May 21–June 21	Air	Mutable
Cancer ♋	June 22–July 22	Water	Cardinal
Leo ♌	July 23–August 22	Fire	Fixed
Virgo ♍	August 23–September 22	Earth	Mutable
Libra ♎	September 23–October 22	Air	Cardinal
Scorpio ♏	October 23–November 21	Water	Fixed
Sagittarius ♐	November 22–December 21	Fire	Mutable
Capricorn ♑	December 22–January 19	Earth	Cardinal
Aquarius ♒	January 20–February 18	Air	Fixed
Pisces ♓	February 19–March 20	Water	Mutable

The Planets

The planets in astrology are the players who make things happen. They're the characters in the story of your life. This story always begins with the sun, the giver of life.

Your sun sign describes your self-expression, your primal energy, the essence of who you are. It's the archetypal pattern of your Self. When you know another person's sun sign, you already have a great deal of information about that person. Let's say you're a Taurus who has just started dating a Gemini. How compatible are you?

On the surface, it wouldn't seem that you have much in common. Taurus is a fixed earth sign; Gemini is a mutable air sign. Taurus is persistent, stubborn, practical, a cultivator as opposed to an initiator. Gemini is a chameleon, a communicator, social, with a mind as quick as lightning. Taurus is ruled by Venus, which governs the arts, money, beauty, love, and romance, and Gemini is ruled by Mercury, which governs communication and travel. There doesn't seem to be much common ground. But before we write off this combination, let's look a little deeper.

Suppose the Taurus has Mercury in Gemini and suppose the Gemini has Venus in Taurus? This would mean that the Taurus and Gemini each have their rulers in the other person's sign. They probably communicate well and enjoy travel and books (Mercury) and would see eye to eye on romance, art, and music (Venus). They might get along so well, in fact, that they collaborate on creative projects.

Each of us is also influenced by the other nine planets (the sun and moon are treated like planets in astrology) and the signs they were transiting when we were born. Suppose our Taurus and Gemini have the same moon sign? The moon rules our inner needs, emotions and intuition, and all that makes us feel secure within ourselves. Quite often, compatible moon signs can overcome even the most glaring difference in sun signs because the two people share similar emotions.

In the section on monthly predictions, your sun sign always takes center stage, and every prediction is based on the movement of the transiting planets in relation to your sun sign. Let's say you're a Sagittarius. Between January 7 and February 4 this year, Venus will be transiting your sign. What's this mean for you? Well, since Venus rules—among other things—romance, you can expect your love life to pick up significantly during these weeks. Other people will find you attractive and be more open to your ideas, and you'll radiate a certain charisma. Your creative endeavors will move full steam ahead.

The planets table provides an overview of the planets and the signs that they rule. Keep in mind that the moon is the swiftest-moving planet, changing signs about every two and a half days, and that Pluto is the snail of the zodiac, taking as long as thirty years to transit a single sign. Although the faster-moving planets—the moon,

Mercury, Venus, and Mars—have an impact on our lives, it's the slow pokes—Uranus, Neptune, and Pluto—that bring about the most profound influence and change. Jupiter and Saturn fall between the others in terms of speed. This year, Jupiter spends the first six months in Taurus, then enters Gemini on June 11 and doesn't leave that sign until late June 2013.

In the section on predictions, the most frequent references are to the transits of Mercury, Venus, and Mars. In the daily predictions for each sign, the predictions are based primarily on the transiting moon.

Now glance through the planets table. When a sign is in parentheses, it means the planet corules that sign. This assignation dates back to when we thought there were only seven planets in the solar system. But since there were still twelve signs, some of the planets had to do double duty!

THE PLANETS

Planet	Rules	Attributes of Planet
Sun ☉	Leo	self-expression, primal energy, creative ability, ego, individuality
Moon ☽	Cancer	emotions, intuition, mother or wife, security
Mercury ☿	Gemini, Virgo	intellect, mental acuity, communication, logic, reasoning, travel, contracts
Venus ♀	Taurus, Libra	love, romance, beauty, artistic instincts, the arts, music, material and financial resources
Mars ♂	Aries (Scorpio)	physical and sexual energy, aggression, drive

Planet	Rules	Attributes of Planet
Jupiter ♃	Sagittarius (Pisces)	luck, expansion, success, prosperity, growth, creativity, spiritual interests, higher education, law
Saturn ♄	Capricorn (Aquarius)	laws of physical universe, discipline, responsibility, structure, karma, authority
Uranus ♅	Aquarius	individuality, genius, eccentricity, originality, science, revolution
Neptune ♆	Pisces	visionary self, illusions, what's hidden, psychic ability, dissolution of ego boundaries, spiritual insights, dreams
Pluto ♀ ♇	Scorpio	the darker side, death, sex, regeneration, rebirth, profound and permanent change, transformation

Houses and Rising Signs

In the instant you drew your first breath, one of the signs of the zodiac was just passing over the eastern horizon. Astrologers refer to this as the rising sign or ascendant. It's what makes your horoscope unique. Think of your ascendant as the front door of your horoscope, the place where you enter into this life and begin your journey.

Your ascendant is based on the exact moment of your birth and the other signs follow counterclockwise. If you have Taurus rising, for example, that is the cusp of your first house. The cusp of the second would be Gemini, of the third Cancer, and so on around the horoscope circle in a counterclockwise direction. Each house governs a particular area of life, which is outlined below.

The best way to find out your rising sign is to have your horoscope drawn up by an astrologer. For those of you with access to the Internet, though, there are several sites that provide free birth horoscopes. www.astro.com and www.cafeastrology.com are two good ones.

In a horoscope, the ascendant (cusp of the first house), IC (cusp of the fourth house), descendant (cusp of the seventh house), and MC (cusp of the tenth house) are considered to be the most critical angles. Any planets that fall close to these angles are extremely important in the overall astrological picture of who you are. By the same token, planets that fall in the first, fourth, seventh, and tenth houses are also considered to be important.

Now here's a rundown on what the houses mean.

Ascendant or Rising: The First of Four Important Critical Angles in a Horoscope

- How other people see you
- How you present yourself to the world
- Your physical appearance

First House, Personality

- Early childhood
- Your ego
- Your body type and how you feel about your body
- General physical health
- Defense mechanisms
- Your creative thrust

Second House, Personal Values

- How you earn and spend your money
- Your personal values
- Your material resources and assets
- Your attitudes and beliefs toward money
- Your possessions and your attitude toward those possessions
- Your self-worth
- Your attitudes about creativity

Third House, Communication and Learning

- Personal expression
- Intellect and mental attitudes and perceptions
- Siblings, neighbors, and relatives
- How you learn
- School until college
- Reading, writing, teaching
- Short trips (the grocery store versus Europe in seven days)
- Earth-bound transportation
- Creativity as a communication device

IC or Fourth House Cusp: The Second Critical Angle in a Horoscope

- Sign on IC describes the qualities and traits of your home during early childhood
- Describes roots of your creative abilities and talents

Fourth House, Your Roots

- Personal environment
- Your home
- Your attitudes toward family

- Early childhood conditioning
- Real estate
- Your nurturing parent

Some astrologers say this house belongs to Mom or her equivalent in your life, others say it belongs to Dad or his equivalent. It makes sense to me that it's Mom because the fourth house is ruled by the moon, which rules mothers. But in this day and age, when parental roles are in flux, the only hard and fast rule is that the fourth belongs to the parent who nurtures you most of the time.

- The conditions at the end of your life
- Early childhood support of your creativity and interests

Fifth House, Children and Creativity

- Kids, your firstborn in particular
- Love affairs, romance
- What you enjoy
- Creative ability
- Gambling and speculation
- Pets

Traditionally, pets belong in the sixth house. But that definition stems from the days when pets were chattel. These days, we don't even refer to them as pets. They are animal companions who bring us pleasure.

Sixth House, Work and Responsibility

- Day-to-day working conditions and environment
- Competence and skills
- Your experience of employees and employers
- Duty to work, to employees
- Health and the daily maintenance of your health

Descendant/Seventh House Cusp: The Third Critical Angle in a Horoscope

- The sign on the house cusp describes the qualities sought in intimate or business relationships
- Describes qualities of creative partnerships

Seventh House, Partnerships and Marriage

- Marriage
- Marriage partner
- Significant others
- Business partnerships
- Close friends
- Open enemies
- Contracts

Eighth House, Transformation

- Sexuality as transformation
- Secrets
- Death, taxes, inheritances, insurance, mortgages, and loans
- Resources shared with others
- Your partner's finances
- The occult (read: astrology, reincarnation, UFOs, everything weird and strange)
- Your hidden talents
- Psychology
- Life-threatening illnesses
- Your creative depths

Ninth House, Worldview

- Philosophy and religion
- The law, courts, judicial system
- Publishing
- Foreign travels and cultures

- College, graduate school
- Spiritual beliefs
- Travel abroad

MC or Cusp of Tenth House: The Fourth Critical Angle in a Horoscope

- Sign on cusp of MC describes qualities you seek in a profession
- Your public image
- Your creative and professional achievements

Tenth House, Profession and Career

- Public image as opposed to a job that merely pays the bills (sixth house)
- Your status and position in the world
- The authoritarian parent and authority in general
- People who hold power over you
- Your public life
- Your career/profession

Eleventh House, Ideals and Dreams

- Peer groups
- Social circles (your writers' group, your mother's bridge club)
- Your dreams and aspirations
- How you can realize your dreams

Twelfth House, Personal Unconscious

- Power you have disowned that must be claimed again
- Institutions—hospitals, prisons, nursing homes—and what is hidden
- What you must confront this time around, your karma, issues brought in from other lives

- Psychic gifts and abilities
- Healing talents
- What you give unconditionally

In the section on predictions, you'll find references to transiting planets moving into certain houses. These houses are actually solar houses that are created by putting your sun sign on the ascendant. This technique is how most predictions are made for the general public rather than for specific individuals.

Lunations

Every year there are twelve new moons and twelve full moons, with some years having thirteen full moons. The extra full moon is called the Blue Moon. New moons are typically when we should begin new projects, set new goals, seek new opportunities. They're times for beginnings. They usher in new opportunities according to house and sign.

Two weeks after each new moon, there's a full moon. This is the time of harvest, fruition, when we reap what we've sown.

Whenever a new moon falls in your sign, take time to brainstorm what you would like to achieve during the weeks and months until the full moon falls in your sign. These goals can be in any area of your life. Or, you can simply take the time on each new moon to set up goals and strategies for what you would like to achieve or manifest during the next two weeks—until the full moon—or until the next new moon.

Here's a list of all the new moons and full moons during 2012. The asterisk beside any new moon entry indicates a solar eclipse; the asterisk next to a full moon entry indicates a lunar eclipse.

LUNATIONS OF 2012

New Moons	Full Moons
January 23—Aquarius	January 9—Cancer
February 21—Pisces	February 7—Leo
March 22—Aries	March 8—Virgo
April 21—Taurus	April 6—Libra
*May 20—Gemini	May 5—Scorpio
June 19—Gemini	*June 4—Sagittarius
July 19—Cancer	July 3—Capricorn
August 17—Leo	August 1—Aquarius
September 15—Virgo	August 31—Pisces
October 15—Libra	September 29—Aries
*November 13—Scorpio	October 29—Taurus
December 13—Sagittarius	*November 28—Gemini
	December 28—Cancer

Every year there are two lunar and two solar eclipses, separated from each other by about two weeks. Lunar eclipses tend to deal with emotional issues and our internal world and often bring an emotional issue to the surface related to the sign and house in which the eclipse falls. Solar eclipses deal with events and often enable us to see something that has eluded us. They also symbolize beginnings and endings.

Read more about eclipses in the Big Picture for your sign for 2012. I also recommend Celeste Teal's excellent book, *Eclipses*.

Mercury Retrograde

Every year, Mercury—the planet that symbolizes communication and travel—turns retrograde three times. During these periods, our travel plans often go awry, communication breaks down, computers go berserk, cars or appliances develop problems. You get the idea. Things in our daily lives don't work as smoothly as we would like.

Here are some guidelines to follow for Mercury retrogrades:

- Try not to travel. But if you have to, be flexible and think of it as an adventure. If you're stuck overnight in an airport in Houston or Atlanta, though, the adventure part of this could be a stretch.
- Don't sign contracts—unless you don't mind revisiting them when Mercury is direct again.
- Communicate as succinctly and clearly as possible.
- Back up all computer files. Use an external hard drive and/or a flash drive. If you've had a computer crash, you already know how frustrating it can be to reconstruct your files.
- Don't buy expensive electronics. Expensive anything.
- Don't submit manuscripts or screenplays, pitch ideas, or launch new projects.
- Revise, rewrite, rethink, review.

In the Big Picture for each sign, check out the dates for this year's Mercury retrogrades and how these retrogrades are likely to impact you. Do the same for eclipses.

CHAPTER 3

Matters of the Heart in 2012

When you're in the throes of a paradigm shift, every area of your life may feel more vulnerable. You may notice a distinct change in what you want and expect in a romantic partnership. You may find yourself attracted to people who are different from people to whom you've been attracted in the past. Whether you're in a new or long-term relationship or are just looking, it's important to keep the channels of communication wide open.

There are, however, some constants to keep in mind with romance and love—which sun signs are most compatible with your own.

Astrology and Carl Jung

In 1950, Swiss psychologist Carl Jung undertook an astrological study about the compatibility of 180 married couples and used 50 aspects—or angles that planets make to each other. This was in the days before personal computers and astrology software that can erect a natal chart and compare several charts in just seconds. The study took several years, and the results were intriguing.

He found three aspects to be the best indicators for compatibility: a sun/moon conjunction, where one partner's sun sign is the same as the sign of the other person's moon; a moon/moon conjunction, where both individuals have their moons in the same sign; and a moon/ascendant conjunction, when one partner's moon is in the same sign as the other person's ascendant. In his book *Synchronicity, An Acausal Connecting Principle,* Jung noted that the first two aspects "have long been mentioned in the old literature as marriage characteristics, and they therefore represent the oldest tradition."

The sun/moon conjunction makes perfect sense astrologically. Your sun sign describes your overall personality; the sign of your moon describes your inner world, your emotions, what makes you feel secure. So if you're a Pisces involved with someone who has a Pisces moon, for example, then there's a beautiful give and take between you. You understand each other. If you have different sun signs, but your moons are in the same sign, then the emotional and intuitive connection is so strong you probably finish each other's sentences.

What about that third aspect, with the moon and ascendant in the same sign? This one also makes perfect sense. The ascendant is the doorway to your chart and describes, among other things, the persona you project to the outside world. So an individual with his or her moon in the same sign as your ascendant feels emotionally secure in your presence and sees the person behind the mask you wear.

Another compatibility aspect includes Venus, the planet that symbolizes love and romance. The most common I've seen are: Venus/sun, Venus/moon, Venus/ascendant; Venus/descendant cusp (cusp of the seventh house of partnerships); and Venus/Mars in the same sign. Another interesting connection I've noted is among couples who have "mirror" charts, where the sign of one partner's ascendant is the same as the other person's descendant. In other words, let's say you have Scorpio rising and your partner has Scorpio on the cusp of his or her seventh house. This aspect brings balance to the relationship.

But because one size doesn't fit all, you and your partner may have other aspects in your charts that make you compatible. For the purpose of this book, we're going to be looking only at sun-sign combinations for compatibility.

Your Best Matches

Aries

Your freedom and independence are paramount to your happiness, so you need a partner who understands and respects your space. But because you're a stranger to compromise, a vital part of any relationship, you may find intimate relationships challenging. Once you're involved, your passions are fierce and can easily topple into the dark extremes of jealousy, possessiveness, suspicion.

Your entrepreneurial and fearless spirit enjoys a partner who can compete with you on any level—on those long hikes into the wilderness, in the boardroom, in the classroom, in the garage out back where you're building your newest invention. You get the idea here, right, Aries? Boredom is your nemesis. So, which signs are good matches for you? Let's take a closer look at some of the possibilities.

Sagittarius. This fellow fire sign will give you all the freedom you crave—and then some. She'll match you joke for joke, drink for drink. If she's the physical type, and many of them are, she'll match you on those hikes. But for a Sadge, those hikes may be in some far-flung spot like Tibet. Like you, Sadge pushes herself, but she's more adaptable than you are. Sometimes she may come off like a know-it-all. But overall, this combination holds great promise.

Gemini. This air sign's wit, versatility, and ability to talk about virtually anything appeal to you. He's generally not possessive, either, a major plus when you're in one of your darker moods. His mind is sharp and lightning quick, and he probably has a vast, complicated network of friends and acquaintances. Also appealing. So what're the negatives? Gemini generally isn't as independent as you are and may spend more time with his friends than he does with you. But overall, this combination is lively, fun, and never boring.

Leo. Another fire sign. On the surface, it looks like a good match. Leo possesses an infinite capacity for enjoyment, which appeals to you. But she also loves having center stage—not just sometimes, but most of the time—and that can be a major turnoff for you.

Libra, Aquarius. Libra is your opposite sign. The match could be fantastic because you balance each other. Where you're the loner, she's the social butterfly. You're independent, she's a networker with more friends than a hive has bees. Whether this works or not depends on the signs of your natal moons, ascendants, and Venus. You and Aquarius could be a winning combination. His independence matches yours, he's as sharp as the proverbial tack, and he pulls no punches in expressing what he wants, when he wants it. Downside? He may not be as physical or competitive and lives much of his life in his head.

What about another *Aries*? Depends on the signs of your moons. Strictly on the basis of sun signs, you're both so independent the relationship may never get off the ground!

Taurus

Stable, dependable, patient. You bring these qualities to any close relationship, and once you commit it's usually for keeps. You aren't into drama, artifice, flamboyance—not for yourself and not in a partner, either. But you enjoy a partner who is physically attractive or who has a particular artistic gift that you appreciate—music, art, a way with words, anything that appeals to your senses.

If you're a Taurus who is into sports and health, and many of them are, then a health-conscious partner is a major plus. But there's another side to you, too, an inner mystic, a quiet, observant Buddha who remains calm and centered, in tune with unseen forces. You would do well with a partner who possesses that quality as well.

Leo, Sagittarius, Aries. Unless you have a moon, rising, or Venus in one of those signs, the fire signs probably won't work for you. Too much drama, boisterous behavior, and anger to suit your tastes.

Virgo, Capricorn. Fellow earth signs. Virgo could be the ticket. She's as practical as you are and, in many instances, just as mystical. Capricorn is focused, as physical as you are, but may not be as mystically inclined.

Scorpio. Your opposite sign, so there may be a good balance. She's secretive and can be vengeful, but she's just as mystical as you are.

Gemini

In a romantic relationship, conversation and discussion top your list. In fact, any potential partner must seduce your mind first—with ideas, information, books, theories that connect seemingly disparate bits of whatever it is that rushes through your head 24/7. You're up front about what you feel, but those feelings could change at a moment's notice, a dichotomy that can be confusing to a partner. And to everyone else around you, for that matter. No wonder your sign is represented by the twins.

For you, everything starts with a single burning question: *Why?* You then set about to find out why, and in the course of your quest you may be distracted by a million other pieces of information that are eventually integrated into your journey. This means, of course, that your journey toward the why of the original ques-

40

tion may not end in *this* lifetime! So you need a partner whose curiosity matches your own.

Sagittarius, Aries. Sadge is your opposite sign. He matches you in curiosity, but may not be up to snuff in other areas. With Aries, there's never a dull moment. She's a match for your quickness and wit, but may not have the curiosity you do about other people.

Libra and Aquarius. Usually compatible in that both signs value information and communication.

Water signs. Oddly, Pisces might be a good match because it's the only other sign represented by two of something, and his imagination will appeal to you.

Cancer

In romance, it's always about feelings first—not the mind, not even the body, but *emotions.* Your partner has to be as dedicated to her inner world as you are to yours, so that your inner worlds can, well, *merge.* That's the ideal. Yet, because you're a cardinal sign, like Aries, Libra, and Capricorn, there's a certain independence in you that demands emotional space. Contradictory, but not to you.

Despite your emotional depth, you tend to avoid confrontations. Like the crab that symbolizes your sign, you retreat into your shell at the first sign of trouble. Yet, how can you smooth out anything in a relationship if you can't discuss disagreements? It's as if you expect disagreements to be ironed out telepathically. So if that's true, then your best matches romantically are probably other water signs. Let's take a deeper look.

Pisces, Scorpio. Both signs are as psychic as you are, but in different ways. Pisces is the softer of the two signs, dreamier. Scorpio might overwhelm you, but gives you the emotional space you need.

Taurus. A good match. This earth sign helps you to ground yourself in the real world and gives you emotional space—maybe more than you need!

Capricorn, Virgo. Cappy is your opposite sign, so the possibility of balance is there. Virgo might be too picky for your tastes, but shows you how to communicate verbally.

Air signs? Fire signs? Not so good, unless you have a moon, ascendant, Venus, or Mars in one of those signs.

Leo

You've got enough passion for all the other signs in the zodiac—and then some. That passion is often linked to the attention of others, which probably explains why so many actors and actresses have a Leo sun, moon, or ascendant. Your life is about drama, and the higher the drama, the deeper your passion. But it's that passion that busts through obstacles, that burns a path toward where you want to go in both life and love.

Your compassion extends to anyone in a tough situation—or to any creature that needs love and reassurance that we humans aren't heartless. So, let's be real here. Your partner, whoever he or she is, probably has to love animals the way you do. Even if there are twenty strays in your back yard, your partner must be amenable to the idea that you feed the multitudes. Not an easy request, says the universe. But there are some strong possibilities.

Sagittarius, Aries, fellow fire signs. Sadge, symbolized by a creature that is half human and half horse, usually has animal companions—not pets, but *companions.* There's a big difference. She's your match in the compassion area. She understands your need to connect to an audience. But she may not stick around to be a part of that audience. The energy match with Aries is great. But unless you've got the moon, ascendant, or Venus in Aries, she may not shower you—or your animal companions—with enough attention.

Gemini, Libra. These two air signs could be excellent matches for you, Leo. You'll enjoy Gemini's lively intellect and Libra's artistic sensibilities.

Virgo

You're the absolute master of details. You collect massive amounts of information, sift through it all with an eye for what works and what doesn't, and toss out everything that is extraneous. Your quest for perfection is never compromised, and it's evident in the inner work you do, honing your own psyche, and in everything you take on in the external world. These qualities can make a romantic partnership somewhat challenging because your partner goes under the same microscope that everything else does.

You're a layered individual and benefit from a partner who understands that and knows how to peel away those layers without making you feel vulnerable or exposed. A partner who enjoys every single one of those layers. So who's your best match?

Taurus and Capricorn. Fellow earth signs. Taurus takes all the time the relationship needs to peel away the layers of your personality so she can find the gold at your core. She's patient, resolute, determined. Capricorn might consider the relationship as just one more challenge to be conquered, but could be a nice balance to your penchant for details.

Cancer, Scorpio. These two water signs complement you. Cancer grasps who you are emotionally, but may not be as willing as you are to discuss elements of the relationship. Since your sign is ruled by Mercury, the planet of communication, that could be a drawback. Scorpio's emotional intensity could be overwhelming, but he'll be delighted to peel away the layers of your personality!

Gemini. Even though air and earth aren't usually compatible, Gemini and Virgo share Mercury as a ruler. Communication in this combination is likely to be strong and fluid, with a constant exchange of ideas.

Libra

There's a certain duality in your psychological makeup that isn't mentioned very often. It's not due to a penchant for secrecy or deviousness, but to a reluctance to hurt anyone's feelings. As a result, you often find yourself paralyzed by indecision. *Who do I really love? A or B?* Since you don't want to hurt either person, you maintain both relationships and make yourself and everyone around you absolutely nuts.

You have a need for harmony and balance in relationships. You dislike confrontation and dissension, so all too often you surrender to your partner's wants at your own expense. So which signs are good matches for you?

Gemini, Aquarius. Fellow air signs understand your psychological makeup. Gemini experiences some of the same duality that you do, but for different reasons. He isn't bothered by dichotomies, since his own life is predicated on them. He appeals to that part of you who needs to communicate honestly. Aquarius may be a bit too rigid for you, insisting that you bend to his desires, but the depth and breadth of his vision attract you at a visceral level.

Sagittarius, Leo, Aries. Any of the fire signs could be an excellent match. Sagittarius never bores you and enjoys you for *who you are*. Leo may want more attention than you're willing to give, but her warmth and compassion will delight you. You and Aries, your opposite sign, balance each other.

Taurus, Virgo, Capricorn. Of the three earth signs, Taurus is probably the best match because you share Venus as a ruler. That means you have similar tastes in music and art and probably share some of the same attitudes and beliefs about money.

Scorpio

As the most emotionally intense sign of the zodiac and one of the most psychic, your powerful and magnetic personality can intimidate even heads of state. Your life patterns are about breaking taboos, digging deeper, looking for the absolute bottom line in whatever you do, in any relationship in which you become involved. You feel and intuit your way through life, and your partner must understand that.

All of this brooding and mulling takes place in the privacy of your own head. The side you show others is light and funny, with a dry wit that can charm, seduce, or spar with the best of them. Yet inside you're always asking, *What motivates him? What secrets does he have?* Given the complexities of your personality, which signs are most compatible with yours?

Pisces, Cancer. Of these two water signs, Pisces matches you in raw intuitive ability, but may be too indecisive to suit you long term. Cancer can be just as secretive as you, but unless you've got a moon or rising in Cancer, this sign could be too clingy.

Taurus, Virgo, Capricorn. The earth signs are compatible matches. Taurus, your opposite sign, brings sensuality to your sexuality and helps to dispel your suspicions about other people's motives. Her earthiness grounds your psychic ability. Virgo's discerning and gentle nature mitigates your emotional intensity. Capricorn's determination appeals to that same quality in you.

Fire signs? *Leos* and Scorpios are both fixed signs, and there seems to be something between them that is powerful. Look at Leo Bill Clinton and Scorpio Hillary.

Sagittarius

You're so multifaceted, with so many different talents, that a relationship presents certain dilemmas—namely, commitment to another person. It's so much easier to commit to, well, your own interests! Also, there's that little ole thing called personal freedom, which you value every bit as much as Aries.

Like Libra, there's a curious duality in your makeup,

best explained, perhaps, by the symbol for your sign—
the mythological centaur. Half-horse, half-human, this
figure might be defined as the wild woman (or man)
versus the conformist. A part of you operates from gut
instinct and the other part of you is acculturated. Which
signs are your best matches?

Aries, Leo, Sagittarius. As remarked under the Aries
section, a relationship with this sign may not go anywhere because you're both so independent. Aries might
want to be in charge all the time, and you get fed up and
hit the open road. Leo could be a terrific choice, particularly if one of you has a moon in the other's sun sign.
Another Sadge would be intriguing.

Taurus, Virgo, Capricorn. Of these three earth signs,
Capricorn is the best match. Even if she lacks your intuitive gifts, her focus, direction, and resolute determination equal yours. Taurus, your opposite sign, could also
be a good match. You share a fascination with the para-
normal, and your energies would balance each other.

Air signs? Water signs? Probably not, unless you have
a moon, rising, or some other prominent planet in those
signs.

Capricorn

You build relationships in the same careful way that you
build everything else in your life—a brick at a time. A
conversation here, a dinner there, a movie, a moonlit
walk, an exchange of beliefs: you're methodical, consis-
tent, disciplined. Pretty soon, the foundation is solid, the
chemistry is exactly right, and you know exactly what
you want.

A relationship, of course, involves the human heart—
not mortar and bricks—and that's where it may get
tricky. You could discover that your methodical approach doesn't work as well in a relationship as it does
with your career. Your success will depend, to a certain
extent, on your compatibility with your partner.

Taurus, Virgo, Capricorn. Taurus's solidity and dependability appeal to you, and he's as private as you are. But his still waters run deep, and he may not express his emotions as readily as you would like. Yet the match would be a good one. Virgo understands what drives you. Another Capricorn, i.e., type A personality, would wear you out!

Scorpio, Pisces. While either of these water signs is compatible with your earth-sign sun, Pisces may too ambivalent for you, too indecisive. Scorpio, though, is a strong match. All that intensity appeals to you at a visceral level, your sex lives would be fantastic, and you share a similar determination. *Cancer*, your opposite sign, might work if the Cancer has a moon or rising in your sign.

Fire signs? Air signs? Again, it depends on the distribution of fire- and air-sign planets in your natal chart.

Aquarius

In love and romance, as in life, your mind is your haven, your sanctuary, your sacred place. It's where everything begins for you. From your visionary, cutting-edge ideas to your humanitarian causes and interests in esoterica, you're a wild card, not easily pigeonholed. It doesn't make any difference to you whether your partner shares these interests, as long as he or she recognizes your right to pursue them.

There's a rebel in you that pushes against the status quo, and that's something your partner has to understand too. Your connections to people and to the world aren't easily grasped by others. Too weird, they think. Too out there. But that's fine. You understand who and what you are, and in the end, that's all you need. So, which signs are your best matches?

Gemini, Libra. Your air sign *compadres* are excellent matches. Gemini suits your prodigious intellect, causes, and ideas. Good communication usually is a hallmark of this relationship, and Gemini is supportive of your causes. With Libra, the focus is on relationships—yours and Libra's connection to five million others. But the right mix exists for a strong partnership. A relationship with another *Aquarius* could be challenging since you'll both insist you're right. But if you can move past that, you'll do fine. Another Aquarius may be like looking in the mirror 24/7. Not for the faint-hearted.

Aries, Leo, Sagittarius. With these fire signs, you enjoy the freedom to be your own person. Life with Aries is never boring and the conversation and adventures are stimulating, but he may not share your humanitarian and esoteric interests. Sagittarius loves your mind and insights, your idealism and rebellion against the establishment. Great compatibility overall. Leo is your opposite sign, suggesting a good balance between your head and his heart.

Earth or water signs? Only if you have prominent planets in either of those elements.

Pisces

It's true that your inner world is often more real and genuine to you than anything in the external world. The richness of your imagination, the breadth of your intuition . . . these qualities create a kind of seductive atmosphere that's tough to move beyond. But because you're a physical being, in a physical world, who has to eat and sleep, work and function, who loves and triumphs and yearns, you have to move beyond it. So you do.

But always there's an inner tension, a kind of bewilderment, a constant questioning. *Where am I going? What am I doing? Do I really want to do this or that?* Your head and your heart are forever at odds, so no wonder your sign is symbolized by two fish moving in opposite directions. In romance and love, this indecisiveness can be problematic. So which signs are most compatible for you?

Scorpio, Cancer. Scorpio's emotional intensity could overwhelm you, but he balances your indecisiveness with his unwavering commitment to a particular path. Intuitively, you're on the same page, a major plus. Cancer's innate gentleness appeals to you, and she appreciates you exactly as you are.

Taurus, Capricorn. These two earth signs appeal to you at a visceral level. Taurus's solid, grounded personality comforts that part of you that is so often torn between one direction and another. Her sensuality is also a major plus. Capricorn's singular vision and direction are a mystery to you, but there's much to learn from her. *Virgo*, your opposite sign, can bring balance.

Fire signs probably won't work for you unless you have a moon or rising in a fire sign. Of the air signs, *Gemini* is probably the most compatible for you. Since you're both symbolized by two of something—two fish, the twins—he understands your dichotomies.

CHAPTER 4

Your Career Choices in 2012

Despite how things may look in the job market, despite the grim statistics about the economy, the housing market, the banks, the plunging dollar, and all the rest of the depressing news that flows into our lives 24/7, many people flourish in economically difficult times. In fact, if you've been laid off from your job, the first thing you can do to turn things around is to look at it as an opportunity. The more positive and upbeat your attitude, the more frequently you view every challenge as an opportunity, the greater the chances that you'll turn things around.

Several years ago friends of ours, a married couple who are both writers, had pretty much hit rock bottom. The wife admitted that she was ready to start cleaning pools just to have a steady income. Then practically overnight everything turned around. Her husband sold a novel that became a popular cable TV show, a producer commissioned her to write a script, and suddenly their bank account fattened, they bought a second home, a new car and a boat, and the world opened up for them. It can open up for you, too.

We create our realities from the inside out. Everything you see around you is a manifestation of a belief that you hold. Some of our beliefs have been passed down to us by well-meaning family members, mentors, teachers, or friends, and we adopt those beliefs because we respect the people who handed them to us. But what do *you* believe about your abilities and talents and your ability to earn your living doing what you love? How do you handle stress? Change?

In 2012, when so much of the world seems to be shifting beneath our feet, we have a chance to delve into those beliefs and get rid of the ones we have adopted out of convenience. We can either go with the flow, change with the times, or we can offer up resistance. The more we resist, the more pain we experience. The more we go with the flow, the greater our capacity to discover where we should be. Which path will you take?

Inventory

One way to prosper professionally during good *and* bad times is to know what you want. So let's take an inventory.

1. Describe your dream job/profession

_____

_____

_____

2. Lay out a strategy for finding/attaining this dream job/profession. Do you need more education, time, additional skills? If so, include those things, and set a goal for attaining them.

_____

_____

_____

3. Set realistic professional goals. Choose a time frame—a month, six months, a year—whatever feels right to you. Ask yourself what you would like to be doing a year from now. Describe it in detail. Make it real!

_____

_____

_____

4. What kind of inner work can you do to make these goals a reality more quickly? Visualization? Take workshops or seminars? Develop your intuition? Describe in detail.

_____

_____

_____

5. What are your greatest strengths? Describe them. Then focus on the strengths you have—not your weaknesses.

_____

_____

_____

Using Synchronicity in 2012

The Swiss psychologist Carl Jung coined the term. It means: the coming together of inner and outer events in a way that can't be explained by cause and effect and that is meaningful to the observer. Or, it's a meaningful coincidence. When it happens to you, don't dismiss it as a random curiosity. A synchronicity can be a navigational tool, a confirmation, warning, or guidance.

For Frank Morgan, an actor who played five different parts in *The Wizard of Oz*, a stunning synchronicity served as confirmation that he was on the right professional track by accepting parts in the movie.

One of the parts he played was the disreputable Professor Marvel. For that role, the director and wardrobe man wanted him dressed in a "nice-looking coat, but tattered," said Mary Mayer, a unit publicist on the film. So they traipsed down to a second-hand clothing store and purchased a rack of coats. Then Frank, the director, and the wardrobe guy all got together and selected one of the coats.

Imagine his surprise when he turned the pocket of the coat inside out and found a name sewn into the lining of the coat: L. Frank Baum, the author of *The Wizard of Oz*. The additional synchronicity here is that both men who wore the coat were named Frank.

In times of stress or major transitions—marriage, divorce, birth, a move, career change or change in employment and income—synchronicities may occur more frequently. Decipher the message if you can, and know that synchronicities indicate we're in the flow, exactly where we're supposed to be.

Your Career Path in 2012

Regardless of what you do for a living, whether you love or detest it or merely tolerate it, you can maximize your strengths and talents to enhance your professional opportunities.

Aries

As a cardinal fire sign, your entire life is about movement, action, doing. You're the pioneer, the entrepreneur, the one who really does march to the beat of a different drummer. Your pioneering spirit is your most valuable asset for navigating any professional changes you encounter this year.

There is no such thing as a challenge for you. You simply rise to the occasion and banish the challenge. You also refuse to recognize defeat. What someone else might see as a setback, you view as an opportunity. In 2011, you learned to follow your passions, wherever they led, and in 2012 that faith starts paying off. Whenever a negative thought enters your mind, change it immediately to something upbeat and positive. Follow the methods that feel right to you.

Taurus

Your senses are so finely tuned that you hear the music of the spheres, poetry flows through your dreams, you have the heart and soul of a mystic. You're the most enduring, taciturn, and physical of the twelve signs. You always finish what you start unless it's just unbearable! In 2011, you learned that your resolute determination is your greatest asset for navigating professional changes. In 2012, you learn to trust your intuition.

Until June 11 this year, Jupiter remains in your sign, a positive and lucky transit that you should take advantage of. Jupiter expands whatever it touches, and every twelve years it touches your sun. You're in the right place at the right time with this transit, so take full advantage of it. Don't shy away from new opportunities that broaden your life.

You already know your own value. In 2012, everyone around you learns it as well, and you keep moving forward and never look back.

Gemini

You're the communicator, your mind buzzing constantly with information that you eagerly share with others.

Some people say you never shut up, that you talk just to fill the silence. Not true. Beneath your chatter lies an insatiable curiosity.

Your ability to multitask and your curiosity are your greatest assets for navigating any professional changes this year. In fact, in 2011 you learned to follow the impulses of your curiosity to see where they might lead, and they led some mighty strange places. But you were in the right place, at the right time. In 2012, your versatility and communication abilities enable you to navigate the paradigm shift that's underway.

Cancer

You're completely attuned to emotions—yours and everyone else's. It's easy for you to slip into someone else's skin and feel what they feel. You hurt as they hurt. You weep as they weep. You laugh as they laugh. Like fellow water sign Pisces, you're a psychic sponge, an empath. Your extraordinary memory is intimately linked to your emotions, and your intuition is remarkable. All of these traits helped you to successfully navigate the transitions of 2011. During the first six months of 2012, when Jupiter is in compatible earth sign Taurus, your hard work last year really begins to pay off. You meet people who not only share your interests, but who are helpful in some way professionally. Your professional options expand. Perhaps you launch a business, write a novel, have a photography exhibit. One way or another, you begin to achieve your dreams, Taurus.

Embrace whatever change comes your way, and trust that the universe works for your highest good.

Leo

You were born to express your creativity through performance. You love the applause, the recognition, the immediate gratification and feedback. Of course, not every

Leo is an actor or actress, but every Leo loves drama. So whether you're on the stage, in front of a classroom, or counseling a patient in therapy, your creative flair moves through you like a force of nature. In 2011, you learned how valuable this asset was in helping you to navigate any professional changes you experienced.

Now, in 2012, especially from June 11, 2012, to late June 2013, you're well positioned for seeing your dreams unfold. Jupiter will be in compatible air sign Gemini, and things should expand explosively for you. Join groups, engage your friends, and offer zero resistance to whatever comes your way.

Virgo

Your gift is details. Whether it's your own life that you're honing, sculpting, and shining like some fine gem, or a particular project or relationship, you can see the finished product in a way that others can't. You also have a particular gift or ability that you're always willing to provide to others, without thought of compensation. These traits carried you through professional changes you may have experienced in 2011.

The first six months of 2012, when Jupiter is in fellow earth sign Taurus, should be fantastic for you, regardless of any doom and gloom around you. Your worldview expands, you may have a chance to travel overseas, perhaps even a publishing opportunity presents itself. It's all preparation for Jupiter's transit through Gemini and your career sector from June 11, 2012, to late June 2013. Now *that* period, Virgo, is going to blow your mind. So prepare yourself for a wild, wonderful career ride.

Libra

You can work a room like a seasoned politician, spreading peace and harmony even among people who can't agree on anything. That's your magic. Yet the very qualities that you can instill in others often elude you. Not that any of us could tell by looking at you. Libra is a master of social camouflage. It seems that nothing ruffles you. But within, you're struggling to maintain harmony without compromising your principles. Your sphere is relationships. More than any other sign, you can see the many sides of an issue and understand that your truth may not be everyone's truth. But you can live with the paradox. It's your gift.

Any professional challenges you encountered in 2011 were undoubtedly overcome by your ability to connect with people. You're in for a real treat from June 11, 2012, to late June 2013, when expansive Jupiter transits fellow air sign Gemini. During this period, your professional opportunities should abound, taking you into new areas and new creative venues and bringing opportunities for foreign travel.

Scorpio

You're the emotional vortex of the zodiac, a spinning whirlwind of contradictions. You aren't like the rest of us, and that's the way you prefer it. You dig deeply into everything you do, looking for the absolute bottom line, the most fundamental truth, and then you excavate everything at the discovery site just to make sure you've gotten it all.

Professional challenges that you encountered last year were met with the fortitude and resilience for which you're known. In 2012, your best bet is to team up with a professional or romantic partner and launch a business or some other endeavor you've always wanted to try. The best time for this is from January 1 to June 11, when expansive Jupiter is in Taurus, your solar seventh house. Your intuition will be spot on during this period. Listen to it.

Sagittarius

You're the life of the party, just like your fellow fire sign Leo. But your approaches are different. Where Leo seeks recognition and applause, you're after the big picture, and it doesn't matter how far you have to travel to find it, how many people you have to talk to, how many books or blogs you must read. When your passion is seized, you're as doggedly relentless as Taurus. One part of you operates from raw instinct; the other part of you is acculturated, aware of how to work the system.

In 2011, the year of transition, you realized that you don't recognize professional challenges. You learned that any bump in a road simply means you take an alternate path to get to where you want to go. Between June 11, 2012, and late June 2013, expansive Jupiter will be in Gemini, in your solar seventh house. To maximize this beautiful transit—and to get the most out of it professionally—team up with a partner, romantic or professional, and try some entrepreneurial venture that suits your soul, Sadge.

Capricorn

You're the achiever, the builder, the classic type A personality whose focus is so tight that everything and everyone becomes part of your journey toward ... well, the top of the hill, the pinnacle of whatever you're attempting to reach. You can build anything, anywhere. A fictional world, a belief system, an invention, a concept, a family, a video world. Name it, and you can build it.

Any professional challenges you encountered in 2011 were undoubtedly tackled the same way that you have tackled any other challenge in your life—by finding a way around it. Or through it. As a cardinal earth sign, you value what is tangible, practical, efficient, and your journey through any obstacle reflects it. In 2011, you learned how not to fear, and that got you through every professional challenge you encountered. In 2012, particularly until June 11, when Jupiter is in fellow earth sign Taurus, your muse is so up close and personal that your creativity soars. Use it to navigate the shifting sands in your world.

Aquarius

You're not easy to pigeonhole. Sometimes you seem to be the paragon of independence. Yet you enjoy the company of groups who share your passions. You're the one who thinks so far outside the box that people close to you may accuse you of communication with aliens, ghosts, goblins, elves. Even if it's true, you just laugh and continue on your journey into the strange, the unknown, on into the heart of the universe.

Any challenges you encountered professionally in 2011 were no major thing for you. You always managed to work your way around the challenge by continuing to explore what interests you. Between June 11, 2012, and late June 2013, Jupiter transits fellow air sign Gemini and your solar fifth house. This should be a huge bonus for you, Aquarius. Your creativity becomes your most valued asset for navigating the paradigm shift. And regardless of how out of the box your professional ideas are this year, you come through it all in great shape.

Pisces

Dreamer, healer, mystic: all these adjectives fit you, Pisces. You live within a rich, inner world that is both a buffer and a conduit to deeper experiences. You don't need anyone else to tell you this. At some level you already know it, appreciate it, embrace it. While it's true that you're a sucker for a sob story, an attribute that can turn you from hero to martyr in the space of a single breath, there's no concrete evidence that you're more of a victim than any other sun sign.

Any professional challenges that came your way during 2011 were met with your powerful intuition, your prodigious imagination, and your unique way of dealing with adversity through faith in your role in the larger scheme of things. The tentacles of your psychic abilities were active 24/7, at your disposal, and awaited your instructions. In 2012, especially until June 11 when Jupiter transits compatible earth sign Taurus, your communication abilities shine. Everything that swirls through your head, in your imagination, can be expressed in ways that others understand. Professionally, this talent alone puts you well ahead of the pack.

CHAPTER 5

Family Stuff

Our birth family is like a mini world. It's with them that we develop psychologically, emotionally, spiritually and intellectually. It's with them that we develop our defenses, needs, expectations, belief systems. They encourage certain behaviors and discourage others. We learn to rebel or conform or just fit in. Family, then, is where it all begins, which is probably why many books and movies deal with dysfunctional or eccentric families.

The paragon of dysfunctional families is probably the Corleones, in the *Godfather* movies. So much drama, violence, and emotion. The emotion is equally intense in *My Big Fat Greek Wedding*, where a young Greek woman falls in love with a non-Greek man. She tries to convince her family to accept him while she struggles to come to terms with her cultural identity. And it's all couched in comedy.

Jeanette Walls, in her memoir, *The Glass Castle,* recalls her bizarre childhood with an alcoholic father and a mother who abhorred domesticity. Jeanette and her siblings gradually made their way to New York. Their parents followed them but chose to be homeless.

Brokeback Mountain, based on a short story by Annie Proulx, is about a forbidden passion between two cowboys in the early sixties and how their love for each other impacts their families.

Your Family

Take a look at your own family. What are the dynamics? Does everyone get along? Are there certain issues that surface time and again? If you have siblings, do they each seem to have different roles in the family? One might be the rebel, for instance, and the other might be the intellectual. What about your parents, partner, and your own kids? If you're an only child, what is your relationship with your parents like?

Families often have commonalities in their respective charts that illustrate the deep connections among them. The parents might have opposing signs, like Taurus/Scorpio, Gemini/Sagittarius, so there's a kind of balance. Then one child might have a moon in Sadge, and the other child has a Gemini sun. There's an infinite number of combinations, and some aren't as obvious as sun or moon signs. But for the purpose of this chapter, let's keep things simple.

Your Style as a Parent

Aries

Your parenting style isn't like anyone else's, that's for sure. Man or woman, you encourage independence in your children from a very young age. You're no control freak. Or, if you are, then it may be due to the sign of your moon. You may be one of those parents who keeps close tabs on your child's growth progress: *7 months, crawling; 9 months, utters first word; age 2, a puzzle prodigy!* Any rules you lay down are in the name of safety rather than an attempt to control your child's every move and decision.

Some Aries wing it as parents. They don't have a clue, really, about what they're doing, so they fine-tune their parenting style at every stage of their child's growth. But even for you, Aries, there are certain constants that probably won't change. In addition to the emphasis on independence, you have a finely honed sense of privacy and probably won't violate your child's unless you have a reasonable suspicion that you should. That's more likely to happen during the turbulent teen years. You give your child plenty of freedom to make his own choices. However, when you do offer guidance or advice, you may blurt it out, which could create some major tension if your child is an adult.

An *Aries mom* can be brash, funny, exciting, unpredictable. Kids enjoy her company because everything with her is an adventure. But she can be fiercely protective—that's the ram who symbolizes her sign—ready to defend her child's turf at the slightest provocation. She isn't nurturing in the traditional sense of the word, i.e., you won't find her slaving over a hot stove preparing the evening meals. She's more likely to have a pizza delivered. But when her child's in need, she's there in a flash.

When an *Aries dad* hangs out with the kids, there's an air of impatience, brashness, restlessness, a kind of *let's get this show on the road!* If he encourages his child to take risks—in sports, love, life—it's because he himself is so fearless. He's terrific at organizing activities, but they happen on the fly. *In ten minutes, we're going on a picnic,* he announces, and then everyone scrambles around grabbing stuff they need. He usually has great pride in and passion for his kids.

In 2012, with Uranus in your sign all year (until March 2019, actually), there may be sudden, unexpected events that impact your parenting style. If you've fallen into a personal rut (unlikely for an Aries, but it does happen now and then), then Uranus whips into your life, turns everything upside down, shakes out what is no longer needed or useful. Your temperament may be erratic, you may be more impatient than usual, your blood pressure could soar at the slightest provocation. Best advice? Sign up for yoga classes with your kids. Meditate with them. Hike with them. Engage them.

Taurus

Your parenting style reflects your stability, determination, and patience. You enjoy your children immensely and strive to nurture their talents, strengths, and gifts. You try to create a beautiful home environment, a place in which everyone delights, where your kids feel comfortable bringing their friends. HOME. In caps.

You probably enjoy music, art, books, movies, and politics, and these interests are reflected in your environment—and are passed on to your kids through a kind of osmosis. So don't be surprised when your son or daughter cranks up the music so loudly it threatens to shatter crystal or when the weekly allowance is blown at the local bookstore!

Since you're the most stubborn sign in the zodiac, that stubbornness certainly surfaces in your parenting. Your child says *yes*. You shake your head *no*. The child keeps saying yes, yes, his voice growing louder and louder until your patience snaps, and the legendary bull's rush seizes you. *No,* you shout, and slam your door. End of story, end of argument, end of struggle.

Since Venus rules your sign, though, your bull's rush usually passes quickly and peace and tranquillity are restored. But you still refuse to change your mind!

A *Taurus mom* is loyal and dedicated to her role as a mother. It won't be her *only* role, but she's likely to consider it her most important role. She's in the line for school drop-offs in the morning, in that same line for pickup in the afternoon. In between she's in court, defending someone like you or me, or she's writing the great American novel, or teaching English to recalcitrant seventh-graders. Or she's selling real estate or jewelry or scooping the next big political story.

The *Taurus dad* works hard and patiently at whatever he does. He finishes everything he starts—and that includes the projects his kids begin for their science classes! He, like his female counterpart, is usually health conscious and watches his diet, exercises regularly, and takes good care of himself. Part of this could be vanity, but whatever it is, his kids pick up on it and sometimes take up the same sports in which dad indulges.

In 2012, Uranus in Aries is transiting your solar twelfth house, that place in your chart that is most hidden and secretive. With Uranus here until 2019, your inner world is shaken up, elements of your unconscious surface abruptly and inexplicably. It's as if you're confronted with psychological archetypes in yourself that you haven't seen before. This kind of turmoil certainly will affect your family and kids—*if* you let it. The bottom line here is that Taurus rarely shows anyone the face of that inner world. The best way to navigate whatever stuff is surfacing is to deal with it and move on.

Gemini

Ideas and communication. That's what you're about, and it's evident in your parenting style. From the time your child is very young, you read to her, talk to her, encourage her to express herself verbally. You buy her puzzles, coloring books, picture books, anything that expands her knowledge and creativity. Your fascination with information and relationships is found in the way you encourage her to reach out to other people, to make friends, to invite them to her house. Don't be surprised, then, if by the time your child is a teen, she has several thousand friends on Facebook!

You're a voracious reader, and it's likely that your home has hundreds—if not thousands—of books. This love of reading is something you pass on to your child, and by the time she's preparing for college, her facility with language and ideas is a major plus. It's said that a typical Gemini is actually two people—the twins are the symbol for your sign—so you're comfortable with duality. This can be confusing to a young child, particularly if you vacillate about what's allowed and what isn't.

With Mercury ruling your sign, any connections between the Mercury in your chart and the sun, moon, rising, or Mercury in your child's chart portend strong communication.

A *Gemini mom* is the supreme multitasker. She can simultaneously pack school lunches, talk on the phone, and be writing a novel in her head. At times she may appear scattered to her kids, but then she suddenly comes out with a zinger of logic or insight that stops them in their tracks. Glances are exchanged, eyebrows shoot up. She's a fount of information and eagerly passes on what she knows to her kids—and their friends and the friends of their friends. If anything, when her kids are with their friends, she must learn to back off and give them space.

A *Gemini dad* is quick, witty, enigmatic. Just when his kids think they've got him figured out, he does or says something that makes him impossible to peg. His intellect is as finely honed as a Gemini woman's, but takes him in different directions. He might be an avid sports fan, for example, a master at chess, a general aviation pilot, or an animal lover. His interests and passions are passed on to his kids.

One thing is certain: a home with at least one Gemini parent in it is never boring!

In 2012, you have several fantastic things going for you astrologically that are sure to bolster your parenting style. First, Uranus in Aries is transiting your solar eleventh house, so you're going to be more involved with friends and groups that support your parenting style. These groups will be kid friendly, too, so it's not as if you have to find a sitter or drop the kids at someone else's place. These group associations may begin and end suddenly, but that's fine with you. They bring an excitement and unpredictability that suit you.

The second transit is fantastic—Jupiter moving

through your sign from June 11, 2012, to late June 2013. This transit enhances all the Gemini qualities of your parenting style—emphasis on communication, books, writing, travel. It will be a period your kids remember as pure fun and enjoyment.

Cancer

You're the nurturer of the zodiac, the one who needs roots, a home, a place or state of mind and spirit that you can call your own. You're a gentle, kind person who takes everything to heart—and this is certainly reflected in your parenting style. Through your example, your kids learn to respect all forms of life, to never hurt others, to treat them as he would like to be treated.

You can be overprotective, for sure, and before your child hits his teens, you'll have to come to grips with how to handle those feelings. Emotionally, you rarely reveal yourself. Like the crab that represents your sign, you tend to move sideways, skirting unpleasant issues, anxious to avoid confrontation, reluctant to discuss the heart of the matter. Your exceptional intuition keeps you in tune with your children, alerting you when they're in danger or happy. You forgive easily, but rarely forget. So if one of your kids hurts your feelings, you'll remember it thirty years from now.

A *Cancer mom* is the prototypical nurturer—always there for her kids, supportive of their wishes and dreams. Yes, if she cooks, you'll find her whipping up delectable dishes that include everyone's favorite foods, whatever they are. Her home is her palace—but it could be the cabin of a boat, a tent in the wilderness, an RV. No matter where she is, she tends to the creature comforts of her family. As a parent, she has rules, but they're emotionally based, just like everything else in her life, so they won't change unless the emotions behind them change first.

A *Cancer dad,* like his female counterpart, is kind,

affectionate, and nurturing, but only to a point. When he feels his personal space is being violated in any way, he backs off, scurries into his crab's shell, and retreats quickly. For a child, he's hard to figure out. Sometimes he's the hero of the child's latest adventure story; other times he's the wet blanket at the party. If he's into metaphysics and alternative healing, then chances are he's in deep, and his kids will pick up on this interest and explore on their own.

In 2012, the period from the beginning of the year to June 11 should be wonderful for you and your kids. You get involved with new groups, your friends become more integral to your life, and in some way, shape, or form you begin to realize your dreams. Your children and family are part of the process. The other transit to watch is Neptune's through Pisces, which begins on February 3 and continues for the next fourteen years. This one brings an emphasis on spirituality and intuitive development that you pass on to your kids. You and your family may travel internationally, but it won't be strictly for pleasure. You'll be on a spiritual quest of some kind. Stonehenge? An ashram in India? Crop circles?

Leo

You love being the center of attention, often surround yourself with admirers, and the world is your stage. But that's just the beginning of your story! You strive to succeed—to shine—at everything you do and to make an impact in every situation. Your personal magnetism draws admirers who are willing to help your cause, whatever it is. You prefer to hang with people whose beliefs are similar to your own, but can get along with just about everyone—as long as no one steals your thunder. Your kindness, generosity, and compassion are nearly legendary.

As a parent, you love unconditionally and fiercely. You tend to instill certain qualities into your children—optimism, loyalty, integrity, honor. When they're toddlers, you enjoy their company and watching them progress to each stage, from crib to crawling to kindergarten. Once they're off to school, particularly by the time they reach middle school and then high school, you may feel marginalized in some way. You really shouldn't. You've got enough interests and passions to fill your next five lives, and your ambitions keep propelling you forward. Generally, you delight in seeing your children fly off into the world, doing what they love.

The *Leo mom* is usually up front about everything—what she feels, why, and for how long. She's definitely disappointed when her kids aren't as forthright, but she gets over it! She likes being at the helm—at home, at work, while traveling—and can be a bit bossy at times. *You and you, do this and that.* Her kids quickly learn to either fall in line or stand up to her. Mom enjoys nice clothes and probably dresses with a flair and style all her own. She's clever at creating impressions and moods through the way she looks and acts (it's the actress in her), but her kids undoubtedly learn to see through it to the gem beneath.

The *Leo dad* is easy to get along with as long as you keep a couple of rules in mind. Never tell *him* what to do, and let him have center stage. If both of your parents are Leos, then the one thing you can count on in your household is plenty of drama! The Leo dad is fun, outgoing, and full of magic. He snaps his fingers and things happen. He has great leadership ability (and not just as a dad), and his energy and frankness endear him to children of any age.

In 2012, two transits will affect your parenting style. Uranus, the planet of sudden, unexpected change, is transiting fellow fire sign Aries, in your solar ninth house. This suggests that your belief system, your worldview, your spiritual beliefs are undergoing radical change. It will be an exciting, unpredictable time, and the whirlwind of events will sweep you and your kids and partner up into a vortex of unpredictable adventures.

The second transit, Jupiter's through Gemini, goes from June 11, 2012, to late June 2013, and emphasizes foreign travel, friends, mental stimulation. Suddenly everything in your life expands, you feel lucky, like you're in the right time and place, and this expansiveness is passed on to your kids.

Virgo

Your mind is lightning quick, just like Gemini's, and you're so mentally dexterous and agile that the competition can't keep pace with you. Due to your attention to detail, to the discerning turn of your intellect, you tend to delve more deeply into subjects than Gemini, and when you gather information it usually has a purpose. You pass this ability on to your children, and it serves you well as a parent, i.e., not much escapes your notice. Your kids will never be able to put anything over on you! Since you're Mercury ruled, like Gemini, you need sufficient outlets for all your mental energy.

You're an attentive parent who does all the expected things—for school, health, your child's happiness—but who may not play by the book. In other words, you probably won't raise your children the way you were raised. If you were brought up in a religious household, for instance, your child won't be. If your parents stressed school over fun, you may do the opposite. If your parents were inordinately strict, you won't be. It's not that you have the heart of a rebel (although you might!) but that your finely honed intellect connects all the dots, and you grasp what's needed for your children to evolve and to achieve their full potential.

The *Virgo mom* is vibrant, upbeat, conscientious, loving. Even though she never *tries* to project a particular image, others sense something different about her, perhaps her softness, her caring. Deep down, she can be a worry wart, fretting about the smallest details, the inconsistencies in life, in her kids, her family. It's part of her insecurity. When she's in that mode, she can be critical—of her kids, her husband, herself. But she can be cajoled out of that mood by lively discussions about ideas, books, travel, any kind of information that seizes her passions. She's generous with her kids and strives to enrich their world through her own wisdom.

The *Virgo dad* is as intellectually curious as his female counterpart. He's a hard worker, detail oriented, with a biting humor that is rarely malicious. He may take his role as dad a bit too seriously at times, but his kids quickly learn how to loosen him up, how to make him laugh. He's an attentive father, the kind who reads to his kids at night, who listens to their dramas and woes as teens, who applauds loudly when they graduate from college. Always with him—and with the Virgo mom— there is tremendous pride in his children, as if he can't quite believe his extreme good fortune.

In 2012, the first six months of the year will be magnificent for you as a parent, for your kids, your family generally. Jupiter will be transiting fellow earth sign Taurus, your solar ninth house. This transit promises international traveling, dealings with publishers and educators, perhaps even living abroad for a while. The living abroad may last longer than the transit because for a year—from June 11, 2012, to late June 2013—Jupiter will be moving through Gemini and your career area. This transit suggests that one possible manifestation is working abroad, and you'll take your loved ones with you.

Libra

You're one of the gentlest souls in the zodiac, usually soft spoken and treading lightly in all matters. You're also deeply romantic about your family and kids. They're your beacons. You love beauty in every shape and form, and when there's no obvious beauty, you find it in what you can imagine. You're an excellent strategist, a natural diplomat, and you often mitigate chaos and drama, dissension and disagreement. Sometimes you assume these roles to your own detriment, just to keep the peace.

As a parent, this tendency to keep the peace at your own expense could be thankless. So strive not to be a martyr, okay? Strive not to bend over backward to please ... well, everyone. Once you can do that, your natural artistic tendencies take over in your parenting. You nurture your children's passions and interests, their gifts and talents as they emerge. You're tuned in to who they are on a soul level and understand how to help them bring that soul into their conscious awareness. Your love of art, music, literature, and every other creative talent is passed on to your kids. Your grasp of the complexities of relationships is translated into language they speak. Facebook, Myspace, and every other social networking group become their community. In short, you usher your children into the finer beauties of the twenty-first century.

The *Libra mom* creates a domestic environment in which her children flourish. But she also has her career, friends, passions, and interests that get mixed up in this collective soup called life and which, in turn, affect her kids. She brings in music, art, gardens, books, and people. Lots of interesting people. She creates moods and atmospheres and invites her children to participate. The lessons they learn, the insights they carry away from these encounters influence them for life. There's no pinning down the Libra mom. Just when you think you've got her figured out, she surprises you. Boring? Never. Not a chance.

The *Libra dad* loves having a team—wife, kids, friends of kids, neighbors, even stray animals, it doesn't matter. Everyone and everything is part of this team. Membership is open. He's an excellent organizer, supportive of his children's endeavors and dreams. But his high ideals can be problematic once his kids are adults, making choices that don't measure up—in his mind—to those ideals. Like the Libra mom, he rarely loses his temper.

Between June 11, 2012, and late June 2013, Jupiter will be transiting fellow air sign Gemini, in your solar ninth house. This transit will lead to an expansion in your educational opportunities, worldview, even in foreign travel. Until October, Saturn will be in your sign. The combination of these two transits should have positive benefits for you as a parent, your family, and kids. Even if you run into restrictions and delays in your personal life or experience sudden events related to your daily work, you come through this period with a stronger grasp of what it means to be a parent.

Scorpio

You're intense, passionate, and strong willed. You often try to impose your will on others, a trait that may serve your children when they're young, but can prove to be problematic as they get older. Like Aries, you're fearless, but you possess an endurance that Aries lacks and can plow your way through virtually any obstacle, any challenge. This trait serves as an example to your children to never give up in their pursuit of what they want.

Your passions are such that you're never *indifferent*. You live in a world of either/or, approval or disapproval, agreement or disagreement, right or wrong. While this trait drives home the importance of values and purpose, it can be challenging for children whose lives are more nuanced. Your ability to dig deeply for the bottom-line answers indicates that you will usually know what's going on in your children's lives.

The *Scorpio mom* places a high value on honesty. It's the foundation of who she is. So it's no surprise that she expects honesty from her children. Even though she herself is secretive, she won't tolerate secrets from her child. She respects their privacy, certainly, but if she suspects something is going on that needs parental intervention, she investigates until she uncovers the truth. She is a loving, devoted mother who is very protective of her kids. At times she may be too protective and strive to shield them from the outside world.

The *Scorpio dad* is as intense as the Scorpio mom. Unless he has a moon or rising in an air or fire sign, he may be just as much of a control freak too. He often has a magnificent talent or interest that he pursues because he's passionate about it and not because he expects to make money at it. He's a nurturing parent, particularly when it comes to his children's talents and abilities and the educational training that helps them navigate life successfully.

In 2012, your role as a parent may shift in unexpected directions. Due to Uranus's transit through fire sign Aries, your work situation may be somewhat erratic at times—or, at the least, unpredictable. This may actually give you more time to spend with your kids, or you may decide to launch a home-based business or to enter a field that gives you more control over your time. With your ruler, Pluto, in compatible earth sign Capricorn until 2024, you're in the power seat when it comes to communication, Scorpio, so start talking to your kids about everything that interests you.

Sagittarius

You're a wild card. There's a part of you who is always looking for the larger picture, the broader perspective, another part who believes you're always right, and yet another part who focuses on the future and the larger family of humanity. You can be very logical, but there's also a mystical element in your psyche that enables you to glimpse the future.

You dislike having your freedom restricted in any way, so you probably don't have a roll call of rules and regulations for your children. You're a loving parent, but expect your kids to find their own way, their own path.

Yet when they make mistakes, you may offer advice that makes you sound like a know-it-all. Your versatility and natural optimism are hallmarks of your parenting style.

The *Sagittarius mom* thinks big. When she suggests a family outing, it isn't just a trip to the next town for a picnic. It's a trip across country or to some far-flung corner of the world, and who cares if it's beyond the family budget? She wears many hats and excels in everything she does as long as she doesn't feel confined, limited, penned in. Her independent spirit radiates from her every pore, and her kids quickly learn to honor it. She offers her children broad guidelines and her own wisdom, but doesn't force her opinions on them.

The *Sagittarius dad* has a broad, sweeping vision about life, love, and the universe. He talks about it freely with his kids, never holding back. He is loving and devoted to his children, but because he expects big things from them may not be satisfied with what they achieve. He enjoys foreign travel and, given his financial situation, exposes his children to foreign places whenever he can. This man is always moving and has dozens of projects going on simultaneously, and his children learn early on that goals are attained through action.

In 2012, Uranus will be moving through Aries and the children area of your chart (which also governs creativity, romance, and enjoyment). This transit will bring about sudden, unexpected events—exciting, unpredictable events—concerning your kids. You'll have to think more outside the box to keep pace with them, but with your vivid imagination and ability to see the broader picture, it'll be a piece of cake for you.

Capricorn

You're the worker bee of the zodiac, industrious, disciplined, efficient, focused. You dislike inertia in others, so it's likely that your children aren't couch potatoes! You probably get them involved in sports when they're young and nurture whatever athletic abilities they have. They learn their work ethic from you and develop common sense, a trait they witness constantly in you.

Even when you were a kid, you had a mature air about you, and as you get older, that maturity is a kind of calm presence, a rock-solid dependability that your children come to expect. Never mind that you're a worrier, that even when you've prepared long and hard and have all the bases covered, you're certain you've forgotten something. Your kids rarely see that side of you. You love them unconditionally—that's what they see.

The *Capricorn mom* always seems to know what she's doing, when, with whom, and what route she's going to take to get there. She appears to be self-confident, certain about who she is, tough as nails. But as her children come to know her as a person separate from her role as mother, they discover she's not tough at all. She simply runs her home and family life as though it's a business and she's the CEO. Even if she has a career—and many Capricorn women do—she's totally devoted to her kids. She might be a little rigid with rules and regulations, but if so, learns that such excessive control results in outright rebellion.

The *Capricorn dad* is as diligent a worker as the Capricorn mom. He's got work ethic written all over him. He prides himself on being well prepared for just about anything, including being a parent. He either has the answers or will find them—for himself, for his children, or their friends. He excels at problem-solving. He can be dictatorial and bossy, but if his kids call him on it, he backs off. For a while, anyway. He's as completely devoted to his kids as he is to his career goals. In fact, one mirrors the other.

In 2012, the period from January 1 to June 11 should be spectacular for you and your kids. Expansive Jupiter is transiting fellow earth sign Taurus then, and everything you and your kids engage in together turns to gold. The Midas touch, Capricorn. In addition, Uranus's transit through Aries and your solar fourth house brings surprising, unexpected events into your home life. A move, perhaps? The birth of another child? Once Jupiter enters Gemini on June 11, where it will be until late June 2013, your daily work schedule will expand and change, and it may be a bit tougher to accommodate your kids. Make time.

Aquarius

You're such an original thinker, a visionary, that of course you apply these talents to parenting. Your household is really atypical. You might live on a boat, in a commune, in the suburbs, in an RV, or hey, maybe even on the space station. Your family structure isn't business as usual, either. But you aren't interested in typical. Everything you do is *different* from the status quo. You think in unique ways, way outside the box, and rarely if ever trust what authority tells you to believe. This ability to think and perceive in new ways is passed on to your children.

Your interests are vastly varied, and any causes in which you get involved are discussed with and communicated to your children. They learn early in life that mom or dad's interests and causes don't have to become theirs, but deserve respect. There probably aren't many rules in your family. Individuality is honored, encouraged, and thrives.

The *Aquarius mom* is a complete paradox. She's a peace-loving rebel who moves against the tide of the status quo, yet conforms when it suits her. She has the patience of a saint—until she doesn't—and can be more stubborn than Taurus unless it suits her purpose to bend with the wind. If her children are as eccentric as she is, then they have learned the value of individuality and probably share mom's love of freedom as well. Mom allows her kids the freedom to make their own decisions, revels in their achievements, and never lets them down.

The *Aquarius dad* considers his family—partner, kids, animals and orphans of all sizes and shapes—to be his sanctuary. Even if he seems undemonstrative and emotionally remote at times, his love for his kids runs deep. He takes every opportunity to expose them to everything that interests him, from ancient sites like Stonehenge and the Nazca lines to books on what the future may look like in a century. If he's a movie buff, his children are exposed to movies at a young age. If he's a traveler, his kids will be well traveled. He's terrific at sharing his knowledge, expertise, and curiosity.

From June 11 to late June 2013, you're in for a treat as a parent. You'll be watching your children's lives expand in unprecedented ways. Whether they're toddlers or adults, you'll delight in what they're learning about themselves and their world. With Uranus transiting compatible fire sign Aries, your communication skills will be sharp, and your conscious mind will be innovative.

Pisces

Your wonderful imagination and remarkable intuition prove valuable in your parenting style. Your imagination enables you to enter the world of your children with ease and playful joy. Your intuition enables you to stay attuned to their emotions even if they don't discuss what they're feeling. Pisces individuals with highly developed gifts—psychics—may have to take a break now and then from parenting just to find their own centers. It's too easy for this type to be overwhelmed with what their kids are feeling.

At times you fluctuate between rigid left-brain logic and that softer intuitive certainty that you're doing the right thing. Try not to set down rules and restrictions when you're feeling like this. Moodiness and ambivalence can cause you to backtrack from your own rules. Guard against being a sucker for a sob story.

The *Pisces mom* often has a strong psychic connection to her children. If they have been together in past lives, chances are she has a grasp on which lives and how everyone's respective roles played out then. She's able to understand what they're feeling even when they're clueless. She is rarely dogmatic with her children, and any household rules she lays down are probably for the sake of safety—and her own peace of mind. Her love for her kids is bottomless. They're her greatest joy, and she just keeps on giving and giving.

The *Pisces dad* is a great listener. His self-containment, gentleness, quiet strength, and the full attention he gives his kids are enviable qualities that enable him to forge tight bonds with his offspring. He encourages and supports his children's artistic interests and may have artistic or musical talent himself. Like his female counterpart, he must learn to balance the demands of his inner life with his responsibilities in the outer world.

2012 should bring some surprises in how you parent and how you view your children. With Neptune in your sign from February 3 onward, your whole parenting approach may become more spiritual, creative, imaginative. Your own intuition is enhanced too during this fourteen-year transit, so you'll be in closer communication with your kids on an unspoken level, able to grasp their personal issues and concerns in a deeper way.

Kids of the Zodiac

Now that we've looked at adults and their parenting styles, let's explore the kids of the zodiac.

Aries

She's the kid who is off by herself, exploring fields and meadows for unusual bugs. Or she's the fearless teen who leaps into a rushing river to rescue a kitten stranded on a rock. Or on the family camping trip where the matches and lighter fluid have been left behind, she's the one who makes a fire by rubbing sticks together or using a magnifying glass to amplify the sunlight. Inventive, independent, entrepreneurial: welcome to the world of the Aries child. And whether she's a toddler or an adult, high drama and action swirl around her.

Taurus

He's the loner. Or he has a small group of friends with whom he hangs out. But whether it's his friends or his family, no one really knows him. Like an iceberg, nine tenths of his personality is hidden. He only shows what he wants you to know. Yes, these still waters run deep. So much goes on inside his head as he figures out where he belongs in the scheme of things that he wouldn't have a clue where to begin verbalizing any of it. So he nurtures his creative gifts, enjoys the sensual pleasures of physical existence, and moves forward at his own pace, patient, certain that the answers will come to him, from somewhere, when he needs them.

Gemini

If Taurus is the loner, she's the social butterfly, flitting from one person to another, one event to the next, and along the way she's passing on what she has learned, what she suspects, what she believes. She's impatient, quick, dexterous. Her life is propelled by a single burning question: *why?* Everything she does, every connection she makes, everyone she knows and loves serves to answer that question. Somehow. In some way. Forget trying to pigeonhole your Gemini child. It just won't happen. When she's young, provide her with an environment where she can learn and explore at her own pace. Nurture her self-confidence and her belief in herself. With those tools, she's well equipped for her journey out into the larger world.

Cancer

She's a tough one to figure out. She feels her way through life, but you may never know about it. She'll talk if she's in the mood, but otherwise nothing and no one will prod her into an explanation about her feelings. As a parent, you sort of have to divine your way through this kid's childhood and beyond. She needs roots. She needs to feel she's an integral part of the family and is appreciated. Much of her life as an adult is based on her childhood memories—the smells and sights and emotions she was feeling at a particular time. If her childhood is happy and secure, then she grows into a happy, secure adult.

Leo

The Leo child is like his own tribe. From the time he's very young, he has dozens of friends and they all hang out at his place. Even as he gets older, his friends are eager to spend time with him, and some of them are orphans and strays attracted by his innate generosity and compassion. Like fellow fire sign Aries, the Leo child is basically fearless. He accepts every dare and takes risks that would leave other kids gasping in awe. Most Leo kids enjoy the company of animals, and their homes tend to have a lot of pets.

Virgo

She's impatient, wants everything yesterday, and is graced with abundant energy. She has questions about everything and is so eager to learn that in the right environment, she explores until she drops from exhaustion. Like Cancer, she can be moody, but these swings usually occur when she doesn't understand something. Her restless mind gnaws away at the puzzle, dissecting it, scrutinizing the details, the minutiae, until she gets it. She has enormous compassion, a quality that is evident at a very young age, and her ability to connect with people is as easy for her as connecting disparate bits of information is for a Gemini. Even when young, Virgo kids show discernment. They may be picky about what they eat, read, or watch on TV.

Libra

The Libra child can be found listening to music in the comfort of his own room, connecting with friends on Facebook and MySpace, or hanging out with friends in some familiar and pretty spot. He isn't the type to play touch football (unless he's got a lot of fire or earth in his chart) or hunt for bugs under rocks or dissect frogs in the lab. As a youngster, the Libra child may have an imaginary playmate or one special friend in whom he confides. He's loyal to his friends, sometimes to a fault, so any friends he has as a youngster are probably going to be friends for life.

Scorpio

She's distinctive in some way—physically, mentally, intuitively. She has fixed opinions even as a youngster, as if she came into life with a particular agenda or belief system. She feels deeply, of course, one of the trademarks of this sign, and the intensity of her emotions may lead to sudden outbursts if her feelings are hurt or she doesn't get what she wants. She flourishes in an environment that is varied and rich, where she can explore her creative abilities. She won't always be forthright about what's going on inside of her, but if you simply come out and ask her, her response may surprise you. She's wiser than her years.

Sagittarius

This kid is Mr. Popularity, and it's evident from the time he's old enough to crawl and interact. He's vivacious and optimistic and makes other people feel good about themselves. It makes him a people magnet. He can be opinionated, though, and blunt. He doesn't think about what he's going to say before he says it. He just blurts it out, a tendency that can be disconcerting to people who aren't accustomed to it. But he needs the freedom to express himself and to know it's okay to defend what he believes. Rules and structure are a good idea as he's growing up. He probably has a fondness for animals, not surprising for a sign symbolized by a figure that is half human, half horse!

Capricorn

From the time she utters her first word, she's as comfortable being and conversing with adults as she is with her peers. Sometimes she has a seriousness about her that is usually evident in her eyes, in the way she watches and appraises you, sizing you up for who knows what reason. Other times, she can be as wild and playful as any other child. Even then, though, her organizational skills are evident, and she can be bossy, no question about it. She is infinitely patient, intent on achieving her goal, whatever it might be.

Aquarius

To this kid, all people truly are equal, so his friends span the racial and socio-economic spectrum. He's an extrovert, eager to know what makes other people tick, what motivates them, but he's also perfectly happy when he's by himself. His mind is as busy as a Gemini's, but in a much different way. Where a Gemini child collects trivia and information, the Aquarian child is immersed in the stuff of the universe. Although he enjoys people and gets involved in all sorts of groups, he's not a follower and will always defend not only his opinions, but his right to have those opinions.

Pisces

She doesn't need many rules. She's so sensitive to her environment and to the people who inhabit it that a cross look from mom or dad keeps her in line. She's a dreamer, this one, whose imagination soars through time and space with the ease of a bird through sunlight. If her intuitive gifts are allowed to develop, this child can become a genuine medium, clairvoyant, mystic, healer. Her strong creative drive manifests itself early.

CHAPTER 6

Your Finances in 2012

Beliefs

Money and relationships are probably the trickiest areas for most of us to navigate successfully. But if we create our realities from the inside out, then in these two areas it's vitally important that we understand our beliefs.

Let's take a closer look. Here are some commonly held negative beliefs about money and relationships. Do you hold any of these?

- Money is the root of all evil
- My relationships never turn out
- Money is nonspiritual
- True love is rare
- The rich have major problems in their lives
- Marriage is a joke
- Money corrupts
- I'm not worthy of (fill in the blank)
- If you have too much money, you have to worry about losing it

You get the idea here. Many of these beliefs we've adopted from family and peers and have held on to them because they're comfortable, we believe they're true, or because we don't even realize we believe them!

So if you're not satisfied with what you're earning, start monitoring how you think about money. Any time you find yourself thinking a negative thought about money, turn the thought around by thinking something more positive. Also, read *Money and the Law of Attraction* by Esther and Jerry Hicks and *You Can Heal Your Life* by Louise Hay.

Now let's take a look at how you can maximize your earning potential in 2012.

Jupiter

From chapter 2, we know that Jupiter represents luck, expansion, success, prosperity, growth, creativity, spiritual interests, higher education, and the law. It also governs publishing, overseas travel, and foreign countries and any of our dealings with them. But for the purpose of this chapter, we're going to focus on Jupiter's impact on our money for 2012.

This year, Jupiter transits two signs. From January 1 to June 11, it's moving through earth sign Taurus. From June 11, 2012, to June 25, 2013, it's moving through air sign Gemini. It will be retrograde in Gemini between October 14, 2012, and January 30, 2013. A Jupiter retrograde simply means that planet isn't functioning at full capacity.

Let's see how these two Jupiter transits this year impact your sun sign.

Jupiter in 2012 and Its Impact on Your Sun Sign

Aries

Jupiter's transit of Taurus, through your solar second house, began in early June 2011, and initially you may have been spending more money than usual. But as the transit stabilized, your income is likely to have expanded in some way. That trend will continue this year, until June 11.

Your second house doesn't just govern your income, but also your values, personal debt, giving and receiving, jewelry, possessions (particularly those that are valuable), reverses in finances, your earning and spending capacity. And with Jupiter in this house, in stable, dependable Taurus, you may be looking for long-term stable investments that will increase your profit and minimize your risk.

If you dislike your job, i.e., the way you earn your daily bread, then Jupiter should bring plenty of new options and opportunities for expansion. You may decide to return to school to update your skills and knowledge, may decide to go to college or graduate school, or may expand your earning possibilities to overseas markets. Since Jupiter governs publishing, law, and higher education, any of these areas are possibilities for increasing your earning capacity.

Once Jupiter enters Gemini for a year-long transit, you'll feel more comfortable because Gemini is compatible with your fire-sign sun. In fact, this transit should be terrific for you, expanding all the areas governed by the third house and Gemini: communication, your conscious mind, daily activities, siblings, short-distance travel. You may write that book you've had in your head for years, build a Web site, start a blog. More frequent travel could be part of your daily activities—car pools, a longer commute. However this transit manifests for you, Jupiter brings luck and expansion, and you, ever innovative, turn it into a potential cash cow.

Taurus

In early June of 2011, Jupiter entered your sign, Taurus, and suddenly life took on a whole new dimension. The trend of expansion and luck that started with that transit continues until June 11 of this year. Whenever Jupiter transits your sign, the ramifications are big—you're in the right place at the right time, luck is your new best friend, your options and opportunities broaden.

Sometimes when Jupiter initially enters your sign, it seems that more money is going out than is coming in. But eventually your net worth rises, you land the dream job, your investments begin to pay off. You tend to be conservative with money, but if there's something you really want, don't hesitate to buy it if you can pay cash for it. You want to avoid credit-card debt during this transit and the one coming up between June 11, 2011, and June 25, 2013. Conserve your resources, but don't be stingy and don't do it out of fear.

When Jupiter enters Gemini on June 11, you're in for another treat. It will be transiting your solar second house of money, so it's likely that your earning capacity will rise, your values will broaden, your opportunities for self-improvement will increase. Jupiter's transits are nearly always fortunate, but there's a risk with excess in some area. When you see a sharp increase in your income, follow your parents' advice—sock some of it away. But again, don't do it out of fear. Any action taken from a basis of fear is likely to attract circumstances that will cause real fear.

Gemini

During Jupiter's transit of Taurus between January 1 and June 11, your unconscious is easier for you to delve into. Dream work, meditation, yoga, or some other kind of mind/body activity benefits you. In fact, you may discover that your dreams hold important information that will help you with issues or concerns that you have. Ideas come to you through dreams and meditations. Consider a past-life regression with a qualified therapist. Everything you learn during this transit is creative fodder, Gemini, and is preparing the way for Jupiter's transit through your sign between June 11, 2012, and June 25, 2013.

Jupiter transits your sign just once every twelve years. So look back to 2000 for hints about what sorts of experiences you may have during this year-long transit. What were your finances like that year? Did you land a new job that paid more? Did you move into a better neighborhood, a larger house? Did you take unnecessary financial risks? All of these areas are possibilities this year.

One thing you definitely want to avoid during this transit is gambling or speculating with your money. Because Jupiter can be excessive, you may feel cocky, as if you can do no wrong. It's smarter to save and to invest in things that further your education, skills, and future.

Cancer

Since last June, Jupiter has been moving through Taurus and your solar eleventh house, a transit that continues until June 11 of this year. This brings an expansion to your social contacts, your wishes and dreams, and opportunities to promote and publicize your work or product or that of your company. Since this transit forms a beautiful angle to your sun sign, other areas of your life will benefit as well, and one of them is your finances.

You might decide, for example, to join an investment group that shares ideas about which stocks or bonds to buy. Or you and a group of friends may invest in rental property or even buy a place together, fix it up, and then sell it for a handsome profit. Any dealing with real estate and homes is a nonbrainer for you, Cancer. It's what you enjoy doing.

Between June 11, 2012, and June 25, 2013, Jupiter will transit Gemini, through your solar twelfth house. It makes it easier for you to delve into your own unconscious, to recall your dreams. If you don't meditate yet, then this transit presents the opportunity to do so. You may discover moneymaking ideas through meditations and dream recall. You may start a blog or build a Web site and find an innovative technique for making money in this way. Use this transit to find out who you are, Cancer. Self-knowledge can lead to a greater understanding about how the universe works, and such knowledge can lead to greater financial stability and more money.

Leo

Jupiter entered Taurus and your career area in June 2011 and won't leave it until June 11, 2012. That gives you six months this year to enjoy the professional expansion—and thus, the financial expansion—of this transit. The last time Jupiter touched this area of your chart was twelve years ago, so look back to 2000 for clues about how the last six months of this transit may unfold for you.

If you would like to change jobs or careers, then it could happen during this transit. Equally possible? Your responsibilities, job description, and salary increase substantially, you launch your own business, sell a book, work overseas. Regardless of the specifics, you will have plenty of opportunities to do what you do best, Leo—shine!

Between June 11, 2012, and June 25, 2013, Jupiter transits compatible air sign Gemini and your solar eleventh house. This transit not only stimulates your social life, but brings you into a whole new sphere of individuals who help you to attain your dreams, whatever they may be. Any groups you join may also prove to be helpful financially.

With Jupiter in Gemini, your communication skills—which aren't too shabby to begin with!—really sharpen. Your mind becomes a steel trap, and you're able to snap out facts, figures, statistics that astound even you. You learn to make money using your ability to communicate and connect with others.

Virgo

When Jupiter entered fellow earth sign Taurus last June, your income probably increased, and that trend will continue until June 11 of this year. It's possible that your work or a quest of some sort takes you overseas, and whatever you learn and experience changes your fundamental beliefs about money. You may suddenly realize, for example, that you're worthy of being rich. Or that your book is just as good as anything on the market and will find the right publisher. In other words, your inner world is shifting, becoming more certain, stronger. As that happens, your life in the outer world will change accordingly.

If you're a writer, this transit expands your publishing opportunities, could bring about significant foreign sales, and makes it easier, generally, to sell what you write. Regardless of what profession you're in, your business could expand to overseas markets. Other possibilities: you head off to college or graduate school, go to law school, or even move overseas.

Once Jupiter enters Gemini and the career area of your chart, you're in for an exciting time. The specifics of this transit vary for each of us, but here are some possibilities: you switch jobs/careers and land something with a larger salary; you work overseas; you sell your novel or screenplay. One way or another, the professional and financial payoff for you is excellent.

Libra

With Jupiter in Taurus until June 11, you and/or your partner may be accruing items like art and jewelry for investments, could delve more deeply into esoteric subjects like ghosts, past lives, communication with the dead, or may combine your resources in some way. Whatever it is, it pays off financially. Let's say that you and your partner have separate homes, then during this transit you may decide to sell one place and move in together. This transit should bring breaks with mortgages, loans, taxes, and insurance.

When Jupiter transits fellow air sign Gemini between June 11, 2012, and June 25, 2013, you have a wonderful opportunity to explore your worldview and spiritual beliefs and to divest yourself of any that are holding you back from achieving your financial goals. The exploration may come through opportunities for foreign travel, to write a book on whatever seizes your passions, or to even go to graduate school to further your skills.

Scorpio

With Jupiter transiting Taurus, your opposite sign, for six months this year, you and your partner may launch a business together, or you may find a business partner for a venture you've had in mind. By combining talents and resources, your income increases, your self-confidence benefits, and you discover that in order to live the way you want, it's important to do what you love.

Air signs aren't compatible with your water-sign sun. However, there's much to learn from this transit—namely, never hesitate to communicate what you believe and why. Don't hide your wisdom; share it with others. On a mundane level, this transit may increase your partner's income, and the two of you may find investments with large payoffs. Your joint finances benefit tremendously.

The trick with this transit is to share—not just money, but resources, time, energy. If you do that, if you go with Jupiter's flow, you'll benefit greatly from everything this planet has to offer.

Sagittarius

Since Jupiter started transiting Taurus in June 2011, your daily work schedule has been exploding like crazy. So much to do, so little time, but yes, you're having fun! Expect that trend to continue until June 11 of this year. If you work out of your home, then it's possible you add a room onto the house or expand your home to accommodate your office. If you work a regular job, then your schedule keeps growing by leaps and bounds until you feel as if you're all over the place. But it suits you. If you own your own business, then you may add more employees or expand your product/services to overseas markets.

Between June 11, 2012, and June 25, 2013, Jupiter transits Gemini, your opposite sign. This transit augurs well for any joint business venture—with your romantic partner or a business partner or both! By pooling talents and resources, anything done in partnership can pay off handsomely. If you're reading this and thinking that you don't have a partner—either romantic or business—don't fret about it. Chances are good that before this transit ends, you'll have both!

Capricorn

Since June 2011, you've been enjoying Jupiter's transit through fellow earth sign Taurus, in your solar fifth house. It is expanding all your creative ventures, your muse is undoubtedly in attendance 24/7, and some days the ideas flow so fast you forget them before you can find a pen or get to your computer to write them down. This trend continues until June 11. So enjoy it while it lasts, and have faith that your creativity is going to increase your bank account!

Jupiter's transit through Gemini and your solar sixth house lasts from June 11, 2012, to June 25, 2013. Buckle up for the wild ride, Capricorn. This transit should expand your daily work routine and schedule to the point where it's bursting at the proverbial seams. You'll have to be more organized than usual during this transit, but the potential benefits in terms of income can be great. With greater responsibility comes a salary boost. With a salary boost comes greater security for you. Even more important, though, is that with this expansion you can build stronger professional goals.

Aquarius

Jupiter has been transiting Taurus and your solar fourth house since June of 2011 and will be there until June 11 of this year. This transit should expand everything to do with your home, family, and the fundamentals of your life. A birth is a possibility. Or you may move into a larger home or expand the home where you currently live. One of your parents may move in with you. Since the fourth house also governs real estate, it's possible that you buy property as an investment.

Between June 11, 2012, and June 25, 2013, Jupiter transits fellow air sign Gemini in the creativity sector of your chart. It's your ticket, Aquarius. The more creative you are, the greater your earning capacity. You may get involved in a creative venture with one of your kids or a new romantic interest, and because it's done from a basis of pure joy, it has a positive effect on your finances.

Pisces

Since June 2011, Jupiter in Taurus, an earth sign compatible with your water-sign sun, has been transiting your solar third house, and it continues this year until June 11. During this period, your communication skills sharpen your conscious mind expands. You suddenly understand how to make money from, well, talking and writing. A blog, your Web site, magazine articles, a book: any of these venues is possible. The Taurus part of the equation helps to ground your imagination, to bring your ideas into the practical daily world.

From June 11, 2012, to June 25, 2013, Jupiter transits your solar fourth house and Gemini. This transit brings luck and expansion to your home life. In terms of finances, you may start working out of your home, doing something you love, and the money follows. Or perhaps you move to a different city or area where your opportunities for employment are better, where your family is happier, where conditions are more conducive to an increase in your income. Since Jupiter is coruler of your sun sign, its transits are nearly always significant for you in some way.

CHAPTER 7

The Structures in Our Lives

Saturn takes two and a half years to go through a sign, so its effects tend to unfold more slowly than those of the moon, which changes signs about every two and a half days. This planet governs the rules and parameters of physical life and represents responsibility, structure, discipline, limitations and delays, obedience, authority, the building of foundations. So by its transit we are confronted, challenged, or helped by Saturn, depending on the angle it makes to our sun signs.

With Saturn occupying two signs this year, the end of Libra and the beginning of Scorpio (which lasts until December 2014), we're all called upon this year to meet our obligations and responsibilities in two different areas. So let's take a closer look at how Saturn's transits in 2012 impact your sun sign.

Aries

Saturn has been opposite your sun sign since October 2009 and finally leaves Libra on October 5 of this year. During this transit, you're learning to structure your personal and professional partnerships and are deepening your understanding of team work and cooperative living. This last part may not be an easy lesson for a spirit as independent as yours, but learn you will. Chances are that your partner—business or romantic—may have met with some restrictions or delays during this transit that have in turn impacted you in some way.

The Saturn opposition to your sun can be a discouraging time—if you let it. You may feel drained physically, so it's important to have a regular exercise routine. It's also important to maintain contact with friends, family, and other people you love. Try not to resist things that are happening to you. Learn to go with the flow.

Once Saturn enters Scorpio, you feel a distinct relief. A weight has been lifted. During this transit, which lasts until December 2014, you'll learn how to accept other people's values, even when those values aren't in line with your own. It may be more difficult to obtain mortgages and loans during this transit, or sources of income you have depended on may dry up. So it's important that you become as self-sufficient as possible before this transit begins.

Taurus

During Saturn's transit through Libra and your solar sixth house, your daily work responsibility has undoubtedly increased. You may be working longer hours, too, but if you're doing something you love and are getting paid more for your efforts, then it certainly isn't a burden. Due to other demands on your time, you're probably learning how to maximize the time you have and are becoming more organized about your daily work schedule. If you're self-employed, then organization and good time use are vital tools.

Once Saturn enters Scorpio and your solar seventh house, you may be dealing with some of the same issues that Aries dealt with during Saturn's transit through Libra. If you allow this transit—an opposition to your sun—to discourage you, if you resist change, then the transit becomes much more difficult. The important lessons with this transit are about learning to cooperate with partners—business and romantic—and to allow relationships that no longer work to fall out of your experience.

Gemini

Saturn's transit through fellow air sign Libra should be quite productive for you, Gemini. Saturn is now forming a harmonious angle with your sun, strengthening your assets, enabling you to find the proper structures for your creative projects, relationships, your life! This transit may bring professional recognition of some kind and a solid boost in your career and creative output. During this transit, it's smart to establish and/or maintain an exercise routine. Although your health should be fine during this transit, you're building up stamina for times when you may have more stress in your life—like during the Saturn opposition to your sun. This transit also helps you to build solid relationships with your children and to find grounded venues of enjoyment.

Once Saturn enters Scorpio and your solar sixth house, your daily work schedule may have to be revamped. More responsibility will bring a greater need for organization and efficient use of your time. If you're self-employed, Saturn in Scorpio will prompt you to always look at the absolute bottom line—costs in terms of money, time, energy, and resources. Be sure to tend to your health during this transit too. Keep exercising and eating responsibly, and stay away from fad diets.

Cancer

As Saturn transits Libra and your solar fourth house, you're learning to balance responsibilities of home and career. This requires you to be more organized and use your time more efficiently. You may have to cubbyhole your life, with an emphasis on family on certain days and an emphasis on career/work on other days. You tend to go with the flow more than other signs, so it's important that you keep doing that. Any time you feel yourself resisting something that's happening, try to understand why and correct it. If you don't know why you feel resistance, then simply reach for a better thought and feeling.

Once Saturn enters fellow water sign Scorpio and forms a beneficial angle to your sun, you're a much happier camper. This transit helps you to solidify all creative projects. Instead of just writing screenplays, for instance, you begin selling what you write. You discover great depth in your own creativity, your relationship with your children, in romance, and in what you do for fun and enjoyment. Maintain an exercise program during this transit, so that when Saturn enters Sagittarius in late December 2014, your physical strength is at a peak.

Leo

Saturn in Libra forms a beneficial angle to your sun, so you're benefiting from this transit. Your communication skills find a proper venue for expression. A book? Blog? Web site? Radio or TV? Whatever it is, you dazzle with your language skills and win accolades from friends, family, peers. If you move during this transit, the place has to be exactly right for you—and your family. Preferably, it should be in the thick of things—theater, restaurants, bookstores. During this transit, you're enormously productive too and enjoy the work.

Once Saturn enters Scorpio and your fourth house, Saturn is opposed to your career area. This transit indicates that you'll have to learn how to reasonably balance your home and work responsibilities. You'll be aware of the absolute bottom line too, in just about everything—with your family, kids, parents, your family's budget. Your intuition should deepen appreciably, and it will be wise to follow any hunches you have.

Virgo

During Saturn's transit through Libra and your solar second house, your financial earnings may be restricted in some way. Or you find the proper structure for your finances through investments, for example, or a pension plan. You may feel that your values are somehow holding you back, preventing you from doing something or going somewhere. The truth is that you're the only one holding you back. During this transit, you're supposed to learn how to conserve your financial resources and to live within a budget.

When Saturn enters compatible water sign Scorpio on October 5, your relief will be palpable. During this transit, with Saturn forming a beneficial angle to your sun, you'll be in a very good position to bolster your communication skills, find a neighborhood that fits your specific criteria, return to school to enhance your skills. Your conscious mind will be able to take abstract ideas and turn them into practical tools. This transit lasts until December 2014.

Libra

Whenever Saturn conjuncts or opposes your sun sign, it's considered to be a major transit—challenging, but filled with potential. During this transit, you divest yourself of relationships and situations that no longer work or which aren't in your best interest. You may change jobs, get divorced or married, or have to provide support for one of your parents. There can be delays, or your freedom is restricted in some way, but the purpose is to slow down your life so that you tend to what is personal and immediate.

Sometimes Saturn conjunct your sun brings about external events that turn your life in a different direction. The more resistance you offer, the more difficult it is. So it's important to learn to go with the flow.

With Saturn's transit through Scorpio and your solar second house from October 5, 2012, to late December 2014, you learn how to conserve your financial resources, how to budget, how to save. If there's a decrease in your earnings during this transit, try not to fret about it. Your intuition should increase. It's the small voice whispering in the back of your mind to go here, do that, try this. Follow its guidance.

Scorpio

During Saturn's transit through Libra and your solar twelfth house, you're being asked to funnel your discoveries about your own psyche and unconscious into some sort of structure. This transit would be a great time to go through therapy, to take up yoga or some other mind/body discipline, and to start meditating, if you don't already. The twelfth house governs not only the personal unconscious, but past lives, institutions, and everything that is hidden. So with Saturn here, you may run into people you have known in previous lives, will have greater access to your dreams and information that comes to you through meditation, and may have contact with institutions like hospitals and nursing homes, even prisons. This doesn't mean *you* will be institutionalized, but that someone you know may be.

Once Saturn enters your sign, you may feel that your freedom of movement is restricted in some way. It could be due to increased responsibility in some area of your life—career, family, work, no telling. The last time Saturn conjuncted your sun was about twenty-nine to thirty years ago. If you're old enough, look back to that time and remember what was going on in your life. Big changes? How? In what areas? One thing you'll have to do is divest yourself of relationships and situations that aren't in your best interest. You may change jobs, move, get married or divorced. Regardless of the specifics, offer no resistance to events. Go with the flow.

Sagittarius

Saturn's transit through Libra forms a beneficial angle to your sun. It brings structure and solidity to your friendships and wishes and dreams. It actually should be easier to attain your dreams during this transit, particularly if you have laid the groundwork and met your obligations and responsibilities to others. If you don't attain your dreams during this transit, then before it ends you'll have a clearer grasp of what you need to clear out of your life to make room for the attainment of these dreams. Saturn's transit through Scorpio and your solar twelfth house should give you the opportunity to do that.

Saturn transits Scorpio from October 5, 2012, to late December 2014. During this period, you benefit from therapy, meditation, yoga, or any other mind/body discipline. Your dreams can be a source of information and insights. Since the twelfth house represents institutions—prisons, hospitals, nursing homes—it's possible that you have more contact than usual with these places. Basically, this transit enables you to clear your life of what no longer works—relationships, situations, belief systems.

Capricorn

Saturn's transit through Libra and your career area is a major transit that could solidify your professional life and bring recognition from peers and bosses. You may assume more responsibility during this period and work longer hours, and there could be some delays or restrictions on your freedom to come and go as you please. Hard work has never bothered you, especially if you're compensated fairly for it. If you're self-employed, then this transit enables you to solidify your business, client base and income.

During Saturn's transit through compatible water sign

Scorpio and your solar eleventh house, you'll be more in your element. Your friendships and any groups to which you belong will be helpful in achieving your dreams and goals. It's important that you learn how to work with groups and to grasp what group dynamics are in a work situation.

Aquarius

During Saturn's transit through fellow air sign Libra and your solar ninth house, you benefit in a major way. This transit solidifies your worldview and spiritual beliefs and enables you to find the right structure for expressing these beliefs. The ninth house also governs higher education, overseas travel, and foreign cultures, countries, and people, so any foreign travel you do will be structured in some way to fit your goals or needs. If you're in a business that sells products overseas, this transit helps to create a good foundation in overseas markets.

Saturn's transit through Scorpio and your solar tenth house brings increased responsibility in your career, longer hours, perhaps recognition by peers and bosses. It could bring about a promotion, or you may decide to launch your own business. If it's the latter, you're going to love the freedom even if it means a lot of hard work and long hours.

Pisces

During Saturn's transit through Libra and your solar eighth house, your access to funds that have been available previously may be restricted or denied you. If you apply for a mortgage or loan, for example, it may be difficult obtaining it. Your partner's income may take a hit. With Saturn here, you're urged to conserve your resources—money, time, energy. This transit helps you to channel your enormous imagination and intuitive ability.

During Saturn's transit through fellow water sign Scorpio and your solar ninth house, you'll benefit from a positive angle that Saturn makes to your sun. This transit should enable you to explore your worldview and spiritual beliefs in a structured way. You may, for instance, travel overseas to various sacred sites on some sort of spiritual quest. Or you may take courses or workshops in metaphysical areas to explore your intuition or alternative healing methods. This transit lasts from October 5, 2012, to late December 2014.

Saturn in Your Birth Chart

Wherever Saturn appears in your birth chart indicates an area where you will learn lessons in this lifetime. It also indicates life issues you may have brought in from previous lives. Saturn's lessons can be harsh, but it teaches us through experience what we need in order to grow and evolve and what our souls intend to accomplish in this life. It shows us our limitations, teaches us the rules of the game. Without it, our lives would be chaos. Individuals with well-aspected Saturns in their birth charts—the angles other planets make to it—have a practical outlook. With a poorly aspect Saturn, growth may be restricted or limited in some way, and the person's outlook could be rigid.

The sign that Saturn occupies shows how we handle obstacles in our lives, deal with authority, and cope with serious issues. The house placement in your natal chart indicates the area of your life that's affected. If you have Saturn in your tenth house, for example, then your career ambition is one of the driving forces in your life, and you'll work tirelessly to succeed. If your Saturn is in Leo, you may need to learn that it isn't all about just *you* and your career.

Every twenty-eight to thirty years, we experience a Saturn return, when transiting Saturn returns to the place it occupied at our birth. The first return, around the age of twenty-nine, brings major life transitions—we get married or divorced, start a family, move, begin a career. The second return, between the ages of fifty-eight and sixty, is considered to be the harvest. We experience major events—retirement, our kids have left home, we downsize, move, inherit money.

Whenever a Saturn transit hits a natal planet, that period should be navigated carefully, with understanding of what's required of you. Saturn takes about twenty-nine years to circle the zodiac. It entered Libra in late October 2009, retrograded from January 13 to May 29, 2010, then entered Libra again on July 22, 2010, and will be there until October 5, 2012. Then it enters Scorpio for a run of about two and a half years.

Natal Saturn in Aries

Your impetuosity and rashness need to be tempered somewhat, so that you think before you act. You consistently encounter circumstances that force you to develop patience and initiative. If you push against these circumstances, then setbacks occur. With Saturn, you can't take shortcuts. This position of Saturn urges you to develop resourcefulness and discipline and to complete what you start. Once you learn these lessons, you're capable of innovative and unique creations.

The downside with this placement is that you're prone to defensiveness and a kind of self-centered attitude that puts people off. Tact and diplomacy will take you farther and, in the end, may be one of the lessons you're here to learn.

Natal Saturn in Taurus

One of your lessons in this lifetime is to develop persistence and resoluteness, an unshakeable belief in yourself and your talents. This belief helps you to win material security and comfort through hard work, discipline, and perseverance. You may not be the fastest-moving person in the world, but you hang in there long after the competition has bitten the dust.

It behooves you to learn how to handle money and your finances. You tend to be frugal even when you don't have to be, but this frugality may become one of your hobbies. You might, for example, hit garage sales, flea markets, any spot where secondhand goods are sold, and could develop a business around it. On the other hand, if this frugality turns to miserliness, you may want to rethink your attitudes and beliefs about money. The downside is a preoccupation with materialism.

Natal Saturn in Gemini

Since Saturn corules air sign Aquarius and is exalted in air sign Libra, it's pretty comfortable in air sign Gemini. It brings discipline and structure to your mental process and suggests that part of what you're here to learn is how to think through problems logically, working them out in detail so that your solutions are practical. Saturn here may restrict a free flowing expression of ideas, but once you've learned to channel your ideas in a pragmatic way, perhaps through writing or some sort of group activity, you reap the benefits. In other words, it's not enough to have a great idea. How can the idea be put into practice to benefit not only you, but others?

Communication is important to you, but it has to be organized, structured in some way, honest, and dependable. That may be one of the lessons you're here to learn. Downside? If you don't do the grunt work this placement demands, your obstacles multiply.

Natal Saturn in Cancer

This placement may restrict your intuitive gifts and your emotions. Or it could provide the proper structure for expressing both. It depends on how you use your conscious desires and intent to create your life. It depends, too, on your deepest beliefs. Do you believe we have free will or that life is somehow scripted, destined? Are events random, or do they rise from some hidden quantum order? While your crablike tenacity helps you to navigate successfully through obstacles, Saturn here urges you to confront obstacles head on, to reveal what's in your heart, and to channel your intuitive talents in a practical, focused way.

Your home and family are important to you. But strive not to impose so many restrictions in this area that the people who are closest to you—and you yourself—feel suffocated.

Natal Saturn in Leo

This placement is all about power and recognition. The desire for both, however, takes many forms. At one extreme, it results in a need to control your environment and everyone inside of it and a hungry ambition that blinds you to everything else. At the other extreme, this placement results in structures that help you to channel your ambition in a constructive, directed way. This placement also suggests that your ego and need for recognition can be your worst enemies, so be aware of that tendency and do whatever you can to mitigate it.

For Boomers born with this configuration, there can be multiple setbacks that prompt you to work harder, put in longer hours, meet all your obligations—and then some. Eventually, though, if you learn patience and resilience, you succeed. You achieve your goals. Cooperative endeavors are beneficial with this placement, i.e., anything in the professional arena in which you have partners, where you're a team player, where your voice is just one among many.

Natal Saturn in Virgo

The tendency with this placement is that you're such a perfectionist you get bogged down in details. You walk into someone else's house, for example, and immediately notice streaks on the cabinets that scream for a dose of Pledge. Or you enter your son's apartment and are overwhelmed by the disorder and chaos. But if you can direct this tendency toward your work and career, you can handle anything, manifest anything, and perform a service that helps many people understand their roles in this lifetime. It's simply a matter of separating the essential from the inconsequential.

Your intuition is highly developed, just waiting for you to pay attention, to connect all the dots. Find humor in everything you do. Take breaks from work. Treat yourself to a trip to Paris or some other far-flung corner of the globe. Learn to revel in your experiences.

Natal Saturn in Libra

Your lesson this time around is to learn the value of cooperation. The success of any partnership, personal or business, involves the ability to compromise. What can you live with to keep the peace? How much can you surrender without giving away your personal power? Your values? Karma is part and parcel of your most intimate relationships, and the sooner you recognize that, the better off you are. The question, though, is how do you recognize which relationships are karmic and which ones are just the luck (or misfortune) of the draw? Well, bottom line, it's about what you feel when in the presence of another person. It comes down to resonance.

The dark side of this placement is a tendency to surrender too much in the hope that you can keep the peace. The real key here is the ability to forgive and forget and move on.

Natal Saturn in Scorpio

In your work, you're as much of a perfectionist as Saturn in Virgo. But in everything else, you're pure Scorpio—after the bottom line, the absolute truth, the real deal. You're secretive in the way you handle stress and difficulties of any kind and must learn how to deal with this stuff in a calm, centered manner. Allow your intuition to guide you. It's an infallible tool. Your persistence, resilience, and determination are among your greatest assets.

That said, there's a proclivity here for incredible discipline in achieving your goals, but you may need help, and help won't be forthcoming unless you ask for it. *Can* you ask for it? Is a request for help even in your lexicon? Check out the sign of your moon. If it's in a water or earth sign, chances are good that you realize you are part of a collective of like-minded individuals. Start there. You won't be disappointed.

Natal Saturn in Sagittarius

Your pursuit of philosophy and/or religious and spiritual beliefs is one of the primary driving forces in your life. You may have a desire to be recognized as an authority in one of the above areas or in higher education, publishing, politics, or the law. You probably have a strict moral code that guides you, but which could stifle creative thinking. Any kind of rigid approach to problem-solving complicates your challenges and problems. It's best to loosen up, to allow yourself the freedom to explore your ideals free of political or religious restraints.

You're happiest if you can structure your life by incorporating your ideals into your daily life in a practical way. Your professional reputation is vitally important to you, but try not to obsess about every little detail, every little word. You're after the big picture. The darker side of this placement is self-righteousness.

Natal Saturn in Capricorn

Saturn rules this sign, so it's very happy here and functions at optimum capacity. Your ambitions are powerful, and from the time you're old enough to understand what a career is, you are pursuing your own. Your talents are varied, and you may be able to integrate all of them in some unique way to achieve what you desire. Your goals are specific; your discipline is astounding.

The usual description about this placement is that the person may appear cold, detached, remote. But I've found this isn't necessarily true. My daughter and her friends, all of them born in 1989 when Saturn was in the early degrees of Capricorn, are among the most joyful group of people I've ever known. But they're also incredibly focused in their pursuit of educational goals, which certainly fits this placement.

Natal Saturn in Aquarius

Saturn, as the coruler of Aquarius, is pretty comfortable here. Your visionary qualities are channeled and expressed in practical ways that benefit others. Your intellect is organized, focused, objective, and capable of innovative discoveries and solutions. With this placement, there's usually mathematical and scientific ability and the ability to conceptualize. The challenge is to integrate your abilities into your daily life and to ground them. You benefit from regular physical exercise that serves to remind you there's more to life than the mind! Yoga, tai chi, or any other mind/body discipline would be a good place to start.

The downside of this placement can be a lack of feeling, intellectual pride, and impersonal relationships.

Natal Saturn in Pisces

The consensus about this placement is that it's difficult. But any challenges can be overcome by channeling your intuitive ability through a structure that Saturn provides. Instead of letting your memories of the past trap you, use memories of past triumphs as a springboard to achieve what you desire. Your psychic ability is the doorway to spiritual and creative development and to higher spiritual truths.

There can be an inordinate amount of worrying that accompanies this placement, so be sure you always allow yourself solitude, a refuge where you can kick back and relax. It helps to practice yoga, meditate, nurture yourself first.

CHAPTER 8

Health and Fitness Tips for the Paradigm Shift

When paradigms shift, it's not just belief systems that are impacted. Our minds, spirits, and physical bodies are also affected. The slowest-moving outer planets exert the most influence over our lives, so let's take a look at the areas of the body these planets rule for hints about how we can take better care of ourselves in 2012.

Saturn

This planet rules bones, teeth, joints, knees, and spine. So during Saturn transits, these are the areas in your body that are most likely to be affected. With Saturn in Libra until October 5, 2011, your lower back, kidneys, ovaries, and sugar levels—all governed by Libra—could be impacted too. Between October 5 and late December, Saturn transits Scorpio, which rules the endocrine system, menstruation, sex organs, and blood, so these areas could be affected too.

Uranus

This planet rules ankles, nervous ailments, miscarriages, reflexes, and sprains. With Uranus in Aries all year, other areas that could be affected are: adrenals, head, insomnia, retinas, scalp.

Neptune

With Neptune in Pisces, the sign that it rules, from February 3, 2012, for the next fourteen years, areas of the body that can be affected are: feet, glandular swellings, eyes, addictions, parathyroid, pituitary, hard to diagnose diseases.

Pluto

Pluto will be in Capricorn until 2024. Possible trouble areas include: enzyme levels, reproductive organs, hemorrhoids. Capricorn rules pretty much the same areas that Saturn does: bones, joints, knees and kneecaps, gout, rheumatism, sprains.

So when you know that one of these outer planets will be forming an angle to one of your natal planets—your sun, moon, and rising in particular—then you can take extra care with the parts of your body that may be more vulnerable. If Saturn is forming a difficult angle to your sun sign, for example, then it would be smart to take yoga regularly to keep your spine and joints flexible.

Your General Health

If you were an alien watching the evening news and the drug commercials that sponsor it, you might get the impression that Americans are a sickly lot in search of the quickest fix. While drugs certainly have their place, more and more Americans are seeking alternative treatments for whatever ails them. From acupuncture to yoga and homeopathy, from vitamin regimens to nutritional programs, we're seeking control over our own health and bodies.

Health and fitness is more than just eating right and getting sufficient exercise. It's also about our emotions, our inner worlds, our belief systems. How happy are you in your job? Your closest partnerships? Your friendships? Are you generally happy with the money you earn? What would you change about your life? Do you believe you have free will or that everything is destined? Is your mood generally upbeat? Do you feel you have choices? Do you feel empowered? By asking yourself these kinds of questions, you can glean a sense of your emotional state at any given time. The state of your emotions may tell you a great deal about the state of your health.

Louise Hay, author of *You Can Heal Your Life* and founder of Hay House Publishing, is a living testament to the impact of emotions on health. As a young woman, she was diagnosed with vaginal cancer. The doctors wanted to operate, but Hay bought herself time—three months—by telling them she didn't have the money. She then took control of her treatment.

As a battered child who had been raped at the age of five, it wasn't surprising to her that the cancer had shown up where it had. She knew that cancer was "a disease of deep resentment that has been held for a long period of time until it literally eats away at the body." She felt that if she could change the mental pattern that had created the cancer, if she could release the patterns of resentment, then she could cure herself.

She set out a program for her treatment—and forgiveness was at the top of her list. She also knew she had to "love and approve" of herself more. In addition, she found a good therapist, a nutritionist, a foot reflexologist, had colonics three times a week, exercised. Her treatment is spelled out in her book. The end result? Within six months, the doctors pronounced her free of cancer.

In her book, there's an invaluable list: next to every ailment and disease is the probable emotional cause and the new thought pattern that will lead to healing. Her techniques may not be for everyone, but when dealing with health and fitness issues, remember that medical science doesn't have all the answers, and you, in fact, may be your own best healer.

The Physical You

These descriptions fit both sun and rising signs. For a more complete look at the physical you, of course, your entire natal chart should be taken into account, with a particularly close look at the sign of your moon—the root of your emotions, the cradle of your inner world.

Aries

Rules: head and face

What You Look Like

Physically these people tend to have ruddy complexions, narrow chins, and arched eyebrows. Sometimes they have a scar or mole on the head or face. Aries men often have profuse body hair, and in both men and women the hair is sometimes tinged with red.

Health and Fitness Tips

Aries rules the head and face, so these areas are often the most vulnerable physically. Headaches, dizziness, and skin eruptions can be common. If you're an athletic Aries, then do more of whatever it is that you enjoy. Competitive sports? Great, go for it. Long-distance runner? Run farther. Gym? Double your time and your workout. Yoga once a week? Do it three times a week. One way or another, you need to burn off your excessive energy, so that it doesn't turn inward and short-circuit your body!

As a cardinal fire sign, you're an active person who gravitates toward daring, risky sports—mountain climbing, rappelling, bungee jumping, trekking through high mountainous regions, leaping out of airplanes. It's probably a great idea to have good health insurance or to have a Louise Hay attitude toward your health—*I'm attracting only magnificent experiences into my life.*

For maximum benefit, you probably should try to eliminate red meat from your diet. Chicken and fish are fine, but a vegan diet would be best. Herbs like mustard, eyebright, and bay are beneficial for you. Any antioxidant is helpful—particularly vitamins C, E, A or Lutein for your eyes, zinc, Co-Q10, Black Cohosh if you're a female in menopause, or Saw Palmetto if you're a man older than fifty. If you pull a muscle or throw your back out of whack, look for a good acupuncturist and avoid painkillers.

Taurus

Rules: neck, throat, cervical vertebrae

What You Look Like

In a Taurus, the neck is usually thick and sturdy and rises from broad, often muscular shoulders that seem to bear the weight of the world. They tend to be attractive individuals with broad foreheads and expressive faces. Yet their faces can be as inscrutable as fortune cookies when they are hiding something or feel threatened in some way. They usually look more youthful than other people their age, the result of good genes and a daily regimen of exercise.

Health and Fitness Tips

Thanks to the sensuality of your sign, you may be a gourmet cook and enjoy rich foods. But because your metabolism may be somewhat slow, you benefit from daily exercise and moderation in your diet. In fact, moderation in all things is probably a good rule to follow.

As a fixed earth sign, you benefit from any outdoor activity, and the more physical it is, the better it is for you. Hiking, skiing, windsurfing, biking are all excellent pursuits. You also benefit from any mind/body discipline like tai chi or yoga. The latter is especially good since it keeps you flexible, and that flexibility spills over into your attitudes and beliefs and the way you deal with situations and people. You probably enjoy puttering in a garden, but because you have such an artistic side, you don't just putter. You remake the garden into a work of art—fountains, bold colors, mysterious paths that twist through greenery and flowers. Once you add wind chimes and bird feeders, nature's music adds the finishing touches.

If your job entails long hours of sitting in front of a computer, your neck and shoulders may be more tense than usual. You would benefit through regular massage and hot tub soaks.

If you're the silent type of Taurus, then chances are you don't discuss your emotions. This tendency can cause health challenges if you keep anger or resentment bottled up inside you. Best to have an outlet—through exercise, for example, or through some sort of creative endeavor. Art, music, photography, writing: any of those would help. Better yet, learn to open up to at least one or two people!

Gemini

Rules: hands, arms, lungs, nervous system

What You Look Like

Geminis generally radiate a lot of nervous energy. It keeps them slender and wiry, and they're always on the move—if not physically, then mentally. They often have twinkling eyes, clear-cut features, a nose that turns up slightly at the end. Some of them have thick hair. They talk and move fast, many are ambidextrous and usually have excellent coordination.

Health and Fitness Tips

You benefit from periodic breaks in your established routine. Whether it's a trip to some exotic port or a trip to the grocery, it's a breath of fresh air, a way to hit the pause button on your busy mind. Regular physical exercise helps to bleed off some of your energy and keeps your already youthful body supple and in shape.

As a mutable air sign, you need intellectual stimulation and a constant array of experiences and information to keep your curiosity piqued. Otherwise it's too easy for all that nervous energy to turn inward and affect your health. The kind of work you do is important in the overall scheme of your health. You do best in non-routine kind of work with flexible hours or, preferably, in a profession where you make your own hours! Any job in communication, travel, public relations, would suit you. When you're passionate about what you do, you're happier. If you're happy, your immune system remains healthy.

With your natural dexterity and coordination, you

would do well at yoga. If you don't take classes yet, sign up for some. Not only will it keep you flexible, but you'll benefit mentally. Meditation would also be an excellent practice for you. Anything to calm your busy head!

Since your respiratory and nervous systems are your most vulnerable areas, your diet should include plenty of fish, fresh fruits, and vegetables. If you live in a place where you can garden, then plant some of these items for optimum freshness. Vitamin C, zinc, the B vitamins, and vitamins E and A are also beneficial for you. With your energy always in fast-forward, it's smart to get at least seven and preferably eight hours of sleep a night. If you're the type of Gemini with a high metabolism, then you benefit from eating several small meals throughout the day rather than just the usual three.

Cancer

Rules: breasts, stomach, digestive system

What You Look Like

Cancers are recognizable because of their round faces. Their bodies are sometimes round, too, though not necessarily overweight. Those who don't have roundness as part of their physical appearance may have some other distinguishing trait—liquid, soulful eyes, a lovely-shaped mouth, generally expressive features. They're moody individuals, and their moods are often reflected on their faces and in the way they walk and carry themselves.

Health and Fitness Tips

As a cardinal water sign, you benefit from proximity to water. If you can live or work close to a body of water, you'll notice a marked difference in your energy and intuition and how you feel and think. Even a vacation close to the water is healing. This seems to hold true not only for Cancer sun signs, but for moon and rising signs in Cancer too. The body of water can be anything—a lake, river, ocean, salt marsh, even a pond!

Not surprisingly, you benefit from any kind of water sport, even a day at the beach or a picnic by the river. The point is that water speaks to you. It feels like your natural element. You might want to read *The Secret of Water* or any of the other books by Masaru Emoto. You will never think of water in the same way again and will be more conscious of how human emotions affect water—and thus our bodies, since we consist of nearly 70 percent water.

Emotionally, you may cling to past injuries and hurts more than other signs or may still be dragging around issues from childhood or even from a past life. Unresolved emotional stuff can lodge in your body and create problems. So it's important that you rid yourself of past resentments and anger. Use hypnosis to dislodge these feelings. Forgive and forget. Have a past-life regression. Read Louise Hay's book *You Can Heal Your Life.*

If you have a moon, rising, or another planet in an earth sign, then consider regular workouts at a gym.

Leo

Rules: heart, back, spinal cord

What You Look Like

From Jacqueline Kennedy to Madonna to Presidents Obama and Clinton, the typical Leo looks regal. Hair that is thick or in some way distinguished, compelling eyes, a smile that can light up the dark side of the moon: these are the Leo hallmarks. Male or female, they project dignity and intelligence and move with a certain elegance. In a crowded room, the Leo is usually the one surrounded by people!

Health and Fitness Tips

Leo rules the heart. So you benefit from a low-fat diet, exercise, work that you love, and relationships in which you are recognized as the unique person that you are. Yes, those last two things count in the overall picture of your health!

Let's talk about your work. Acting, of course, is what you're known for. And performance. And politics. And, well, anything where you can show off your abundant talents. So if right now you're locked into a humdrum job, are the low person on the bureaucratic totem pole, and don't receive the attention you feel you deserve, then your pride and ambition are suffering. That, in turn, creates resentment that could be eating you alive. Turn the situation around by finding a career or an outlet where your talents shine and you're appreciated and recognized. You're a natural leader whose flamboyant style and magnetism attract the supporters who can help you.

You have a temper, but once you blow, that's it. Unlike Cancer, you don't hold on to grudges or harbor resentments or anger from childhood. You tend to be forward looking in your outlook, and your natural optimism is healthy for your heart and immune system. Anything you can do to maintain your cheerful disposition is a plus. When you feel yourself getting down, rent comedies, find books that make you laugh out loud, blog about your feelings.

Virgo

Rules: intestines, abdomen, female reproductive system

What You Look Like

Their physiques are usually slender and distinctive in some way—beautifully sculpted fingers and hands, for instance, nice legs, gorgeous teeth. They're physically attractive as a rule, which they enhance through their fastidious attention to detail. Their eyes may be unusual in some way, and their features tend to be sharp, clearly defined. They're fastidious about personal hygiene.

Health and Fitness Tips

If you're the type of Virgo who worries and frets a lot, then the first place it's likely to show up is in your digestive tract. You might have colic as an infant, stomach upsets as a teenager, ulcers as an adult. The best way to mitigate this tendency, of course, is to learn how NOT to worry and to simply go with the flow.

You do best on a diet that includes plenty of fresh fruits and vegetables, fish, and chicken. Try to stay away from fried or heavily spiced foods. Red meat might be difficult to digest. If you live in a place where fresh fruits and vegetables are difficult to find during the winter, then supplement your diet with the appropriate vitamins and minerals. If you're a fussy eater—and some Virgos are—then the vitamin and mineral supplements are even more important.

You benefit from hot baths, massages, anything that allows you to relax into the moment. Yoga, running, swimming, gym workouts, any of these exercise regimens benefit you. Some Virgos, particularly double Virgos— with a moon or rising in that sign—have an acute sense of smell. If you're one of those, then be sure to treat yourself to scented soaps and lotions, fragrant candles and incense, and any other scent that soothes your soul.

Virgo is typically associated with service, and you may find that whenever you do a good deed for someone, when you volunteer your time or expertise, you feel better about yourself and life in general. The more you can do to trigger these feelings, the healthier you'll be. You have a tendency toward self-criticism that's part and parcel of your need for perfection, and whenever you find yourself shifting into that critical frame of mind, stop it in its tracks. Reach for a more uplifting thought. This will help you to maintain your health.

Libra

Rules: lower back, kidney, diaphragm

What You Look Like

Even in a crowd of beautiful people, they stand out in some way. As a Venus-ruled sign, they have distinctive features—beautiful eyes, gorgeous skin, well-formed bodies, expressive mouths. They're often slender, good-looking. They enjoy beauty—in their partners, their surroundings, their aesthetic tastes. So it isn't surprising that they often dress beautifully and have homes that are boldly colored and uniquely decorated.

Health and Fitness Tips

If your love life is terrific, then your health probably is too. You're happiest when you're in a relationship, preferably a committed, lifetime relationship. When things between you and your partner are on an even keel, your energy is greater, your immune system works without a hitch, you sleep more soundly, and you're more apt to have a healthier lifestyle.

You prefer working in an environment that's aesthetically pleasing, where there's a minimum of drama with congenial people. If your work situation doesn't fit that description, then it could affect your health—and for the same reasons as a love life that is lacking. Emotions. Your lower back, kidneys, and diaphragm are vulnerable areas for you, and unvented emotions could manifest in those areas first. If it isn't possible to change jobs or careers right now, then find an artistic outlet for your creative expression. Music, photography, art, writing, dance, any area that allows you to flex your creativity.

You benefit from yoga, walking, swimming, and any kind of exercise that strengthens your lower back muscles. Meditation is also beneficial, particularly when it's combined with an awareness of breathing.

The healthiest diet for you should consist of foods with varied tastes, plenty of fresh fruits and vegetables, organic if possible, and a minimum of meats. Anything that benefits your kidneys is good. Drink at least eight glasses of water a day, so that your kidneys are continually flushed out.

Scorpio

Rules: sexual organs, elimination

What You Look Like

The body types vary, but the eyes ... well, the eyes are nearly always compelling, intense, piercing. They rarely reveal what they're feeling and are masters at disguising their expressions. Their masks are carefully honed through years of hiding their emotions. Many Scorpios have thick eyebrows, sharp noses, seductive mouths. Their voices are often husky and low.

Health and Fitness Tips

As a fixed water sign, you probably benefit by a proximity to water every bit as much as Cancer does. Lake, ocean, river, pond, salt marsh: take your pick. If none of these is available, then put a fountain in your backyard or somewhere in your house and create a meditation area. It's important that you have a quiet center where you can decompress at the end of the day, particularly if you have a busy family life and a lot of demands on your time.

You tend to keep a lot of emotion locked inside, and if the emotions are negative—resentment, anger—they fester and affect your health. So try to find someone you can talk to freely about your emotions—a partner, friend, family member. Or pour these feelings into a creative outlet. One way or another, get them out.

Scorpio rules the sexual and elimination organs, so these areas could be where ill health hits first. Be sure that you eat plenty of roughage in your diet and enjoy what you eat while you're eating it. Stay away from the usual culprits—fried or heavily processed foods. You do best with plenty of fresh food, but may want to consider eliminating red meats. Consider colonics treatments for cleaning out the bowels.

For your overall health, it's important to enjoy sex with a partner whom you trust. Avoid using sex as a leverage for power in a relationship.

Sagittarius

Rules: hips, thighs, liver

What You Look Like

They tend to come in two types—tall and broad through the shoulders or shorter and heavier. The second description comes in part from Jupiter, which rules the sign and causes them to indulge their appetites. They look athletic and have high foreheads that get higher in men as they age and their hair recedes. They move quickly, but not necessarily gracefully.

Health and Fitness Tips

As a mutable fire sign, you can't tolerate any kind of restriction or limitation on your freedom. You must be able to get up and go whenever you want. If you work in a job that demands you punch a time clock, where your hours are strictly regulated, or are in a relationship where you feel constricted, then you probably aren't happy. For a naturally buoyant and happy person like you, that could spell health challenges. Sadge rules the hips, the sacral region of the spine, the coccygeal vertebrae, the femur, the ileum, the iliac arteries, and the sciatic nerves, so any of these areas could be impacted health-wise.

You benefit from any kind of athletic activity. From competitive sports to an exercise regimen you create, your body craves regular activity. You also benefit from yoga, which keeps your spine and hips flexible.

If you're prone to putting on weight—and even if you're not!—strive to minimize sweets and carbs in your diet. The usual recommendations—abundant fresh vegetables and fruits—also apply. If you're the type who eats on the run, then you may be eating fast or heavily processed foods and should try to keep that at a minimum or eliminate it altogether. Even though your digestive system is hardy enough to tolerate just about anything, the fast foods and processed foods add carbs and calories.

Antioxidants are beneficial, of course, and these include vitamins C, A, and E. Minerals like zinc should be included in your diet and also a glucosamine supplement for joints.

Capricorn

Rules: knees, skin, bones

What You Look Like

As a cardinal earth sign, these individuals understand the benefits of exercise, and their bodies show it. While they generally aren't muscular—some are, but not as a rule—they look to be in shape. Their bodies are often angular and slender, and their faces, regardless of their age, have a maturity about them.

Health and Fitness Tips

Since you seem to have been born with an innate sense of where you're going—or want to go—it's likely that you take care of yourself. You know the routine as well as anyone—eat right, stay fit, exercise, get enough rest. But there are other components to living long and prospering (to paraphrase Spock!), and that's your emotions.

You, like Scorpio, are secretive, although your motives are different. For you, it's a privacy factor more than anything else. You keep your emotions to yourself and may not express what you feel when you feel it. This can create blockages in your body, notably in your joints or knees. It's vital that you learn to vent your emotions, to rid yourself of anger before it has a chance to move inward.

You're focused, ambitious, and patient in the attainment of your goals. But your work—and your satisfaction with it—is a primary component in your health. If you feel you've reached a dead end in your career, if you're frustrated more often than you're happy with what you do, then it's time to revamp and get out of Dodge. By taking clear, definite steps toward something else, you feel you're more in control of your destiny and mitigate the possibility of health challenges.

Since your knees are vulnerable, running is probably not the best form of exercise for you, unless you do it only once or twice a week and engage in some other form of exercise the rest of the time. For a cardio workout that isn't as tough on your knees, try a rowing machine. For general flexibility, there's nothing like yoga!

Aquarius

Rules: ankles, shins, circulatory system

What You Look Like

Tall and slender or short and round, their body types are as different and varied as they are. But many have deeply set eyes and classic profiles. Many of them move as quickly as Geminis; others move like molasses. Most aren't particularly coordinated, but some are. So, bottom

127

line, it's tough to spot these individuals in a crowd. But as soon as you listen to them for five minutes, they're easier to peg. They talk eloquently about their ideas and ideals, and you'll recognize them by their discussions of alternative foods, alternative fuels, alternative lifestyles, alternative everything.

Health and Fitness Tips

Let's start with the effect of Uranus ruling your sign. It sometimes can set your nerves on edge—too many sounds, too much chaos around you, loud noises deep into the night, the backfiring of cars, the incessant drone of traffic, even a crowd at the local mall. You're sensitive to all of that. It's part of what makes it important for you to have a private space to which you can withdraw—a quiet back yard filled with plants, a room inside your house with an altar for your Wiccan practice filled with scents from candles or incense that soothe your frazzled nerves. Or perhaps a book on tape can shut it all out. But shut it out you must to protect your health.

Because you live so much inside your own head, exercise is definitely beneficial for you. It doesn't have to be anything complicated—yoga done in the privacy of your own home, long walks, regular bike rides. But do *something* to ground your body, to get your blood moving, to silence the buzz inside your head. It will all benefit your health.

Nutrition? Well, for an Aquarian, this can go any number of different ways. You enjoy different types of food, so that's a place to start—with what you *enjoy*. The foods are likely to be unusual—organically grown, for instance, prepared in unusual ways, or purchased from a local co-op. If you live in the city, then perhaps you purchase food from a grocery store you've been frequenting for years. The idea here is that *you* know what's best for your body, what you can tolerate, what you need. Even though Aquarians aren't generally as in touch with their

128

bodies as earth signs, they have an intuitive sense about what works for them. In the end, that's all that matters.

Pisces

Rules: the feet, is associated with the lymphatic system

What You Look Like

Common wisdom in astrology says there are two types of Pisces—the whale and the dolphin. And this goes for the sun, moon, or rising in Pisces. The whale is, well, large, but also tuned into everything and everyone on the planet. The dolphin type is slender, sleek, quick, joyful, graceful. But both body types usually have extraordinary eyes that are not only soulful, but seem to be able to peer through time.

Health and Fitness Tips

Let's start with emotions. Let's start with the fact that you're a psychic sponge, able to absorb other people's moods and thoughts with the ease of magnet attracting every other piece of metal around it. Yes, let's start there. It's why you should associate only with optimistic, upbeat people. The negative types steal your energy, wreck your immune system, and leave you in a tearful mess at the end of the rainbow with nothing to show for your journey.

Like your fellow water signs Cancer and Scorpio, you probably benefit from proximity to water. Whether you live near water, work near it, vacation near it, water refreshes your soul, spirit, intuition, and your immune system. Read Masaru Emoto's books on how water responds to emotions and intent. You'll never think about water in the same way again. You'll never think about your sun sign in the same way again, either.

You benefit from any kind of exercise, but try something that speaks to your soul. Swimming. Rowing, but in an actual boat, on an actual river instead of in a gym. Even a hot tub where you kick your legs is beneficial. Pay attention to the water you drink. Is your tap water filled with fluorides? Then avoid it and look for distilled water. Drink at least eight glasses a day. Indulge yourself in massages, foot reflexology, periodic dips in the ocean. Any ocean.

Meditate. Find the calm center of your storm.

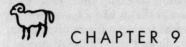

CHAPTER 9

Aspects

Throughout this material, we've talked about beneficial or challenging angles that a transiting planet makes to your sun sign or that transiting planets make to each other. These angles are called *aspects*. Think of them as a symbolic network of arteries and veins that transport the blood of astrology. In a natal chart, these angles connect our inner and outer worlds, accentuate certain traits and play down others. Each aspect represents a certain type of energy, so there really aren't any good or bad aspects because energy is neutral. It's what we do with the energy that counts. It comes back to free will. When transiting planets make angles to each other, energy is also exchanged.

For instance, every year there is at least one very lucky day when the transiting sun and transiting Jupiter form a beneficial angle to each other—a conjunction (same sign and degree), a sextile (60 degrees apart), or a trine (120 degrees apart). The lucky day in 2012 falls on May 13, when the sun and Jupiter are exactly conjunct. This means that the sun's life energy and Jupiter's expansive energy combine and create, well, some magic for all of us! It's especially good for Taurus and other earth signs, but since we all have Taurus somewhere in our charts, everyone benefits.

If you look back to the presidential election in November 2008, Saturn in Virgo and Uranus in Pisces formed an exact opposition to each other. They were 180 degrees apart, an aspect that is like a tug-of-war. In this case, the tug-of-war was between the candidate that represented the old paradigm, the established order—Saturn—and the candidate who symbolized sweeping change—Uranus.

Aspects are most powerful as they are approaching exactness. So even though a conjunction, for example, is 00 degrees of separation or a square is technically 90 degrees of separation, many astrologers use *orbs* that can be as wide as five or ten degrees. Some astrologers use small orbs, but others assign larger orbs for the sun and moon and smaller orbs for other planets. The closer the orb, the more powerful the combination. If you're sensitive to transits, then, you may be feeling lucky for several days before May 13!

In terms of a natal chart, any transiting planet that is approaching an aspect with one of your natal planets is also most powerful on its approach. The traditional aspects have been used since the second century A.D. They are the conjunction, sextile, square, trine, and opposition. These aspects are considered to be the major or hard angles and are also the most powerful. There are other minor aspects that astrologers use, but for the purpose of this chapter, we'll only talk about the traditional aspects.

At the end of this chapter is a natal chart. We'll be referring to it as we go through the aspects.

Conjunction, major hard aspect, 0 degrees

This aspect is easy to identify—clusters of planets within a few degrees of each other, usually but not always in the same sign and house. But it's a complex aspect because energies combine, fuse, merge. Think of it as power, intensity. So if you have conjunctions in your natal chart, the astrologer who reads for you should address what it means and how you can use it to maximize your potential.

Let's look at the young woman's chart. With her Saturn—♄—and Neptune—♆—conjunct in her tenth house of career, there's already a tension and power in her chart. Saturn builds structures and boundaries and seeks to hold back, restrict. It's about rules and responsibilities. Neptune urges us to allow boundaries to dissolve, to release the ego, to reach for higher ideals. So this woman will confront these dualities in her career— her tenth house.

With Uranus—♅—thrown into the mix, these experiences and dualities will come at her out of the blue, suddenly and without warning. Her career will be unusual, strange, filled with idiosyncratic people and defined by strange experiences—the Uranus influence. Uranus shakes up the status quo and when it's conjunct Saturn—even widely, by 7 degrees in this case—she will feel conflicted at times about which path to follow, which choices to make.

In this same chart, notice the close conjunction between the moon—☽—and Mars—♂—in the sixth house. One degree of separation. One possible repercussion is that her emotions are especially intense, even volatile at times, when it comes to her daily work routine and the maintenance of her health. Her health stuff may occur in fits and starts—one week she'll run two miles a day, the next week she's a couch potato, and the next week she meditates and practices yoga. It's the same way with her work. Erratic, moved by the spirit and passion of the moment. But because Mars is in Virgo, she's diligent, a hard worker at whatever she takes on.

Since Mars is within a degree of the seventh-house cusp, this passion she has spills over into her personal and business partnerships.

Sextile, major soft aspect, 60 degrees

Again, look at the young woman's chart. An example of a sextile occurs between her sun—⊙—at 8 degrees Virgo in her sixth house and her Jupiter—♃—at 5 degrees Cancer in her fourth house . The orb, according to the aspect grid, is 2 degrees and 41 minutes. Close enough to have significant impact.

A sextile is a point of ease. It represents a free-flowing energy between the planets involved. No tension. The sextile is a kind of buffer, a shield against turmoil, indecision, instability. But if there are too many sextiles, then the person may be too passive!

In the young woman's chart, her Pluto in Scorpio in the eighth house—12♀♏49—is closely sextile her Neptune in the tenth, within 5 degrees of her Saturn in the tenth, within a 6-degree orb of her Virgo Mars in the sixth, and within 5 degrees of her Virgo moon in the sixth. That's a whole lot of energy stacked in her favor and suggests that whatever she does on a daily basis with her work somehow feeds into the larger picture of her career. During her college years, she was able to manifest jobs out of thin air while in school and during the summers.

When she was in high school, for instance, she and her parents vacationed in windsurfing spots in the Caribbean and South America because her dad is a windsurfer. So she learned to windsurf and became so proficient at it that she was able to teach windsurfing at her college, through the sailing club, to any students who were interested. The college paid her ten bucks an hour. Gas money! Food money!

From the time she was old enough to walk, she enjoyed horseback riding and loved working with horses, being around them. She lived near an equestrian community, so becoming a barn rat was not a tough thing to do. During the summer of her freshman year, with her parents breathing down her back about getting a job, she manifested a job teaching riding at an equestrian summer camp.

These examples are precisely the kinds of experiences that accompany the sextiles in her chart. That Pluto in Scorpio, a sign that planet rules, gives her enormous power and ability to hone in on what she needs and wants and make it happen.

Square, major hard aspect, 90 degrees

Friction, angst, *oh my God, the sky is falling*: that's how squares feel in a natal chart. The sky, of course, is never falling, but the friction and angst are quite real and act as triggers for action, forward thrust. They force us to develop, evolve, and reach aggressively for our desires.

How's this play out in real life? Look at the young woman's chart. She has three squares to her natal Mercury in Libra, in her seventh house of partnerships, all of them from that cluster of planets in her tenth house of career. Her natal Mercury—05☿♎33—is square to those tenth house planets from between 2 to 4 degrees. Ouch. The need to achieve something professionally is very strong. But it's not just about achieving. She wants to make her mark on the world, to leave something behind, some sort of legacy, something unique that bears *her stamp*. Because Mercury rules communication and this young woman enjoys writing and is good at it, that could be one of her signatures.

Mercury is also square her Jupiter in Cancer in the fourth house, suggesting that she may try to take on too much—in her writing, her life, her partnerships. Hit the pause button, breathe, ask for guidance through imagination, visualization, your family (fourth house), and dreams.

Squares spur us to action.

Trines, major soft aspect, 120 degrees

This aspect works like a sextile, linking energies in a harmonious way. It's associated with general ease and good fortune. Again, though, if there are too many in the chart, passivity may result.

Look at the chart again. The young woman's 8-degree Virgo sun in her sixth house is closely trine to both Neptune and Saturn in Capricorn. The Saturn/Sun trine enables the young woman to set realistic goals and to attain them. The Neptune/Sun trine gives her deep compassion, psychic and artistic ability. She's able to attract the right opportunities for her career. The trine to Uranus is a bit wider—7 degrees—but is still significant. It suggests that her profession is or will be unusual and that her freedom is important to her. It's doubtful this young woman will be found in an office, confined to a 9 to 5 job. Whatever she does is likely to be unique.

Opposition, major hard aspect, 180 degrees

This aspect feels like a persistent itch that you can't reach and usually involves polarities—Taurus/Scorpio, for example, or Aries/Libra. It brings about change through conflict and sometimes represents traits we project onto others because we haven't fully integrated them into ourselves.

In the woman's chart, her natal Jupiter in Cancer is opposed to all three planets in her tenth house. Jupiter expands everything it touches, so with Saturn, the woman's professional success comes about through persistence and dedication and by working with her beliefs in a constructive, positive way. With her Jupiter opposed to Uranus, the freedom to call her own shots, make her own schedule, to do her own thing, is paramount. In a chart that lacks direction and focus, this aspect can lead to involvement with revolutionary groups or religious cults. In a strong chart like this one, however, the Uranus/Jupiter opposition can indicate involvement in humanitarian efforts. The Neptune/Jupiter opposition can indicate utopian ideals, getting suckered by a sob story or trusting smooth talkers with a devious agenda. But it can also lead to great spiritual awareness and enhanced psychic ability.

Some other minor aspects that astrologers use are:

- the semi-square, 45 degrees. It creates irritation and friction between the planets involved.
- the septile, 51 degrees. Indicative of harmony and union in a nontraditional way. Can suggest spiritual power.
- the quincunx or inconjunct, 150 degrees separation. Indicates a need for adjustment in attitude and beliefs.

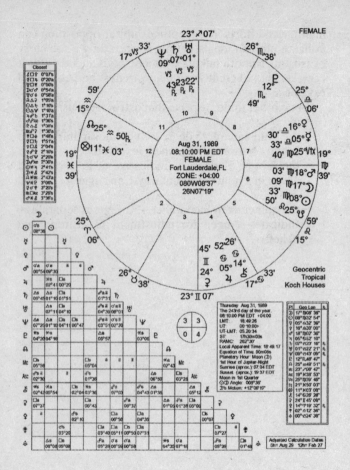

CHAPTER 10

The Astrological Neighborhood

Whether you're just learning astrology or are a seasoned pro or somewhere in between, the Internet is a wonderful tool for studying astrology. You can Google anything—a planet, an aspect, some obscure detail about astrology—and some Web site or blog undoubtedly has the information you're looking for.

Astrology sites offer a vast spectrum of services, from free natal charts, daily transits, and monthly horoscopes to political and world predictions—it's all at your fingertips. Here are some of the best sites:

www.astro.com: Enter your birth data and obtain a free natal chart. This site is also chocked full of information about astrology. Great for the beginner, the intermediary, and the advanced astrologer. Something for everyone here. There are also some terrific articles by well-known astrologers.

www.astrologyzone.com: Susan Miller's site is a favorite for neophytes and pros alike. Every month she writes around three thousand words per sign about what you can expect in the upcoming month. Her predictions are eerily accurate!

www.moonvalleyastrologer.com: Celeste Teal is *the* expert on eclipses, a specialized area of astrology that few have researched the way she has. Her two books on eclipses are seminal works.

www.astrocollege.com: Lois Rodden's site is extraordinary. This woman spent most of her life collecting birth data and then created a piece of software that is invaluable in research. This site also rates and sells astrology software. Lois has passed on, but her work survives.

http://astrofuturetrends.com: Author and astrologer Anthony Louis does just what the site says. He predicts future trends, covers political stuff, and provides an overall view of astrology.

www.starlightnews.com: Click on Nancy's blog. Here you'll find the latest predictions and insights about world affairs. Nancy's predictions about politics have been right on. Before the 2004 election, she made some predictions about tight senatorial races that were totally accurate. She also called the presidential race in 2008. We've been following her closely ever since.

www.astro-yoga.com: This site combines astrology and yoga. We created it and this system of yoga.

www.tjmacgregor.com: Here you'll find monthly astrological predictions for writers.

www.ofscarabs.blogspot.com: About synchronicities— what they are, how they show up in our lives, what they might mean, and hundreds of stories.

Software

Computers have transformed everything about astrology. In the days before, you had to figure all this stuff by hand, through complicated mathematical formulas that left you gasping.

Our first piece of software was a really simple program we found at some computer store for ten bucks. It erected a chart in about sixty seconds. There it was— rising, moon, sun, planets, the houses—everything set up on the computer screen as if by magic. In the late 1990s, we bought our first really terrific astrology software from Matrix for about $300. In the years since, http://www.astrologysoftware.com has supplied us with endless data and information and revolutionized the study of astrology.

But it's not just enough to have a great piece of software. When your computer crashes, when you receive updates that screw up, when windows updates to a new system, you call the Matrix help line and their people walk you through it until everything works. The employees on their help lines aren't outsourced. You won't reach India. You'll talk to someone in Michigan who is not only an astrologer, but a computer geek who knows how to fix your problem. If by some fluke they can't fix your problem, they'll credit you for one of their other terrific programs.

The only complaint we have about Matrix is that to activate the software, you have to call or contact them through the Internet to receive a special code. If your computer crashes, if you buy a new PC or laptop . . . well, it's annoying. When you pay this much for software, you shouldn't have to obtain a special access code.

Another great piece of software is SolarFire. Astrologers are as dedicated to this program as they are to Matrix's software. Check out http://www.alabe.com for current prices. While the two programs offer similar features and capabilities, preferences seem to be individual. Both Matrix's Winstar and astrolabe's SolarFire offer many alternative features—like reports for natal, transit, and progressed interpretations.

Kepler's astrology program—http://www.astrosoftware.com—is beautiful in its rendition of charts, interpretations, and just about anything any astrologer could use or need. We like it for its ease, its beauty. But it's not a Winstar or SolarFire.

If your exploration of astrology takes you deeper, there are other software programs that take you there. Bernadette Brady is the undisputed mistress of fixed stars. Her software program, Starlight, is remarkable not only for its accuracy, but for its presentation. You will never think of fixed stars in the same way once you play with this program. What won't make sense in a natal-chart interpretation suddenly snaps into clarity when you use Brady's software. Be sure to download a print to file version for the software—through a PDF file—so that you can maximize usage. Their Web site: http://www.zyntara.com.

Lois Rodden's AstroDatabank is the software that Lois Rodden developed. It contains over thirty thousand birth records, "carefully documented and coded for accuracy with the popular Rodden Rating system. AstroDatabank includes intriguing biographies, revealing personality traits, important life events, and significant relationships." For the curious, the researcher, the neophyte and pro alike.

Both Winstar and SolarFire produce computerized report software. These reports are handy for when a friend of a friend is in a fix and you don't have the time to interpret transits and progressions for the person's birth chart. Winstar also produces software on the tarot and numerology.

Day Watch, another Winstar program, is forecasting software that is invaluable for astrologers. From their site: "Certainly it creates personalized astrological calendars, a great tool for professional astrologers and those who have an understanding of astrological terms, symbols, and technique. But Day Watch also contains a full range of onscreen and printable interpretations of events that even someone with absolutely no astrological training can read, understand, and immediately put to use in their daily lives."

At the beginning of every month, we bring up our personalized calendars that tell us what is happening daily in our natal charts and also lists which planets are changing signs in that month, on what date, and which planets are turning retrograde or direct. Each month includes an ephemeris and lunar charts for the new and full moon. The program also offers various types of reports.

Getting a Reading

So now you're ready for an astrological reading. But where do you start? Which astrologer should you use?

The best way to find an astrologer is through soeone who has gotten a reading and recommends the individual. If you don't know anyone who has had an astrological reading, then the next best course is to head over to the nearest bookstore and look through the astrology books. Browse through titles that interest you. Note the author's style. If the author uses a lot of astro jargon or seems to write in a depressing or heavy-handed way, move on. Once you find an author whose book you like, check to see if he or she has a Web site and get in touch with the person.

Rates for a reading vary from one astrologer to another and usually depend on what you want. Would you like just an interpretation of your natal chart? Would you like a forecast for the next six months or a year? Do you want a compatibility chart for you and your partner? Some astrologers prefer to do phone readings and record the reading. Others prefer to work through e-mail. If the astrologer you've chosen lives close to you, all the better. Have the reading done in person.

What to Expect During a Reading

Every astrological reading begins with your natal chart, so an accurate birth time is essential. It should come from your birth certificate or a parent's memory. An approximate time means the entire reading won't be as accurate.

This reading differs from a daily horoscope you find in a newspaper or on a Web site because it's tailored to your specific chart rather than just to your sun sign. If you're getting a reading only on your birth chart, then the astrologer interprets the entire chart, not just pieces of it. The astrologer looks at the signs and house placements of the various planets and the angles the planets make to each other.

Think of a natal chart as a holographic depiction of who you are. It's an organic blueprint, where the parts fit together in certain ways. In a reading, the signs of your sun, moon, and rising are where most astrologers begin. The sun represents your total personality, the moon symbolizes your inner world, and your rising sign is the doorway to your chart—the portal through which all your experiences enter. So an astrologer would look at the mix of these planets and then look at how they meld or oppose, facilitate or challenge other planets in your chart.

In addition to planets and aspects, astrologers also look at some other things in natal charts: the Nodes of the moon, part of fortune, various asteroids, Chiron, Vertex, and Sabian symbols. The Nodes are discussed in the next chapter, so let's go through the other parts of the list.

Part of fortune ⊗ **:** This is the most commonly used Arabic part, of which there are dozens. Its placement by sign and house designates where your "pot of gold" lies. It's your luck factor.

Asteroids: There are probably hundreds of asteroids, but astrologers use only a handful of them. Thanks to the work of astrologer Demeter George, four asteroids are the most commonly used: Vesta, Ceres, Athena, and Juno. Here are their general meanings:

Vesta ⚶ **:** This asteroid's position in a natal chart describes where we are dedicated and how we can use our energies to bring about the greatest change in the larger world.

Ceres ⚳ **:** How were we nurtured and how do we nurture others? That's what Ceres shows us, according to the sign and house position.

Pallas Athena ⚴: How do you fight for what you want? How do you pursue what you desire? Pallas, the warrior queen, describes the battles we choose to fight.

Juno ⚵: The asteroid of marriage. It generally describes the romantic/marriage partner we need and get.

Chiron ⚷: Known as the wounded healer, this planetoid describes where we are wounded and how healing this wound, which often stems from early childhood, can lead to greater wisdom and the healing of others.

Vertex: It's a point that describes agreements we made prior to being born into this life, a point of destiny. Since we have free will, we can choose not to keep these appointments, but it's probably a good idea if we do. Often the sign of our Vertex is the sign of someone to whom we're close—parent, partner, child, friend, mentor.

Sabian Symbols: Back in the early part of the twentieth century, astrologer Marc Edmund Jones spent hours with a clairvoyant, Elsie Wheeler, who gave him psychic impressions of each of the 360 degrees of the zodiac. The impressions are usually couched in metaphors, but over the years have proven to be eerily accurate. To test it, go to one of the sites listed in this chapter and get a free birth chart. Then go to www.cafeastrology.com, search for Sabian symbols, and look up the degree of your sun sign.

There are other points and asteroids that astrologers use, but when you're just starting out in your interpretation of your own chart—or of someone else's—keep the chart as clean as possible. Stick to the planets. Once you've got those meanings down, start adding other elements to the chart.

🐏 CHAPTER 11

Your Soul's Agenda

The Soul

There are various ways to look for spiritual aspects in a chart. Some astrologers use Neptune and the angles it makes to other planets. Others use the moon and its aspects. We use the North and South Nodes of the moon.

The Nodes aren't planets. They're points formed by the moon's orbit around Earth that intersect with the Earth's path around the sun. They're always separated by 180 degrees, so they form an axis of energy. If your North Node falls in Gemini, then your South Node falls in Sagittarius, the sign that is six away from Gemini. If you haven't done so already, turn to the appendix, locate the time span that includes your birth date, and find out the sign of your North Node. Then look at the table below to find your South Node.

The South Node represents our comfort zone, the accumulation of characteristics, attitudes, and talents that we bring into this life from other lives or—if you don't believe in reincarnation—that are laid down early in childhood. We retreat to our South Node when we're hurt, feel sick or threatened, or perhaps when we're in a new relationship and aren't sure yet where things are going. We also retreat here when we feel unsure of ourselves. The South Node is the psychological equivalent of comfort food.

The North Node symbolizes the direction we should move in this life to fulfill our talents and potential and to evolve spiritually. It represents the soul's agenda this time around, the qualities, traits, and experiences our higher selves felt that we need to evolve spiritually and to reach our potential.

LUNAR NODES

If your north node is in	*your south node is in*
Aries	Libra
Taurus	Scorpio
Gemini	Sagittarius
Cancer	Capricorn
Leo	Aquarius
Virgo	Pisces

The sign of your North Node describes the types of experiences you should strive for in this life. It can also describe the psychological bent, potential, and talents that you should try to develop, to reach for, in order to attain your soul's agenda and to achieve your creative and spiritual potential. The sign of the South Node describes all of the above, but from previous lives. It's "been there, done that, and still feel comfortable here."

The house placement of your South Node describes the area that is your comfort zone. The house placement of your North Node describes the area where your greatest potential and talent can be achieved and the way in which you can evolve spiritually.

Take a look at the natal chart at the end of chapter 9. The woman's South Node in Leo—☋12♌32—falls in her fourth house of the home, her domestic environment. Her North Node in Aquarius—☊12♒32—falls in her tenth house of career. These signs suggest that to evolve spiritually, to achieve her full potential, she should strive to create a career that helps others. Aquarius is the sign of the humanitarian, who often works with groups to achieve a common goal.

She feels most comfortable when she's in the spotlight, or when she's involved in some drama involving her family and personal environment. She's such a warm, caring person that she's a people magnet (South Node in Leo). The house placement of her South Node suggests that she feels most comfortable in her personal environment. But the path to her spiritual evolution and to her achievement lies in the public arena.

Nodes Through the Signs

Aries North Node

Your soul craves independence. But your comfort zone lies in the embrace of others. You're at ease in most relationships, within groups, and seek balance in everything you do. Sometimes your need for balance is so great that you bend over backward to accommodate others and end up compromising your own values. That's your comfort zone—Libra South Node—speaking.

It's your South Node, too, that constantly sends you off in search of the perfect partner, the elusive soul mate. But you probably won't find the ideal partner until you know who *you* are and what you believe separate from your parents, family, authority figures, and anyone else who seeks to define you. That's where your Aries North Node comes in, where you must reach for your independence and freedom.

This node is about *you*—your independence rather than your codependence, about following your impulses, passions, and hunches rather than pressing the pause button on all that and doing something to please someone else. You're here this time to develop independence in thought, action, words, deeds. You're here to define your values according to who *you* are rather than through group consensus. Don't hesitate to take risks. Live like the *Star Trek* motto, boldly going where no man (or woman!) has gone before. Spiritually, you must sprout your wings and fly.

Easier said than done because it begins with solitude, a state of being that is foreign to you. As you begin to carve time for yourself, your Libra South Node may throw a major tantrum and urge you to get out and about, to hurry to that party, that get-together, that crowd of friends and strangers so that you can work the room. Resist those temptations, regardless of the comfort they promise. Ignore the criticisms of others—a difficult challenge because Libra South Node can't abide disapproval. The moment it detects disapproval, it causes you to run around apologizing to everyone, making excuses, laughing, oh, you were just kidding, really, and how about if we all get together tomorrow night for another party?

While your Libra South Node seeks to smooth things over with family, friends, coworkers, and everyone else who disapproves, your Aries North Node coaxes you to continue following impulses and forging your own path. It urges you to be spontaneous, to take off at a moment's notice with just a backpack and your ATM card and head for parts unknown. It demands that you become an individual separate from the collective called family, relationships, the community. It pushes you beyond consensus reality to test the limits of your soul. Once you're able to do that, you can successfully draw on your Libra South Node for harmony and balance.

Examples: Ram Dass, Jay Leno, Neil Armstrong.

Taurus North Node

Your soul seeks stability. With this fixed earth-sign node, your mission this time around is to define your values and realize your potential through everything the physical universe has to offer. It's a magnificent banquet of sensual delights, glittering beauty, unimagined riches. Your playground is physical reality, and you're supposed to build something meaningful and lasting while you're here. You're supposed to do it patiently, with resilience to any obstacles in your way, and whatever you tackle isn't done until it's done!

But your Scorpio South Node resists. It demands that you merge with whatever you're doing, that you become the project, the relationship, the ideal, and that you control it. It urges you to work privately, in secrecy, never letting on what your real agenda is. Your South Node investigates, researches, digs for answers and truth, and does it with a kind of terrible impatience and intensity. Your North Node asks that you take some things on faith and trust, that you let your soul speak, and allow events to unfold naturally, organically.

The Scorpio South Node suggests that in past lives, you've dealt with crisis, calamity, excessive sexuality, suspicion, deceit, profound transformation. This time around, one of your callings is to find the calm center of the storm. While everything is collapsing around you, while people you care for are losing their minds and swept up in high drama, you are as still and centered as Buddha.

To achieve this requires enormous practice and patience. Start meditating. Have a physical exercise routine that grounds you completely in physical reality. Yoga, running, swimming, tai chi, biking, the gym: do anything that heightens your awareness of your physical body. And be selfish. Yes, that last part sounds strange because we're taught from a young age to practice the opposite. But for the Taurus North Node, selfishness is self-empowerment. It means you put your own needs and desires first. You're a survivor. Once you do that, you won't feel the need to manipulate and control others.

The sensuality part of the Taurus North Node can be

troublesome because all too often you're working from the raw sexuality of your Scorpio South Node. Try to balance your sensuality. Instead of leaping into sexual relationships, ease yourself into sensual relationships. Experiment, follow your passions in areas other than sex. Otherwise, the seductiveness of the Scorpio North Node takes you into the really dark places—excessive sex, drugs, eating, spending, booze. Kurt Cobain, heroin addict and suicide, is the dark example of this nodal axis. Jacques Cousteau, underwater explorer, and J. R. R. Tolkien, author and creator of the Hobbit world, are more evolved examples. They built legacies and worlds and touched the lives of millions.

Other examples: Greg Allman, Lucille Ball, Pearl Buck, Harry Houdini

Gemini North Node

Your soul seeks diversity and wants to tell everyone about the journey. It is as if you're searching for a unified theory of the universe. Why, why, why? Your insatiable curiosity urges you to gather information to answer these burning questions and then to disseminate what you learn in any way you can, through many venues simultaneously. That's why you're here this time around. As one of the two signs symbolized by two of something, you multitask with ease.

Your Sagittarius South Node practically guarantees that you have a worldview or belief system that serves as a solid foundation in your life. It enables you to take in other people's belief systems and to compare and contrast them with your own. But when you're deep inside this comfort zone, you may think *your* belief system is the only truth. You may become intolerant of other people's spiritual and political beliefs and become a self-righteous stick in the mud.

It's likely that someone in your immediate circle of family and friends holds a belief system radically op-

151

posed to yours—parent, friend, partner, sibling, other relative, neighbor, coworker. This opposition probably leads to heated discussions and arguments. You're intent on convincing the other person that you're right, but this only creates further dissension. Instead, look at this person as your teacher. What can you learn from him or her? Listen with an open mind—and *really* listen. Also listen to what your soul whispers in the silence of your own mind and body. All too often, you're so intent on what you're going to say next that you're deaf to what the other person is saying and dismiss the whispers of your soul as nonsense.

Once you're aware of this pattern within yourself, you can catch yourself before it happens. Here are some guidelines to help you along:

Maintain your curiosity. It's one of your most valuable resources. When someone says something that pushes your buttons, ask yourself why you feel the way you do. Resistance is usually a clue to something within yourself that you should explore and strive to understand.

Always believe in yourself. Yes, this can be challenging for a Gemini North Node person. The twins that symbolize Gemini indicate a duality in your personality. One twin urges you to reach for the seemingly impossible and the other twin is laughing into her hands, snickering, *Yeah, right.* The best way to reconcile this duality is to develop a firm certainty about your talents that gets you through both good times and bad.

Examples: Susan Sarandon, Deepak Chopra, Bill Clinton

Cancer North Node

Your soul searches endlessly for someone or something to nurture—a person, a cause, a mission. You're here to navigate the world of your emotions and intuition, to learn to nurture others as you have nurtured yourself in past lives. You need to discover what makes you feel emotionally secure and to establish that security in your life in order to achieve your potential.

Your Capricorn South Node brings clear goals and ambitions. But because work, goals, and ambition are your comfort zone, you may feel you have to control everything and everyone within your environment. You have a heightened sense of responsibility too, believing that you must assume all the responsibility—at work, at home, with your family. Your desire to achieve and be recognized for those achievements suggests that you work extremely hard. But since these traits come from your South Node, you may not make significant progress until you're living from a centered, emotionally secure place.

If you can stay in tune with your emotions, they will act as an infallible guide. When a negative emotion surfaces, don't just shove it aside, but don't obsess about it, either. Take note of it—then release it and let it flow out of you. In the same way, you should release your need for control too. Control of others is an illusion fostered by your South Node. The only person you can control is yourself—your own thoughts, actions, choices, your home and personal environments. You can't control what others think, and do, and believe.

The Cancer/Capricorn axis is about how we live our private and public lives. Home and family versus career and profession, right brain versus left brain, the inner world versus the outer world. The Cancer North Node urges you to open your heart, to listen to the whispers of your intuition, to lower your defenses. As a cardinal water sign, this node also urges you to explore the unknown.

Examples: Elisabeth Kübler Ross, Erma Bombeck, Daphne du Maurier

Leo North Node

Your soul craves recognition, so baby, let the good times roll! You're here this time around to explore all forms of creative expression. You're supposed to learn what you love, what you truly desire, to have fun and be happy and how to manifest all of it. Along the way, you're also supposed to learn how to give and receive unconditional love. Sounds like a Disney movie, right?

Thanks to your Aquarius South Node, you're tolerant of people who are different from you, understand group dynamics, believe that we're all created equal. Your comfort zone is the world of ideas, the mind, the intellect. In fact, you may be more comfortable with ideas than you are with people or more comfortable putting the group before the individual, friends before partner and family. But your Leo North Node urges you to reach beyond ideas, beyond the group, to plunder the depths of your creativity and express yourself as an individual.

To navigate your Leo North Node successfully, here are some essentials:

- Nurture your creativity on a daily basis—not just whenever the spirit moves you. Once you learn to do this out of sheer enjoyment, your heart opens wide, and you start to realize that it's okay to be recognized for your achievements. It's okay to stand out from the group, to step out into the limelight and announce who you are.
- Ignore peer pressure. Whether this is difficult or easy depends on your age, of course, and the type of work you do.
- Create your life consciously. This requires awareness of your internal patterns. If you dislike some of the patterns you find, then reshape them or break them altogether.
- Don't depend on others to make you happy. Whenever you find yourself doing this, break the habit by

making a conscious decision to create your own joy. Then go do exactly that.

The beauty of the Leo North Node is about *you*—as an individual separate from any collective, any tribe. Love yourself first so that you're whole enough to love others.

Virgo North Node

Details, perfection: that's what your soul hopes to find this time around. You're the Swiss watchmaker, immersed in the details of creating the best watch in the world. All those intricate levers, the beveled glass face, the tiny little hands. Somehow you bring all these parts together and do it with utter perfection. Now apply the watchmaker analogy to your life. Somehow you're supposed to bring all these disparate bits and pieces together, analyze your experiences, and then manifest your beliefs and ideals in a practical way. The heart of your journey is self-perfection.

Your Pisces South Node offers some of the tools you need—a deep compassion, magnificent imagination, excellent intuition and healing ability. But when your inner critic is screaming, and you retreat into your Pisces South Node out of fear, then it's easy to become trapped in a victim consciousness. You know the routine—you're not good enough, not quite up to the task, there are others more qualified . . . and so on. First, silence the inner critic and resolve not to quit. Once you do that, the rest becomes easier.

When you feel that coiled serpent of fear in the pit of your stomach, tackle it. When you feel unable to make a decision, take a few deep breaths and try to explore your resistance. Don't obsess about the fear or tear it apart, scrutinizing every bit of it. Just acknowledge it and try to move through it.

Share your knowledge and skills with others, without

thought of compensation, but do so only because you want to, not because you feel obligated. By performing a service out of compassion rather than obligation, you mitigate the risk of victim consciousness.

Remain in the moment. Or, as Ram Dass said, *Be here now.* By being fully rooted in the moment, fear can't choke you. Read Eckhart Tolle's *The Power of Now.* By doing this, you also mitigate self-criticism. Any time you find yourself falling into this frame of mind, tell yourself that you're perfect as you are. *Love and approve of yourself.*

Your Virgo North Node urges you to navigate your daily life with reason, logic, and attention to detail. Once you're able to do this, you can draw on the South Node's power of imagination and intuition and can manifest virtually anything you desire.

Examples: Harrison Ford, Michael J. Fox, Kurt Vonnegut Jr.

Libra North Node

Your soul seeks balance: that's what this lifetime is about. Specifically, you're here to learn how to balance your needs with those of your partner, kids, friends, parents, and just about everyone else. You do it by walking in the other person's shoes.

Your comfort zone, of course, is the exact opposite of everything in the first paragraph. When you're afraid or uncertain, hurt or not feeling well, you retreat into an independent, *I can do it myself* frame of mind. You become selfish, intolerant of people who are different from you, and aren't open to any kind of compromise.

This *me first* attitude can be tough to overcome. But a good first step is to put others first. Yes, balk all you want, but it's the perfect place to start. Try it in small increments at first. Perhaps your partner needs the car at the same time that you're scheduled to have lunch with someone. Instead of insisting that you should get the car, make other arrangements. Or once a week or once a month, put someone else before yourself—let someone else go before you in the grocery store line, at the theater, the gas station. When you start doing this on a regular basis, then you're moving along the path of your North Node.

The Aries South Node prompts you to act decisively, impulsively, rashly because you assume you know what's going on, that you've got the right information and the right answers, and it inadvertently hurts someone. Better to pace yourself, ask questions, interact with people around you, and gather the information you need. Use tact and diplomacy rather than the blunt force of words and actions.

Once you're able to embrace the art of relating to others, then you can successfully draw on the independence and fearlessness of your Aries South Node.

Examples: Madonna, Frédéric Chopin, Anaïs Nin

Scorpio North Node

Your soul cries out for personal power. You're here to learn about using that personal power and magnetism in a positive, constructive way. Through intense experiences, you learn to purge your life of the nonessential or of whatever is stagnant in any area—relationships, jobs, careers, belief systems, habits. Then you can draw on your Taurus South Node to build what is durable, lasting.

You've got plenty of help on this journey. Your South Node gives you ample physical energy, practicality, and a stubborn determination that can see you through anything. Your Taurus South Node urges you to collect things—old books, stamps, art, jewelry—and it whispers, *I want to be surrounded by comfort and beauty.* But when you become obsessively attached to these possessions, to comfort and beauty for their own sake, you may attract a situation that teaches you possessions are just stuff we own.

Your work ethic is stellar, nose to the ground, immersed in whatever you're doing, for as long as it takes. But you make some things harder than they need to be. That's when you know you're being resistant to change. Yet change is part of what you're here to learn.

When change knocks at your door, invite it in for coffee and a chat. If you can't learn to do that, then circumstances will force change and it will be something profoundly transformative and probably not pleasant. Again, take small steps. Once a week, do something you've never done before. If you're terrified of heights, then the step could be something as dramatic as skydiving or as small as walking to the end of a high diving board.

Empower others by supporting their creative endeavors, spiritual values, raises and promotions, or anything else that is important to them. Use your exceptional intuition to gain insight into others—who are they in the privacy of their own hearts? What are their dreams, motives, and hopes? Use your intuition as often as you can. It's like a muscle. The more you use it, the stronger it becomes.

When you feel fear that threatens to send you scampering back to your comfort zone—to the nearest mall to shop for anything, to the comfort of rich foods, booze, drugs, the entire physical spectrum of sensual delights—stop. Breathe. Then investigate. What are you afraid of? Has it happened yet? Or are you afraid of something that *may* happen? Once you become aware of the pattern, you can break it, and when you break it, you're truly advancing along the path of your Scorpio North Node.

Examples: Tiger Woods, Edgar Allan Poe, Francis Ford Coppola

Sagittarius North Node

Your soul is seeking truth—specifically, your personal truth. It may sound like a major undertaking, but you can achieve it by using your intuitive ability to grasp the big picture rather than collecting endless, disconnected facts. The emphasis for you in this lifetime is on right brain, intuition, and imagination rather than logic and reason.

Your comfort zone—the Gemini South Node—is about information, facts, and figures. You can talk to anyone about anything, have terrific communication skills, and are one of the most social creatures in the zodiac. But when you feel threatened and afraid, you retreat into the darker aspects of your South Node—you talk when you should be listening, second-guess what people are thinking and feeling, make up facts, change rules in the middle of the game.

To use your North Node energy successfully, learn to trust yourself. To trust that inner voice of your intuition rather than the voices of everyone you consult before you make a decision. Strive to be more spontaneous. By allowing yourself freedom to take off at a moment's notice for an exotic port, to call in sick to work so you can attend your kid's play at school, to run off and get married in Vegas—well, it's part and parcel of the Sadge North Node. Honor it! Spontaneity is the manifestation of your intuition.

Strive to be more patient. Yeah, your Gemini South Node won't want to hear about it, but patience leads you to realize there are no quick fixes, and what's the big rush about, anyway?

Your North Node urges you to explore the unknown, to delve into spiritual, political, and metaphysical issues that people around you may not want to discuss. Just resist the temptation for self-righteousness and go about your business. This journey doesn't belong to anyone else. It's *yours.*

159

Examples: Drew Barrymore, Colin Powell, Zelda Fitzgerald, Angelina Jolie

Capricorn North Node

This time around, your soul seeks to control its own destiny. That's it in a nutshell, that's why you're here this time around. Already, your Cancer South Node is sobbing in a corner for that orphan on the news tonight, for the starving animals roaming the ruins of the latest disaster, for the most recent genocide somewhere. She doesn't want to hear about your ambitions, about you taking charge, about you controlling your destiny. So she pouts, she plunges you into a depression, and here *you* now sit, worrying yourself into a frenzy about stuff that hasn't even happened yet.

Let's back up. Your Cancer South Node offers plenty of tools for your journey—intuition and compassion, a sense of personal history, deep emotions that are your gauge to what's really going on in your life. Your South Node knows how to comfort anyone and anything in need that's hurting, that needs a shelter for the night—or for a year. This includes strays—cats, dogs, birds, whatever finds its way to your doorstep. The problem arises when you nurture and heal at the expense of your own needs or when you nurture others without first nurturing yourself. That's when your South Node becomes an impediment to achieving your potential. That's when you become like Rapunzel, trapped in her tower.

Your Capricorn North Node urges you to reach for everything you want and to achieve your potential through careful planning, strategizing, and hard work. But your Cancer South Node keeps hurling up images of your past mistakes, the issues you dealt with in childhood, how your mom or dad or family might object to what you're doing. You stop in your tracks, suddenly paralyzed and filled with doubt.

So your first order of business is to release the past.

The present is your point of power. The present is the place from which you write the script of your life. Honor the past, certainly, but recognize that your childhood, your parents, the bully in the sixth grade have no say over your life now.

Your second order of business—and imagine this as a Power Point presentation—is to stay tuned in to your feelings. But don't use your emotions to manipulate or control others. When you feel negative, don't dwell on it. Let the negativity wash through you, put one foot in front of the other, and move forward again.

Third point? Always express what you feel, when you feel it. Don't keep it all bottled up inside, as your South Node would like. Let it all out. Not only will you feel better, you'll be advancing on the path of your North Node.

By the way, you are in illustrious company! Examples: Indira Gandhi, Robert Redford, Oprah Winfrey

Aquarius North Node

Your soul searches for the collective experience, so this time around, you're here to learn about the importance of groups. Whether it's your family group, your community, a social circle, a political or spiritual movement, or some massive humanitarian effort that impacts the family of man, you're supposed to learn you can't always be the center of attention.

Your Leo South Node won't be happy about this development. It basks in applause and recognition. Yet your South Node also confers a terrific personality, great warmth and magnetism, and such radiant joy for life that if you can direct those qualities toward something larger than yourself, you will succeed at everything you do.

Your ego is well developed, thanks in large part to your Leo South Node. But ego alone won't do the job this time around. You're called upon to reach beyond the self, to extend yourself into the larger world, into the family of man, where you can make a tremendous difference, an integral component in a paradigm shift. You may do this through any number of creative venues, through your career, through volunteering, through your family life or the way you earn your living. But there are some definite steps you can take toward embracing your North Node, and foremost among them is to minimize drama.

Your South Node, see, is all about drama—in temperament, relationships, activities. In every single phase and area of your life there may be drama that your South Node stirs up, stokes. So strip away the drama, and what do you have? Someone with great talents and potential who can achieve that potential through shifting focus from self to the group, the tribe, the community, whatever it is.

Use your Leo South Node to cultivate and nurture your creative passions. If you can pour your emotions into a creative outlet, especially one that brings insights and pleasures to a larger group, you're well on your journey into your North Node.

Examples: Leonard Cohen, F. Scott Fitzgerald

Pisces North Node

Your soul wants to sink into the depths of imagination and intuition to discover the larger spiritual and creative picture that governs your life. This lifetime is about unearthing everything that is hidden in your life—power you have disowned, secrets that are kept in family vaults, in genealogy books, in the deepest reservoirs of your DNA. Your life is about bringing all this stuff into the light of day.

Your Virgo South Node brings a lot to the table for this journey—a discriminating intellect, a penchant for details, a remarkable ability to connect the dots in any situation, event, crisis, relationship. You name it, the Virgo South Node grasps how all the connections are made. Your South Node is terrific in any situation where rapid solutions are needed, where connections must be made at the speed of light, and where everything—all the information and details—are *correct*.

But, *correct* aside, this is the life where you go with the flow, avoid self-criticism, trust the universe to deliver what you need and desire, and develop your spiritual beliefs. All of this can be done through your daily work, but in terms of the big picture, the larger canvas of possibilities, the forest as opposed to the trees. Maybe you blog about your experiences. Maybe you set up a Web site that sells a particular product or service that helps others to reach their highest potential. The bottom line about the Pisces North Node is, ultimately, unknown and unknowable, too mystical to penetrate unless it's your conscious path, and too complex to decipher unless your intuitive skills are remarkably developed.

But remember this. When your Virgo South Node slaps its ruler across your desk in ninth grade and demands that you memorize how to conjugate the verb "to be" in Latin, Spanish, French, and German, it's your Pisces North Node that hurls your arm upward, knocking that ruler away, and says, "Chill. I'm on my own path to enlightenment."

Examples: Matt Damon, Naomi Campbell, Isadora Duncan

CHAPTER 12

By the Numbers

Even though this is an astrology book, we use numbers in some of the daily predictions because we're attempting to remain true to what Sydney Omarr did. The legendary astrologer was also a numerologist and combined the two forms in his work. So let's take a closer look at how the numbers work.

If you're familiar with numerology, you probably know your life path number, which is derived from your birth date. That number represents who you were at birth and the traits that you'll carry throughout your life. There are numerous books and Web sites that provide details on what the numbers mean regarding your life path.

But in the daily predictions, what does it mean when it's a number 9 day, and how did it get to be that number? In the dailies, you'll usually find these numbers on the days when the moon is transiting from one sign to another. The system is simple: add the numbers related to the astrological sign (1 for Aries, 2 for Taurus, etc.), the year, the month, and the day.

For example, to find what number June 14, 2011, is for a Libra, you would start with 7, the number for Libra, add 4 (the number you get when you add 2011 together), plus 6 for June, plus 5 (1+4) for the day. That would be 7+4+6+5 (sign + year + month+ day) = 22= 4.

So June 14, 2011, is a number 4 day for a Libra. It would be a 5-day for a Scorpio, the sign following Libra. So on that number 4 day, Libra might be advised that her organizational skills are highlighted, that she should stay focused, get organized, be methodical and thorough. She's building a creative future. Tear down the old in order to rebuild. Keep your goals in mind, follow your ideas.

Briefly, here are the meanings of the numbers, which are included in more detail in the dailies themselves.

1. Taking the lead, getting a fresh start, a new beginning
2. Cooperation, partnership, a new relationship, sensitivity
3. Harmony, beauty, pleasures of life, warm, receptive
4. Getting organized, hard work, being methodical, rebuilding, fulfilling your obligations
5. Freedom of thought and action, change, variety, thinking outside the box
6. A service day, being diplomatic, generous, tolerant, sympathetic
7. Mystery, secrets, investigations, research, detecting deception, exploration of the unknown, of the spiritual realms
8. Your power day, financial success, unexpected money, a windfall
9. Finishing a project, looking beyond the immediate, setting your goals, reflection, expansion.

Simple, right?

CHAPTER 13

Love and Timing in 2012 for Aries

If it's true that timing is everything, then it behooves you to be informed about when love may come knocking at your door. If you're already in love and in a committed relationship, this sort of timing can also be useful—to romance the one you love, to plan a trip together, to know when conditions are favorable to start a family, to move.

Venus is the planet that governs love and romance, Mars governs sexuality, and Mercury governs communication. Love+sex+communication: that looks like part of the winning ticket. But we'll include new and full moons in the equation, too, since the moon rules our inner worlds, our intuitive selves. New moons generally usher in new opportunities, and full moons bring insights, news, and a touch of craziness!

For the Single Aries

You love your independence. Everyone around you knows this. But you're also an incurable romantic, Aries, admit it. You want the earth to move (Hemingway), you want longing looks across a cafeteria (*Twilight*), you want the whole package, no matter how strange or odd (*The Time Traveler's Wife*). The best dates for meeting someone who fits this ticket fall between September 6 and October 3, when Venus transits dramatic Leo and your solar fifth house. So make yourself available during this time period. Accept all social invitations. Get out and about doing what you enjoy doing; be open to the experience of meeting someone. Your focus will help to attract the right person.

Good backup dates fall earlier in the year, when Venus transits your sign: February 8 to March 5. This transit increases your self-confidence, and others see you as attractive and fascinating, as a leader, as someone on the cutting edge.

If you're not interested in a long-term romantic relationship and are just looking for a quick fling with no strings attached, then the period from October 6 to November 16 looks promising. Mars transits fellow fire sign Sagittarius during this period, so you're in the right place at the right time and the place could be somewhere overseas. Or perhaps you connect with this person through a social networking site.

Another period to watch is when Mercury enters your sign or fellow fire signs. These periods increase the chances of excellent communication with a romantic partner. However, this year, all the Mercury retrogrades occur in fire signs, Aries, so be particularly aware of the retrograde dates. The Leo dates: June 25 to July 14, when Mercury then turns retrograde until August 8, then continues transiting Leo until August 31. Aries dates: March 2 to April 4 and April 16 to May 9. From March 12 to April 4, Mercury will be retrograde. Mercury enters Sagittarius on October 29, retrogrades on November 6, turns direct in Scorpio on November 26. On December 10, it enters Sadge again until December 31.

For the Committed Aries

Read the section above for the single Aries. These dates are also good for a committed Aries, but for different reasons. For instance, when Venus is transiting Leo and your solar fifth house or your own sign, plan something special for you and the one you love. Get out of town for a few days to some romantic spot that you and your partner will enjoy. Treat yourselves to a special dinner, bring your partner flowers, a book he or she has been wanting to read, a piece of jewelry or something else that is significant.

When Venus transits Sagittarius from December 15, 2012, to January 9, 2013, take a trip abroad, visit a sacred site, or do something else with your partner that involves a quest.

Marriage on your mind, Aries? Be sure to set the date for when there are no retrogrades of Mercury, Venus, or Mars. The Mercury retrogrades are listed under single Aries. The Venus retrograde to avoid is in Gemini and falls between May 15 and June 27. There are no Mars retrogrades this year. And since Uranus is in your sign this year, it would be smart to avoid a Uranus retrograde as well, which falls between July 13 and December 13. That immediately knocks five months off the year. So let's look for dates that might be beneficial for a marriage:

- On or after the new moon in Taurus on April 21. No retrogrades then, either, so this date looks very good. Venus is in compatible air sign Gemini on this date—another plus.
- On or after the new moon in your partner's sign
- Any time after June 11, when Jupiter enters compatible air sign Gemini. Use this alternative in the event that family members prefer a marriage later in the year!
- For a summer wedding, on or after the new moon

168

in Leo would be good in spite of the Uranus retrograde
- For a fall wedding, on or after the new moon in Libra, your opposite sign

For All Aries

Keep in mind that any relationships that begin this year will be impacted by Uranus in your sign. Uranus, as the planet of sudden, unexpected events, can lead to sudden, unexpected attractions, relationships, and affairs. These relationships will certainly be tremendously exciting, but may not be the most long-lived.

Also, with Uranus in your sign for the next seven years, the emphasis on your freedom and individuality will be pronounced. So whether you're single and looking or in a committed relationship, it's important that your partner gives you a lot of freedom. By the same token, you must allow your partner an equal amount of freedom. All too often, your passions in a relationship are so encompassing that you can become possessive and jealous. That won't work during the long Uranus transit in your sign.

Another detail to consider is that Saturn is in Libra, your opposite sign, until October 5. The Saturn opposition to your sun can be a somewhat discouraging time if you allow it to be. Your mind-set tends to be more serious.

The third point to consider is Jupiter. The planet of expansion and luck enters Gemini on June 11, bringing a positive boost to your conscious mind that can mitigate the sobering influence of the Saturn opposition. With Jupiter in your solar third house, you and your partner would have good luck finding a wonderful neighborhood to start your lives together.

Other Considerations

Strange events and feelings are triggered by eclipses. The solar eclipse in Gemini on May 20 occurs in your solar third house. It could bring about new opportunities for love and romance with someone with whom you share great communication. It's possible that the person lives in your neighborhood or that you meet this individual through a sibling or other relative.

The lunar eclipse in fellow fire sign Sadge that occurs on June 4 should be quite positive for you. You could get involved with someone from another country or whose belief system is radically different. You could meet someone while traveling.

The solar eclipse on November 13 falls in Scorpio, in your solar eighth house. With this one, a new opportunity could surface to share your expertise, time, money, or energy, and the recipient of your generosity is someone with whom you become involved. Or it brings you closer to your current partner.

The lunar eclipse in Gemini on November 28 brings up feelings that you want to express to a partner. Or there could be news concerning a partner. With Jupiter forming a conjunction of five degrees to the moon, any news you hear should be positive and expansive and make you feel lucky.

CHAPTER 14

Career Timing in 2012 for Aries

You don't think like other people. You're the trailblazer, remember? You're the entrepreneur, the one who finds a professional niche—and then fills it. If you've ever wanted to be self-employed (and most Aries probably have had that desire at one time or another), then 2012 is the year to set that dream in motion. Let's take a look at why and how you can maximize the energy of the transiting planets to create a professional life that you love.

Why 2012?

Most metaphysical teachers talk about the importance of being fully present, fully grounded in the moment. In *The Power of Now, The Law of Attraction,* and *Seth Speaks,* the message is the same: our point of power is the present. We may cling to the past and yearn for the future, but neither will bring us the power we have in this moment, in this breath, in a present action.

So before this year is already behind you, make a list of your professional goals and dreams. Then ask your-self: *What's holding me back?* Chances are that the only thing holding you back is . . . well, *you.* Your fear. Your insecurity. Your belief, perhaps, that you aren't quite up to the task. Sometimes, even for an Aries, it's easier to maintain the status quo than to forge ahead, because at least the status quo is *known*. But if you always stick to what is known and familiar, you'll always wonder what if ... *What if* you had taken that leap of faith, *what if* you had launched that business, *what if* you had taken the plunge, what if, what if. So for 2012, Aries, don't be a *what if* person. Take the leap. Believe in yourself. Express who you are, and be proud of it.

Dates to Watch For

Pluto entered Capricorn and your solar tenth house in 2008, so that's when your career path began to transform. Perhaps you resigned from a job or were fired. Perhaps your company was downsized or went out of business. Maybe your company moved overseas. However the events unfolded for you, change was in the wind. Change is still in the wind, but you're more in control of things now.

Pluto will be retrograde in Capricorn between April 10 and September 17, so during this time it's wise to remember that Pluto won't be functioning at full capacity. You may be revisiting power issues that have risen in the last few years. That said, there are times this year when Venus forms a beneficial angle to Pluto and to your career area. These times are good for pitching new ideas, launching your own business, and garnering the support you need. They also favor raises and promotions.

March 5 to April 3: Venus in Taurus forms that beneficial angle mentioned above. With Venus transiting your financial sector at this time, it looks as if your income ticks upward. Raise? New job that pays more? Both are possible.

October 3 to 28: Venus in Virgo forms a beneficial

angle to your career area and to Pluto. As Venus transits your solar sixth house, your daily work schedule and routine are highlighted. Things flow your way with employees, bosses, and work generally.

June 11, 2012, to June 25, 2013: Jupiter's transit through compatible air sign Gemini is a definite boon for you, Aries. It enhances your communication abilities, expands your curiosity, and may take you overseas or into new areas, like higher education and publishing.

January 8 to 27: Mercury transits Capricorn and the career area of your chart. This transit favors communication with bosses, peers. It's the time to push your own agenda forward, to ask for a promotion and a raise. It's also a good time for submitting resumés and applications for new jobs, if you're so inclined.

November 16 to December 25: Mars transits Capricorn and your career area. During this period, everything about your professional life is energized, active. You could conflict with bosses and authorities, though, so be measured in your responses, Aries. Think before you speak. If you do that, then this period should allow you to move ahead, to make significant strides professionally and with projects in which you're involved.

What the Moons Say

As discussed earlier in the book, new moons are related to new opportunities, and full moons are connected to news, insights, activity. So let's see what the lunations this year have in store for your career.

The new moon in Capricorn occurred at the end of 2011, but there's a powerful full moon in your career area on July 3. This moon, with Pluto positioned closely to it, brings professional news that should put you squarely in the driver's seat, Aries, exactly where you like to be.

April 21: The new moon in Taurus and your solar second house should be extremely lucky for you. A raise or promotion may come through that's directly related to your professional work.

September 15: The new moon in Virgo, in your solar sixth house, ushers in new opportunities in your daily work. A higher level of efficiency and perfection will be required with this opportunity, but if you take it, you do so because it interests you. And when you're interested, you go the extra mile.

Once a year, there's a new moon in your sign, Aries. It's important because it sets the tone of your life for the next year. In 2012, it falls on March 22, and both Mercury and Uranus form close conjunctions to the moon. This suggests that new opportunities that surface do so quickly out of the blue and could involve communication, travel, education. You'll have to be on your toes to seize the opportunity, but to be forewarned is to be forearmed!

Saturn's Movements

Until October 5, Saturn is in Libra, your opposite sign. We've talked elsewhere about why this is a major transit, but let's take a look at what it may mean for your career.

With Saturn in your partnership area, there could be delays in business partnerships. If you're self-employed, for example, and have a business partner, then you may have to assume more responsibility because your partner, for whatever reason, isn't up to snuff. Or if you depend on someone in your business to call the shots, things may be challenging. Just try not to get discouraged and remember that you write the script of your life from the inside out. So if you sense that things aren't working out the way you hoped and planned, go to plan

B. If you don't have a plan B, create one. You'll find your way one way or another because there's little in the known universe that keeps an Aries down!

From June 11 onward, you've got Jupiter in Gemini on your side, mitigating some of Saturn's influence. In fact, Jupiter and Saturn are forming a beneficial angle to each other. This angle suggests that the professional structures you set up should help you to expand creatively and attract helpful people and opportunities.

Parting Thoughts About Career Matters

Whenever you feel discouraged about your career or anything else this year, get out and do something physical. Many Aries are active, athletic individuals, and you always feel better while you're moving. Whether you're climbing mountains, skiing, swimming, or jogging a solitary few miles, do it with the intention of improving how you feel. Once you feel better, the experiences and people you attract will be more positive. Yes, it may sound simplistic, but don't knock it until you've tried it.

Once you feel better, figure out what caused or contributed to your discouragement. If it's a relationship, then it may be time to reevaluate whether you still want that person in your life. If the cause is a situation, then perhaps it's time to release the situation.

Get the idea?

CHAPTER 15

Navigating Uranus in Aries in 2012

As an Aries, you generally seek excitement, a rush of adrenaline in just about everything you do. But Uranus's transit of your sign for the next seven years may be a bit more than you bargained for.

Not only is Uranus the planet that symbolizes sudden, unexpected change, but it rules innovation, rebellion, individuality, genius, eccentricity, and lightning. It ushers in change in an abrupt manner, with events that literally seem to come out of the blue. You rarely see Uranian events headed toward you. The purpose? Shake up your status quo so that the old can fall away, making room for the new.

Most of us have areas of our lives that are relatively stable—a relationship, a job, our family situation, our finances, our careers, our beliefs. Whatever it is, that's the area that is probably going to be impacted during the seven years of Uranus's transit through your sign. Granted, predictability is less of an issue for Aries than it is for some of the other signs, but even an Aries can get stuck. So for starters, take an honest appraisal of your life and pinpoint the area or areas that feel the most stable and predictable. If it's a relationship, job, or living situation, what would you change? Once you know that, you can begin to implement change in that area and perhaps mitigate some of the challenging effects of the Uranus transit so that you can enjoy its benefits.

Take a look at the possibilities that may unfold with this Uranus transit. Whether these changes are challenging or ultimately beneficial depends on your particular situation and attitude.

Possibilities

1. Loss of a job
2. You land a dream job
3. Loss of income
4. Your income soars
5. Loss of a relationship
6. Better relationship materializes
7. You take more risks
8. The risks pay off
9. You start your own business
10. You move
11. Child leaves home
12. Child returns home
13. Loss of a parent
14. You invent something
15. You find a gap in the market that your product or services fill
16. Retirement
17. Your creativity flourishes
18. Unusual psychic or spiritual experiences
19. Your marital status changes
20. You inherit money, win the lottery, or earn more than you dreamed possible

These possibilities are some of the most common. To really grasp the possibilities germane to you, get out your natal chart. Look at the house where Aries is found in your chart. Look for any planets you have in Aries. These areas—plus your sun—are the ones that will be impacted by Uranus's transit through your sign.

Turn to the natal chart at the end of chapter 9. This woman is a Capricorn with a tenth-house sun, has a Leo moon in the fifth house, and has Aries rising at 19 degrees and 54 minutes—19♈54. The rising is the cusp of her first house, which governs the self. So Uranus has been in her twelfth house since it was at 17 degrees and 16 minutes of Pisces—17♓16—the cusp of her twelfth house.

During this period, with Uranus stirring up all the hidden stuff in her unconscious, she got married and divorced, landed a great job in an assisted living facility as the wellness director (she's an RN), was nearly forced to resign by an abusive boss, fought it, held onto her job, and got a raise. All three of her sons left home during this transit—to jobs and college. She moved twice.

As of this writing, in 2010, she is now accustomed to this Uranian energy and is planning to branch out as a consultant in her field, helping other men and women to navigate the labyrinth of health care and options for their aging parents and grandparents. In other words, she sees a gap in the health-care market and is figuring out ways she might fill that gap. That's the innovation part of the equation.

Once Uranus enters Aries in March 2011, it will be on its approach to her rising—an important, major life transit. The rising, as the portal to our charts, is where our experiences enter into our lives. The closer Uranus gets to her ascendant, the more unpredictable, exciting, and high energy her life will become. The conjunction is exact in March 2016, but she may start feeling it as early as the summer of 2012, when Uranus reaches 8 degrees Aries (eleven degrees from her rising) before it turns retrograde. It turns direct again in early December 2012 and gets to within seven degrees of her ascendant by July 2013, before it retrogrades again. By July 2014, Uranus gets to within three degrees of her rising before it retrogrades once more. In late May 2015, it hits her rising.

What all this means is that each year, as Uranus inches closer to that exact hit on her rising sign, she feels a progressively stronger urge to break free of any restrictions that are holding her back. The closer it gets to her rising, the closer it also gets to forming beautiful angles—trines—to her South Node in Leo (fourth house)—☋12♌32, and her natal moon and Pluto in Leo in the fifth house—☽21♌48 and ♇22♌54. So while she's feeling this tremendous urge for freedom, Uranus is making it easier for her to bring about major changes in her emotional, inner life (moon). A new relationship could enter the picture, and it will be one wild, wonderful ride, different from anything she has experienced before. She might move.

With Pluto thrown into the mix, she has a marvelous opportunity to understand her innermost being—the unconscious beliefs and attitudes that have resulted in negative situations or relationships in the past. The trine to Pluto from Uranus gives her enormous personal power. One of her sons (fifth house) may get married. She might do or create something so innovative that she is recognized for it by peers. The trine to her South Node and sextile to her North Node in Aquarius in the eleventh house—☊12♒32—suggests that people she has known in the past (this life or others) may surface. She will have an opportunity to attain her dreams.

These possibilities are due to the transit of just one planet, Aries. So when you look at your natal chart to see where Uranus's impact will be felt most strongly, look beyond your sun sign. Look at other planets and points, too.

Dates to Watch For

March 22: We mentioned this date before because it's the day of the new moon in your sign. With Uranus within two degrees of this new moon, expect the unexpected. Embrace everything that comes your way, every opportunity. Try it on for size, see how it feels, let your emotions guide you. If it feels good, go for it. If it doesn't, walk away without regrets.

April 21 to 23: Not only is the twenty-first a new moon in Taurus—i.e., new financial opportunities for you—but Mercury in Aries is approaching an exact conjunction with Uranus. It becomes exact on the twenty-third. This aspect stimulates your conscious mind. All kinds of innovative ideas flow through you. Write them down; scrutinize each one. Can you make them practical? Insomnia could tag you during this period because it will be difficult to shut off your head.

June 19: The new moon in Gemini features an exact and beneficial angle between Uranus and Venus. This aspect stimulates your creativity, your love life, and perhaps even your finances, too. Because Venus is retrograde and then turns direct, there's another exact hit for this aspect during the first week of July.

August 17: The solar eclipse in fellow fire sign Leo also features Uranus forming favorable angles to Mercury and to Jupiter. This trio, with the new moon, heightens communication, luck, and expansion and ushers in new opportunities that come out of nowhere.

Late August to early September: A potentially challenging aspect (square between Uranus and Pluto) that could set off fireworks as change is ushered in rapidly and unexpectedly.

November 28: The lunar eclipse in Gemini features Uranus forming beneficial angles to the moon, the sun, and Jupiter, suggesting a high-energy day, with unexpected news that is cause for celebration.

CHAPTER 16

Aries and Mars in 2012

Since the publication of H. G. Wells's *War of the Worlds* in 1898, Mars has been part of our collective imagination and popular culture. The story idea for the novel is simple. Mars is dying and the Martians flee their world and invade Earth, planning to take over the planet and all its resources. Their first attack, on London, with advanced weaponry seems to ensure their victory. But they're defeated by germs—Earth germs.

In 1911, Edgar Rice Burroughs wrote *A Princess of Mars*. It was the first of eleven novels about the red planet and featured John Carter, a confederate Civil War veteran who ends up being transported to Mars. Over the course of the eleven books, he settles into life on his adopted planet—he gets married, becomes involved in Martian politics, and fights the good fight.

Ray Bradbury's *Martian Chronicles*, published in 1951, twists the theme of Martian-as-invader in a new way. Human settlers arrive on Mars, and the Martians are killed by the bacteria that the humans bring with them. But these Martians capture our hearts because they are beautiful people of an ancient civilization.

Robert Heinlein, with his 1961 publication of *Stranger in a Strange Land*, brought another twist into the Martian theme. His story centers on a human born on Mars, the only survivor of the first manned space mission to the planet. The protagonist, Valentine Michael Smith, is raised and educated by Martians then returned to Earth when he's a young man. He has the sensibilities of a human, the perspective of an alien, and incredible psychic powers.

In terms of TV, there was *My Favorite Martian* and in film a host of many forgettable movies. An exception was *Total Recall,* based on a Philip K. Dick short story, in which Arnold Schwarzenegger plays a man haunted by suppressed memories—specifically, journeys to Mars. The story has all the complex hallmarks of Philip K. Dick—paranoia, duplicity, deep and powerful secrets, and plenty of corrupt bad guys. The ending takes place on Mars, when atmospheric gases and water are freed from deep within the planet's rocks.

Part of our fascination with Mars is that it bears some similarities to Earth and may have been habitable at one time in the past—and may be in the future. Its surface has been dramatically changed by volcanism, impacts by asteroids, meteors, and other celestial bodies, violent movements in its crust, and great cyclonic dust storms that frequently swallow the entire planet. Its polar ice caps grow and recede, like ours, with the change of seasons. Near the poles, the layered soil indicates that the planet's climate has changed more than once. Its ancient volcanoes, once powered from the heat of the Martian core, rise against the starkness with a kind of fierce purity. The largest volcano, Olympus Mons, is seventeen miles high and may be the largest in the solar system. There's also a titanic canyon about the size of the distance between New York and L.A.

Thanks to the Mars Odyssey spacecraft, it's now believed that billions of years ago Mars was inundated by the largest floods in the solar system. No one knows where all that water went, but the Mars Odyssey detected substantial quantities of water mixed into the soil about three feet down, near the Martian south pole.

So far, the mystery about water on Mars hasn't been

solved. How much is frozen in the polar ice caps? How much of it may be locked in ice beneath the red surface? The answers may hold vital information not only about the Martian past, but also about the formation of Earth and other planets in the solar system.

The Mars Reconnaissance Orbiter has been studying Mars since 2006. In October 2009, NASA released high-resolution photos of the Martian surface that were taken from 233 telescopic observations. These images indicate a variety of surface shapes and textures.

On a clear night at certain times of the year, you can walk outside after dark and glimpse Mars in the sky, a speck of rose-tinted light between 56,000,000 and 399,000,000 kilometers from Earth. Its diameter is a little more than half that of Earth, the length of a Martian day is 24.6 Earth hours, a Martian year is 1.88 Earth years, and gravity on the surface is about a third of Earth's. The atmosphere is unbreatheable. Ninety-five percent of it consists of carbon dioxide. It has two moons, both so small that they may not be moons at all, just rock that got trapped in the planet's gravitational pull. They are named after the two squires who served Ares, the Greek god of war: Phobos, which means "fear," and Deimos—"panic."

Mars in Astrology

To the ancient Greeks he was Ares, a savage god who was little more than a bloodthirsty son of a bitch. In the *Iliad,* Zeus finds Ares, his son, completely odious because he enjoys nothing but "strife, war, and battles." On Olympus, he is intensely disliked for his blind violence and brutality.

This theme is beautifully illustrated in the movie *Gladiator.* Times are brutal, and brute strength is held in such high esteem that the populace turns out to watch men kill each other in the stadium. Not surprisingly, Aries Russell Crowe won an Oscar for his performance. Now skip ahead a couple thousand years. In *The Running Man,* one of the novellas that Stephen King wrote as Richard Bachman, this same theme is repeated, but now the protagonist (Arnold Schwarzenegger in the film) is running for his life on national TV and surviving by his wits and brute strength. Same theme, different century.

But aggression, survival, and war are only one side of Mars. The Greek side. On the Roman side, he was called by the name we know him as: Mars. He was first and foremost the god of agriculture—the protector of cattle, the preserver of corn—and was associated with the woodpecker, the horse, and the wolf. As the husband of Rhea Silvia, a vestal virgin, he fathered Romulus and Remus, who were suckled by a wolf.

The connection between Mars and sex probably came about as a result of Ares's affair with the goddess Aphrodite. She was married to a cripple, Hephaestus, and compared to him Ares was handsome, dashing, courageous—all the things the Olympians looked for in a mate. Ares, of course, took advantage of the situation, and their lustful encounters on the "marriage couch" became well known to the other gods when Hephaestus ensnared the adulterous couple in an invisible net.

In 2012, Mars makes it through six signs and less than a week of a seventh sign. Let's explore the possible ramifications of these transits for you.

Important Dates

January 1 to July 3: Mars in Virgo, your solar sixth house. This transit ramps up the intensity of your daily work. You may have additional responsibilities now and have to work longer hours or use your time more efficiently to get everything done. Virgo is an earth sign, and you may feel smothered at times by this transit, unless you have a lot of earth and water signs in your natal chart. That said, the way to make this transit work for you is to tend to details and be sure a project, paper, or whatever you're working on is as perfect as you can get it before you turn it in.

July 3 to August 23: Mars in Libra, transiting your solar seventh house. This transit brings about a lot of activity and movement with romantic and business partnerships. You'll be searching for ways to balance your responsibilities to yourself and others. You'll discover that a little patience and cooperation take you much farther than dissent and arguments.

This transit should certainly stimulate your sex life, Aries. Whether you're single or in a committed relationship, this transit suggests that subtle seduction is best. Take your partner out for a quiet, romantic dinner. Go to a café afterward or a bookstore or both. Set the stage for romance, and the rest will follow!

During this transit, Jupiter is in Gemini, a fellow air sign of Libra, so any business dealings in which you become involved should expand your creative venue and relationship opportunities.

August 23 to October 6: Mars in Scorpio, a sign it co-rules. This transit may be emotionally intense, giving rise to passions you weren't aware of within yourself. You're after the bottom line in everything you take on and do in every relationship and situation. It's as if your intuitive antennae twitch constantly during this transit. Part of your focus may be on psychic phenomena or past lives, as well as mundane issues like taxes, your partner's income, and mortgages/loans.

October 6 to November 16: Mars in Sagittarius, a fellow fire sign. This transit should be spectacular for you, Aries. It speeds up activity related to education, publishing, foreign travel, your worldview and spiritual beliefs—all ninth-house activities. Mars will be forming a beneficial angle to your sun, heightening all the attributes for which you're known: fearlessness, trailblazing, out-of-the-box thinking, daring, a certain recklessness! But this transit will enable you to get things done.

November 16 to December 25: Mars in Capricorn, your career sector. This transit galvanizes your professional life and deepens your ambition and could bring confrontations with bosses or other authority figures. It's possible to push your professional agenda forward at this time, as long as you do it in a measured, thoughtful way instead of rushing into something.

Capricorn is symbolized by the goat, an animal that can climb virtually anything, but moving only at its own pace. It can't be rushed or hurried—unless that's what it wants. So to make the most of this transit, move as the goat moves. Know where you're going and what your end point is. Have a plan B.

December 25 to February 2, 2013: Mars in Aquarius, an air sign compatible with your fire-sign sun. This transit should be a good one, triggering a lot of activity in your social life. You may have opportunities, perhaps through groups to which you belong, to achieve or at least to get closer to achieving your dreams. Be sure to get out and about and accept all social invitations. You never know who you might meet.

CHAPTER 17

The Big Picture for Aries in 2012

Welcome to 2012, Aries. This year highlights your work, creativity, originality, personal unconscious, and many sudden, unexpected events. Let's take a closer look.

Mars, your ruler, begins the year in Virgo, in your solar sixth house, where it will be until July 3, thanks to a long retrograde. While it's moving direct, your daily work life should be hectic, but you'll have the physical energy to get things done. You may have to schedule your time more efficiently, however, so everything on your agenda receives the attention it deserves.

Pluto, the snail of the zodiac, starts off the year in Capricorn, where it has consistently been since November 2008. You're accustomed to its energy now. Its transit, which lasts until 2024, is bringing profound and permanent change, evident in the economic challenges that now face the U.S. Most institutions are in the throes of great change—the health-care industry, petroleum and insurance industries, mortgages/lending, housing, aviation, even the Internet. You name it, and Pluto's fingerprint can be found.

On a personal level, this planet's transit through the career sector of your chart until 2024 probably started bringing about professional change in 2008. That trend will continue.

Neptune entered Pisces and your solar twelfth house

on April 4, 2011. But by early August 2011, it had slipped back into Aquarius. On February 3, 2012, it enters Pisces again and won't move on until January 2026. For hints about what this may mean for you, look back to that period in 2011 when Neptune was in Pisces.

Neptune symbolizes our higher ideals, escapism, fiction, spirituality, and our blind spots. It seeks to dissolve boundaries between us and others. One possible repercussion of this transit is prolonged religious wars, which proliferated during Uranus's transit in Pisces in early 2003. On a personal level, though, Neptune's transit through your twelfth house is likely to increase your intuitive ability. It will be easier for you to recognize other people's motives and hidden agendas—and to recognize your own. You may be scrutinizing your spiritual beliefs more deeply, perhaps delving into your own past lives and taking workshops or seminars to develop your intuitive ability.

That brings us to Uranus, which entered your sign in March 2011. Undoubtedly, you've already found this transit to be a wild, unpredictable ride. Uranus's job is to shake up the status quo, to move us out of our ruts and routines, to wake us up so that we recognize where we have become rigid and inflexible. For an Aries, this will be an exciting time that will last until March 2019. Few elements in your life will be predictable during this transit. Relationships will begin and end suddenly. What was certain yesterday will be uncertain by tomorrow. You'll attract idiosyncratic individuals into your life. These people are apt to be highly creative, unusually bright, or even geniuses at what they do. During the seven years of this transit, you'll experience many changes—in your job and career, personal life, and living situation.

Saturn begins the year in Libra, your opposite sign. It has been there since the summer of 2010 and will be there until October 2012. This transit brings structure to business and personal partnerships, can cause delays and restrictions, and prompts you to strive for cooperation and balance in your relationships. During this opposition to your sun, you may feel discouraged at times because it seems that nothing is moving in your direction. You could encounter problems with bosses and other authority figures, and if you resist what's going on, you could suffer from health problems. That said, this transit teaches you to "go with the flow," whatever that flow may be, and to continue to reach for your dreams, to move forward even when you're discouraged, and to simply put one foot in front of the other and believe in yourself.

Once Saturn enters Scorpio in October, your spouse or partner's income may be restricted in some way. There could be delays or difficulties in obtaining mortgages or loans. However, with any metaphysical work, you find the right structures for studying and pursuing intuitive development.

Expansive Jupiter begins the year in Taurus, your solar second house. This transit, which lasts until June 11, should plump up your bank account and expand your moneymaking options. You may have opportunities to travel internationally, perhaps as a result of new business deals. Then on June 11, Jupiter enters compatible air sign Gemini and your solar third house. This transit, which lasts until late June 2013, should be fabulous for you. Your communication abilities expand, you may move to a neighborhood that suits you better, and, depending on your age, you may see the addition of a brother or sister to your family.

They say that timing is everything, so with that in mind, let's look at some specific areas in your life.

Romance/Creativity

The most romantic and creative time for you all year falls between September 6 and October 3, when Venus transits Leo and the romance/creativity area of your chart. If you're not involved before this transit begins, you probably will be before the transit ends. And if you're not, it won't matter because you're having too much fun. Or you're deeply immersed in a creative project that consumes a lot of your time and energy. Great backup dates: February 8 to March 5, when Venus transits your sign. Things really seem to flow your way then in many areas, but particularly with romantic and creative ventures.

The best time for serious involvement and deepening commitment in an existing relationship occurs when Venus transits Libra and your seventh house from October 28 to November 21. You and your partner may decide to move in together, get engaged, or get married. Just be sure that you don't do any of this under a Mercury retrograde period. Take a look under the appropriate section below to find out when Mercury will be retrograde this year.

Other good backup dates: July 3 to August 23, when Mars transits Libra and your solar seventh house. This stirs up a lot of activity with a partner.

Career

Usually, Venus and Jupiter transits to your career area are the times to look for. But those transits don't happen this year. However, between November 16 and December 25, your ruler, Mars, will be in Capricorn, moving through your career area. This is the time to push your professional agenda forward, to make new professional contacts, and to keep your nose to the grindstone, completing projects and brainstorming with coworkers for new ideas. Also, between January 1 and June 11, when Jupiter is transiting Taurus, it forms a harmonious angle to your career area, so your professional life should run smoothly with expanding options and greater pay.

When Venus is in Capricorn and your tenth house between February 4 and March 1, don't hesitate to pitch
ideas, submit manuscripts and screenplays, and ask for
a raise. It's also an excellent time to launch a Web site,
start your own business, or make new professional contacts. Other people will be receptive to your ideas. A
great backup period falls between April 2 and May 11,
when Mars transits your sign.

Best Times For

Buying or selling a home: August 7 to September 6,
when Venus is in Cancer and your fourth house; June 7
to 25, when Mercury transits Cancer.

Family reunions: Any of the dates above.

Financial matters: The period from January 1 to June
11, when Jupiter transits your house of money. Also,
March 5 to April 3, when Venus moves through the
same area.

Signing contracts: When Mercury is moving direct!
More on this later.

*Overseas travel, publishing, and higher-education
endeavors:* December 15 to January 9, 2013, when Venus transits your solar ninth house and fellow fire sign
Sagittarius.

Mercury Retrogrades

Every year, Mercury—the planet of communication and
travel—turns retrograde three times. During this period,
it's wise not to sign contracts (unless you don't mind re-
negotiating when Mercury is moving direct). It is wise
to check and recheck travel plans and communicate as
succinctly as possible. Refrain from buying any large-

ticket items or electronics during this time too. Often, computers and appliances go on the fritz, cars act up, data is lost . . . you get the idea. Be sure to back up all files before the dates below:

March 12–April 4: Mercury retrograde in your sign. Ouch!

July 14–August 8: Mercury retrograde in Leo, your solar fifth house of romance and creativity.

November 6–26: Mercury retrograde in Sagittarius, your solar ninth house. This one impacts publishing, higher education, and foreign travel.

Eclipses

Solar eclipses tend to trigger external events that bring about change according to the sign and house in which they fall. Lunar eclipses trigger inner, emotional events according to the sign and house in which they fall. Any eclipse marks both beginnings and endings. The solar and lunar eclipse in a pair falls in opposite signs. If you're interested in detailed information on eclipses, take a look at Celeste Teal's excellent and definitive book, *Eclipses: Predicting World Events & Personal Transformation.*

If you were born under or around the time of an eclipse, it's to your advantage to take a look at your birth chart to find out exactly where the eclipses will impact you.

Most years feature four eclipses—two solar, two lunar, with the set separated by about two weeks. In November and December 2011 there were solar and lunar eclipses, so this year the first eclipses fall during May and June.

May 20: Solar eclipse at 0 degrees Gemini, in your third house. This one brings new opportunities in communication, travel, and your neighborhood and with your siblings.

June 4: Lunar eclipse in Sagittarius, your ninth house. This should be a positive eclipse for you and bring news from abroad.

November 13: Solar eclipse in Scorpio in your solar eighth house. New opportunities in shared resources. Your partner or spouse could see a raise on or around the time of this eclipse. Deep emotions surface.

November 28: Lunar eclipse, Gemini. Jupiter forms a five-degree conjunction to the eclipse degree, suggesting that whatever news comes your way, it's positive and you're in an upbeat, expansive mood.

Luckiest Day of the Year

Every year there's one day when Jupiter and the sun meet up, and luck, serendipity, and expansion are the hallmarks. This year that day falls on May 13 with a conjunction in Taurus, your money house!

Eighteen Months of Day-by-Day Predictions: July 2011 to December 2012

Moon sign times are calculated for Eastern Standard Time and Eastern Daylight Time. Please adjust for your local time zone.

JULY 2011

Friday, July 1 (Moon in Cancer)   Today's new moon in Cancer should usher in new opportunities related to your home and family. In the market for a new house? Hoping to have a child? This new moon creates a perfect environment for these events. This moon also receives a harmonious angle from Jupiter in Taurus, which makes it likely that you'll have the financial means to use this moon to your advantage.

Saturday, July 2 (Moon into Leo, 5:44 p.m.)   Mercury enters Leo and your solar fifth house. This transit lasts until July 28 and should bring about lively discussions and communications about your spiritual beliefs and educational goals. You may be talking about an overseas trip. Just keep in mind that Mercury will be retrograde between August 2 and August 26, so travel on either side of those dates.

Sunday, July 3 (Moon in Leo)   You've got a chance to shine today, and it isn't even something you have to work at! People notice you and recognize your accomplishments in some way. This moon also forms a terrific angle to Uranus in your sign, suggesting that you're on a major roll today, Aries. Make it count.

Monday, July 4 (Moon into Virgo, 9:16 p.m.)   Venus enters Cancer and your solar fourth house, a transit that should create a pleasant atmosphere at home, just in time for the July 4 holiday! Venus remains in your fourth house until July 28, indicating that you may be beautifying your home in some way. If you're married or living with your partner, your love life should be quite satisfying during this transit.

Tuesday, July 5 (Moon in Virgo)   If you're back at work today, you may have to pay closer attention to details. Employees or coworkers could have issues that demand your attention. You may find yourself in an uncomfortable position, trying to mitigate the impact of these issues without really having the full story. If possible, wait a day or two to make decisions.

Wednesday, July 6 (Moon into Libra, 11:54 p.m.)
The moon enters your opposite sign. Your emotional focus shifts to partnerships and finding balance between your professional and personal life. Balance isn't easy for an Aries, unless you have a lot of planets in Libra. But today you have an opportunity to strive for the very thing that challenges you.

Thursday, July 7 (Moon in Libra)   This moon forms a harmonious angle to Mercury in Leo, emphasizing your communication abilities and your insights into a romantic relationship or a creative endeavor. You're able to pitch your ideas with great conviction today. Get busy!

Friday, July 8 (Moon in Libra)   You and your partner may get away for a long weekend. Or you shut yourselves away for the weekend, enjoying each other's company and amusing yourselves with movies you've wanted to see and books you've wanted to read.

Saturday, July 9 (Moon into Scorpio, 2:32 a.m.) Uranus turns retrograde in your sign until December 10. During this period, you could have a number of unusual psychic experiences. These could range from telepathy to precognition to spontaneous recollection of a past life. You may be scrutinizing the direction of your life, and you could find a unique path!

Sunday, July 10 (Moon in Scorpio)   Most of the time, you probably aren't very good at keeping secrets. The exception is when the moon is in Scorpio. Someone may confide in you, and you'll have to keep the information to yourself. You can do that part just fine. When you give your word, it means something.

Monday, July 11 (Moon into Sagittarius, 3:47 a.m.) The Sadge moon, like the Leo moon, fits you well. You're in the mood for the open road, and there may be no stopping you! So satisfy the travel itch through some virtual travel this evening. Figure out where you want to go, what it will cost, and then plan ahead! Okay, so it lacks the spontaneity of the Sadge moon. But you'll get to your destination!

Tuesday, July 12 (Moon in Sagittarius)   Your varied talents come into play today. A relationship or an event prompts you to seek the larger canvas, and you probably like what you find. How can you integrate your discoveries into your daily life? Can you gather the support you need among friends, family, coworkers?

Wednesday, July 13 (Moon into Capricorn, 10:14 a.m.) The moon joins Pluto in the career sector of your chart.

If there's a professional issue you need to deal with, then today is the day to do it. Your sense of personal power comes from some deep inner place, and the people around you respond to it.

Thursday, July 14 (Moon in Capricorn)   Feeling the effects yet of tomorrow's full moon in Capricorn? You are if the day is crazier and more rushed than usual at work. Just take things in stride, put one foot in front of the other, delegate when necessary, and don't sweat the small stuff. By the end of the day, things shake out in your favor.

Friday, July 15 (Moon into Aquarius, 4:30 p.m.)   Today's full moon in Capricorn sheds lights on a professional issue, relationship, or challenge. If you feel you haven't had all the information you need to make an informed decision, then today the information comes your way. This moon is the second of three lunations this month and is known as the "Buck Moon."

Saturday, July 16 (Moon in Aquarius)   Emotionally, you're feeling just about as good as it gets. These feelings help to attract upbeat and positive experiences and people. Remember how you feel today so that if a day comes up when you're not at your peak, you can conjure these emotions and turn your attitude around. You may want to practice what Esther and Jerry Hicks call "rampaging appreciation," where you verbally express appreciation for whatever moves you. A flower. A sunny day. An unexpected check.

Sunday, July 17 (Moon in Aquarius)   You're working your way toward the new moon in fellow fire sign Leo on July 30. It's not too early to think about the new opportunities you would like to manifest in terms of creativity, romance, and what you do for fun and pleasure. Do you have a manuscript you would like to sell? A screenplay? A collection of photos to exhibit? Thinking about starting a family? All are possible with the new moon in Leo.

Monday, July 18 (Moon into Pisces, 1:13 a.m.)   The moon enters your twelfth house. By now, you should have a pretty clear idea about the kinds of emotional experiences this moon attracts. With your intuition so much stronger, psychic experiences are a given. Be sure to follow your hunches. There's a flow to your emotions, too, and it may surprise you. Make a symbolic gesture to welcome the moon entering your sign on Wednesday—i.e., clean out your closets, your attic, or your garage!

Tuesday, July 19 (Moon in Pisces)   You may be trying to change the mind of someone close to you. Heated arguments won't work. Appeal to the person's spiritual side, to their better half. Let's say that the topic is universal health care. You're for it, the other person is against it. "But it's socialized medicine," the person argues. And to that, you might say, "Isn't it right to take care of society's most vulnerable individuals? Kids? The elderly?" A response like this could work miracles!

Wednesday, July 20 (Moon into Aries, 12:26 a.m.) Two power days—today and tomorrow—mean that you can move your own concerns, agendas, and goals forward much more quickly. Organize your thoughts and goals, figure out a strategy, and go for it. With Uranus retrograde in your sign right now, you've got plenty of cutting-edge ideas.

Thursday, July 21 (Moon in Aries)   Even if there are barriers that stand between you and what you're trying to achieve, you don't recognize them as barriers. You simply push on through them, intent on your goal, focused on your direction. This is how change occurs,

Aries. Apply this energy to any area of your life that needs a breath of fresh air.

Friday, July 22 (Moon into Taurus, 12:59 p.m.) With Mercury still in fellow fire sign Leo, Mars in compatible air sign Gemini, and the moon in Taurus, you're poised to make waves today. You're busting up the status quo. While there could be some discontent initially, you discover you've got plenty of supporters who are also ready for change.

Saturday, July 23 (Moon in Taurus) Stick to what you know, what you feel to be true in your bones, Aries. Don't flip-flop or betray yourself. You could be more focused on your finances today, perhaps tallying your expenses and comparing them to what you actually earn. Are you in the red? If so, take steps to reverse that trend.

Sunday, July 24 (Moon in Taurus) Time to pay the piper. Credit card bills may be coming due. Once you have paid them off, keep just one credit card, and cancel the others. Today, try to pay for your purchases in cash. That way you're aware of what you're really spending.

Monday, July 25 (Moon into Gemini, 12:35 a.m.) The moon joins Mars in Gemini, so you're a powerhouse of mental energy. You've got the ideas, the ambition, and the direction to makes these ideas a reality. All you need is the proper venue. A book, perhaps? If you have writing aspirations, then get busy! Make time to write.

Tuesday, July 26 (Moon in Gemini) You could be running around today, tying up loose ends, doing errands, scheduling appointments that you've put off. Use your time in the car wisely. Listen to self-improvement tapes. Listen to news shows. Catch up with what's going on in the world.

Wednesday, July 27 (Moon into Cancer, 9:12 p.m.)
The moon joins Venus in Cancer, bolstering your love life, your intuition, and your ability to nurture others—and to be nurtured in return. Venus changes signs tomorrow, so if there's something in particular you want to do around your house, in your yard, with your family, get it done today.

Thursday, July 28 (Moon in Cancer)   Mercury enters Virgo and your solar sixth house, and Venus enters Leo and your solar fifth house. The first transit lasts into late August because Mercury turns retrograde on August 2. The second transit, which lasts until August 21, marks the beginning of one of the most romantic and creative times for you all year. Just about everything in your love life should hum along nicely during this period. If you're not involved at the beginning of the transit, you probably will be by its end.

Friday, July 29 (Moon in Cancer)   Read the big-picture section on Mercury retrograde to understand what that planet will be doing during August. For today, focus on home and family obligations, and get ready for tomorrow's new moon in the romance sector of your chart! What kinds of relationships and creative endeavors would you like to manifest? Give it careful thought. Back your desires with emotions.

Saturday, July 30 (Moon into Leo, 2:16 a.m.)   Today's new moon in Leo is close to Venus—a major plus for you! If you do nothing else today, have fun and do things that bring you pleasure. In many ways, this new moon is a gift from the universe that reminds you life is supposed to be joyful!

Sunday, July 31 (Moon in Leo)   With yesterday's new moon in this sign, expect new opportunities to show up in romance, creative endeavors, and with children. If you've thought about starting a family, this new moon certainly favors it!

AUGUST 2011

Monday, August 1 (Moon into Virgo, 4:42 a.m.) A perfect moon for the beginning of the week. You're on target, and you have a very good idea what needs to be done. You may not yet know how to implement what you have in mind, but perhaps you should wait a while for that. Tomorrow, Mercury turns retrograde in Virgo. So wait until after August 26 to figure out the rest of your strategy.

Tuesday, August 2 (Moon in Virgo) Mercury turns retrograde in your solar sixth house of daily work and health. Read about this retrograde in the big-picture section. With the moon also in Virgo today, you may be somewhat out of sorts, feeling irritated or annoyed for no particular reason. Use this retrograde period to revise and review. Don't start anything new.

Wednesday, August 3 (Moon into Libra, 6:05 a.m.) Mars enters Cancer and your solar fourth house, where it remains until September 18. During this transit, you may be initiating home-improvement projects, looking for a new house or apartment, or experiencing changes at home. Children move out or back home; a parent moves in or needs additional support. You get the idea. This transit spells a lot of activity related to home.

Thursday, August 4 (Moon in Libra) Your social skills are called upon today. You may have to act as an ambassador or diplomat for your company. You'll have to listen to various sides of a story or issue, not take sides, and make your best determination. You and your partner may be rehashing old issues. Don't worry about it too much. Once Mercury turns direct again, it will all get straightened out.

Friday, August 5 (Moon into Scorpio, 7:57 a.m.) This moon is among the most secretive and passionate, and may prompt you to take a closer look at a partner's finances. Whether you're self-employed or you work for a company, you may be considering financing for a project of some kind. Look around all you want. Just don't make a decision until after August 26, when Mercury will be moving direct again.

Saturday, August 6 (Moon in Scorpio)   If you find yourself detouring today into the weird and inexplicable, blame the Scorpio moon! You actually may find mysterious topics that intrigue you. Astrology, for example, could be one possibility. Other possibilities include life after death, communication with the dead, reincarnation, and mediumship.

Sunday, August 7 (Moon into Sagittarius, 11:21 a.m.) Here's that fire-sign Sadge moon that you enjoy. Today, it brings a wider canvas to your emotional life. You're able to lift yourself up into a positive, forward-thinking mood. Make a list of the people and conditions in your life that you truly appreciate.

Monday, August 8 (Moon in Sagittarius)   There are right and wrong ways to do a given task. You know the difference. If you're tempted to take shortcuts, keep in mind that you may pay for it down the road. Since Mercury is still retrograde, it's smart not to sign contracts until after August 26.

Tuesday, August 9 (Moon into Capricorn, 4:38 p.m.) Professionally, you should be on a roll—not just today and tomorrow, but through the end of the year, while Jupiter forms a harmonious angle to your career area. You have the ability now to plan well and effectively, to set long-term goals, and to manifest what you want. So get busy, Aries!

Wednesday, August 10 (Moon in Capricorn) Your ambitions may blind you to what's really important. Move cautiously today through your work and relationships. Take time to notice the minutiae of your life. Everything around you is a faithful reflection of your deepest beliefs. If there's something you dislike, then change the belief that it reflects.

Thursday, August 11 (Moon into Aquarius, 11:48 p.m.) If you're hanging out with friends today, take note of who is the most genuine. Which friend supports you unconditionally? With whom do you feel the most comfortable? Your findings may surprise you.

Friday, August 12 (Moon in Aquarius) Tomorrow is a full moon in Aquarius, and you could be feeling the impact today. Is your phone ringing off the hook? Is your cell phone filling with text messages? Is your in-box overflowing? If so, then expect more of the same tomorrow. Social invitations flow in.

Saturday, August 13 (Moon in Aquarius) You have your pick of parties and things to do today. Neptune forms a wide conjunction to this moon, so you may need more information before you decide what to do. The information could be anything from the location of the party or event to the time and guest list. You gain insights into a friendship or into a group to which you belong.

Sunday, August 14 (Moon into Pisces, 8:55 a.m.) Take it easy today. You've earned it. Kick back with a good book or a favorite movie, take a yoga class, or do something else that relaxes you. It would behoove you to spend a few minutes meditating at some point during the day. The Pisces moon loves it!

Monday, August 15 (Moon in Pisces)   Clearing the tables, right, Aries? That means you need to get rid of clutter, clean up the papers on your desk, and generally prepare yourself for the moon entering your sign tomorrow. By now, you know that means it's going to be a power day. Be ready for it so you can make the most of it.

Tuesday, August 16 (Moon into Aries, 8:03 p.m.) With the moon in your sign again, you're on a roll once more, certain of your steps, your decisions, your agenda, and your goals. It's easy to gather the support you need for an idea or project. On other fronts, this lunar transit should spice up your love life or attract unusual people into your life.

Wednesday, August 17 (Moon in Aries)   With the moon linking up with Uranus retrograde in your sign, you may find innovative ways of making money. It's a matter of recognizing a gap in the market and filling it. You may want to brainstorm with a friend or coworker or with someone who is an expert in the field you're studying.

Thursday, August 18 (Moon in Aries)   With the dog days of summer starting to wind down, you may be looking ahead to the fall and the last quarter of 2011. What would you like to achieve before the end of the year? What would you like to enjoy, experience, and do before then? Make a list. Post it where you'll see it often. Think of it as a wish list.

Friday, August 19 (Moon into Taurus, 8:37 a.m.) The moon joins Jupiter retrograde. The combination of planets prompts you to think about money you may be spending—or want to spend—this weekend. Since you can be an impulsive spender, be sure to pay in cash so that your expenses are real to you. It would be a good idea to tuck cash away somewhere in your house.

Saturday, August 20 (Moon in Taurus) Feeling stubborn today? Blame the Taurus moon. The one thing you have to watch with this transit is that you aren't stubborn just to be contrary. If you dig in your heels about something, be sure it's worth your while. Choose your battles carefully, Aries.

Sunday, August 21 (Moon into Gemini, 8:53 p.m.) Venus enters Virgo and your sixth house, where it remains until September 14. During this period, your work life should unfold smoothly, as long as you're on top of things. Pay close attention to details. An office flirtation may heat up, Aries. Try not to break any hearts!

Monday, August 22 (Moon in Gemini) Some days, your life is about action, doing, moving forward. Other days, it's about feeling your way intuitively through events. Today, your mind just won't quit. You've got a million ideas zipping around in your head. Be sure to record the ones that seem worthwhile—the ones that strike you as unique, cutting-edge.

Tuesday, August 23 (Moon in Gemini) In three days Mercury turns direct and you'll be able to pack your bags and hit the road, if you're so inclined. Until then, do as much virtual traveling as you like, but don't buy tickets until after August 26. That office romance may start to really heat up with the new moon in Virgo on August 28. If romance isn't what you're interested in, then give some thought to the new opportunities you would like to see manifested in some other area of your life.

Wednesday, August 24 (Moon into Cancer, 6:31 a.m.)
This moon forms a harmonious angle to Venus's present position, but a challenging angle to your sun sign. The best way to navigate the challenge is to allow your intuition a full voice and to follow its guidance. It's especially true when dealing with romantic relationships and relationships with your parents. You'll need plenty of patience today.

Thursday, August 25 (Moon in Cancer)   Nurture yourself and your own abilities. Sometimes, you get so caught up in doing and acting that you neglect your inner life, Aries. Then you're forced to slow down due to a cold or a virus, and this stresses you out. Look inward before your body forces you to do so.

Friday, August 26 (Moon into Leo, 12:09 p.m.)   Mercury turns direct today, liberating you! Time to hit the road, sign contracts, and get started on everything else you postponed during this retrograde. This movement should help your love life, Aries, particularly when it comes to communication.

Saturday, August 27 (Moon in Leo)   Another gift from the universe. The Leo moon encourages you to get out and have some fun. If you've got something creative going on in your life now—a script, a novel, photography, dance, art, any or all of the above—then by all means dive into that project. In one way or another, it's your day to shine and feel good about yourself and your life.

Sunday, August 28 (Moon into Virgo, 2:13 p.m.)   Today's new moon in Virgo brings new opportunities to your daily work life and to the way you maintain your health. You may, for instance, join a gym or start taking yoga. You may have a chance to change jobs, hire new employees, or land a lucrative contract for your company. Venus is close to the degree of this new moon, suggesting that romance and the arts also play prominent roles.

Monday, August 29 (Moon in Virgo)   Read the fine print. That's one thing the Virgo moon urges you to do consistently. If you follow that rule, then this moon certainly works in your favor. The one possible drawback is a tendency toward criticism—of others or of yourself. Instead of criticizing, look for qualities you can appreciate in others.

Tuesday, August 30 (Moon into Libra, 2:26 p.m.) Jupiter turns retrograde in Taurus, in your financial sector, until December 25. This movement prompts you to look more deeply within concerning what you value. Do you spend your hard-earned dollars according to your beliefs? If you're antiwar, for example, do you buy from corporations who support war?

Wednesday, August 31 (Moon in Libra)   Balance is everything today, and what a fine line you walk. You usually seek to leap ahead, to scoop up life and all its experiences in one fell swoop. But the Libra moon asks for a more gentle approach. Be circumspect but exuberant. Be present.

SEPTEMBER 2011

Thursday, September 1 (Moon into Scorpio, 2:48 p.m.)   Get ready today for the long Labor Day weekend that begins tomorrow. Clear off your desk, get your agenda in order for next week, and return phone calls and e-mails. Be sure your insurance payments are up-to-date. If you've got something brewing that isn't common knowledge yet, keep it secret until the moon enters fellow fire sign Sagittarius on Saturday afternoon.

Friday, September 2 (Moon in Scorpio) There are many ways to go about obtaining what you want. Today, you discover a secret path into the heart of what you desire. Be sure that if you follow this path, no one will be hurt or put in a tough spot. You'll know. You have those kinds of instincts.

Saturday, September 3 (Moon into Sagittarius, 3:04 p.m.) Here's that wonderful Sadge moon again. It's a weekend, and you've got plenty of free time. Mercury is moving direct again; life is looking very good. Start planning your vacation, Aries. You've got the desire for some far-flung destination. Make it happen.

Sunday, September 4 (Moon in Sagittarius) If you're a writer in search of a publisher, then this transit could brings news from them or could prompt you to mail off your manuscript. Presumably, you've done your homework and narrowed your list of publishers so that you know to whom you should submit. If you're returning to college or graduate school, a whole different set of expectations and events is in motion.

Monday, September 5 (Moon into Capricorn, 10:04 p.m.) The moon joins Pluto in your career sector. Once again, these two pair up, which they'll be doing a lot between now and 2024. The combination creates powerful emotions, the kind of emotions that can shatter barriers and smash through obstacles. So use the energy wisely to push your ambitions forward.

Tuesday, September 6 (Moon in Capricorn) This earth-sign moon forces you to focus on the practical and the efficient, and to organize yourself for maximum use of your time. If you resist doing this today, you may find the day a bit more difficult than it could be otherwise. So always try to go with the lunar flow. The day will feel like less of a roller coaster.

Wednesday, September 7 (Moon in Capricorn)   If yesterday was your day to organize, then today is the day to implement. Think of it as a wheel—you're not reinventing it, only making the pieces fit in a better way. You should have the support you need, but even if you don't, you've never been afraid to strike out on your own.

Thursday, September 8 (Moon into Aquarius, 5:43 a.m.) Your social calendar fills rapidly for the weekend, and you'll have your choice of invitations. Even if you already have plans for the weekend, consider at least one invite. It never hurts to expand your circle of friends and acquaintances. If there's a decision you've put off making, today may be the day to revisit it. You'll have the emotional detachment you need.

Friday, September 9 (Moon in Aquarius)   You may join a group that supports your interests, or you could volunteer for a community charity involved in causes you like. Stay focused on your goals, Aries, rather than shooting off in a dozen different directions. You're great at launching projects but often lose interest midway through and drop the ball in someone else's lap.

Saturday, September 10 (Moon into Pisces, 3:27 p.m.) It's time to treat yourself to a past-life regression or a session with a psychic or medium and to begin your exploration of the truly mysterious, the unknown. Have your questions and issues lined up in your mind. Allow your intuition to speak, and listen closely to what it whispers.

Sunday, September 11 (Moon in Pisces)   Deep down, you've got the answers you need. Your challenge, Aries, is to access that deeper part of yourself so you can find those answers. One access point is your dreams. Ask for insight and information before you fall asleep, and make a suggestion that you'll awaken at the end of the dream so that you can record it.

Monday, September 12 (Moon in Pisces)   Today's full moon in Pisces sheds light on something that is hidden. You suddenly grasp what the actual situation is and can now make a fully informed decision. Jupiter forms a wide but beneficial angle to this moon, suggesting that you benefit from this information and that it somehow expands your creative venue.

Tuesday, September 13 (Moon into Aries, 2:50 a.m.) The moon enters your sign, and you're ready to move forward. Whether your focus is career, family, relationships, or money, you're in the groove, Aries, and can manifest just about anything that you set your sights on.

Wednesday, September 14 (Moon in Aries)   Venus enters your opposite sign, where it will be until October 9. This transit marks an excellent time to deepen your commitment in some way to your partner. You move in together, get engaged, or get married. If you're uninvolved when this transit starts, you could meet someone special before the transit ends. Or your business partnerships find an even keel.

Thursday, September 15 (Moon into Taurus, 3:25 p.m.) It's a money day. And lucky you, Jupiter still forms a beneficial angle to this moon—and to your career sector—which suggests that you're in a good place to request a raise, to land a promotion, or to do something else that brings in more money.

Friday, September 16 (Moon in Taurus)   Pluto turns direct in Capricorn, in your career sector. This should improve your professional life. Anything that has been delayed these last months will now move forward. You have a much clearer idea now about your career goals and in particular about what you would like to accomplish professionally by the end of this year.

Saturday, September 17 (Moon in Taurus)   You may be straightening out financial issues that have been mixed up since Mercury's retrograde. Be sure to check and recheck all banking statements. You could find an error in your favor. If you don't use financial software yet, you may want to invest in Quicken or some other program so you can track your finances and expenses more easily.

Sunday, September 18 (Moon into Gemini, 4:06 a.m.) Mars enters Leo and your solar fifth house, where it will be until November 11. This transit should spice up your love life considerably, with a lot of your energy going into enjoyment, pleasure, romance, creativity. Mars in Leo forms a beautiful angle to your natal sun, so your physical energy is boosted as well. Consider starting a regular exercise program of some kind. Mars in Leo will love that.

Monday, September 19 (Moon in Gemini)   You and your siblings or neighbors may get together for some sort of joint community venture. It could be a volunteer project for a charity event, or it could just be beautification in your own neighborhood. A lot of discussion ensues through e-mail and text messages.

Tuesday, September 20 (Moon into Cancer, 2:54 p.m.) This moon is opposite Pluto in Capricorn, so it could create tension between your obligations at work and your responsibility to your family. The tension seems worse than it actually is, so step back and breathe through it, Aries. Then take an honest and emotionally detached look at what's really going on.

Wednesday, September 21 (Moon in Cancer)   Who or what are you nurturing? Are there ways to increase your nurturing of others without sacrificing yourself? These are some of the questions you may be asking yourself today. You may not find all the answers, but the process of exploration will be able to unfold now and will flesh out your understanding of who you are and where you're headed.

Thursday, September 22 (Moon into Leo, 9:56 p.m.) The moon joins Mars in your solar fifth house. This intriguing combination of planets feeds your need for recognition and attention. You aren't the type who craves attention just for itself, but for your achievements, insights, and knowledge. If you approach this with an attitude of playfulness, things will turn out in your favor.

Friday, September 23 (Moon in Leo)   Your creative adrenaline is pumping hard and furiously, and your muse is up close and personal. So dive into your creative projects, Aries, and relish the fact that your creative drive is pushing you to attempt new venues and to excel in areas that are new to you.

Saturday, September 24 (Moon into Virgo, 10:50 p.m.) You and your partner may be involved in a pursuit that requires not only time but close attention to detail. Whether this is a creative project, a financial endeavor, or something else, the Virgo moon demands a certain level of perfection that requires patience.

Sunday, September 25 (Moon in Virgo)   Mercury joins Venus in Libra, in your seventh house, and will be there until October 13. This combination of planets indicates that you and a partner—romantic or professional—will be discussing your relationship. Who expects what? Which strategies are best? How can you both find balance in this relationship?

Monday, September 26 (Moon into Libra, 12:51 a.m.)
With Mercury, Venus, and Saturn all in Libra, Mars in fellow fire sign Leo, and Uranus in your sign, today could be nearly overwhelming in terms of obligations. But you're an Aries, which means you can whip through it all with your eyes shut. You wing it and leave the competition in the dust.

Tuesday, September 27 (Moon in Libra) Today's new moon in Libra should usher in new opportunities in romantic and business partnerships. If you're already involved, then you and your partner should do something special together this evening. If you're not involved, don't worry about it. You'll be enjoying yourself regardless. If you've considered starting your own business, then today is the perfect time to iron out the details.

Wednesday, September 28 (Moon into Scorpio, 12:06 a.m.) Other people's resources come into play today. Your partner's finances could be one area that surfaces. Just as likely, however, is that you and your partner draw up your wills or are dealing with insurance issues, banks, or mortgages—all the domain of the Scorpio moon. There could be an element of secrecy to some events. Wait until the moon is in Sadge to explore those secrets.

Thursday, September 29 (Moon in Scorpio) If things that go bump in the night interest you, then you may want to hit your local bookstore and head straight to the metaphysics section. You can stock up on books that deal with reincarnation, life after death, or mediumship. If you're short on money right now, explore the Internet. One way or another, you will increase your knowledge about these areas.

Friday, September 30 (Moon into Sagittarius, 12:42 a.m.) This moon forms a great angle to Mars in Leo.

You're ready for an adventure. You may not be sure what kind of adventure you want, but trust that the universe will toss some interesting options your way. Your temptation will be to sample them all simultaneously!

OCTOBER 2011

Saturday, October 1 (Moon in Sagittarius)   With a solid lineup of planets in fellow fire signs and compatible air signs, you're in a perfect place for the beginning of October and the countdown through the last three months of the year. Your physical, intellectual, spiritual, and emotional energy is humming along. So get out and do something you enjoy. Anything. Remind yourself that life is supposed to be fun and beautiful.

Sunday, October 2 (Moon in Sagittarius)   For all the times you've wondered how far you can take an idea, today is the perfect time to find out. And it begins with one step. And then another and another. Since you have the big picture, you can afford to take the time to plot your course toward your destination. Not everything has to be done in quantum leaps on the fly.

Monday, October 3 (Moon into Capricorn, 4:16 a.m.) Take stock. That's what sort of day it is. Pick an area of your life and determine if it's moving the way you want. If not, determine how to turn things around. If you already know which area of your life you would like to be different, then work on that area through the use of positive affirmations and expressing appreciation for everything in your life that is perfect.

Tuesday, October 4 (Moon in Capricorn)   By now, you already have a sense of the kinds of experiences you have when the moon teams up with Pluto. Your emotions tend to be more powerful—and not always in a positive sense—and you can find yourself in power plays with other people. So when you wake this morning, be sure to start your day with as many upbeat emotions as you can conjure.

Wednesday, October 5 (Moon into Aquarius, 11:19 a.m.)   Detachment is the name of the game today. Once you detach emotionally—from an issue, relationship, concern, or whatever it is—you're able to think more clearly about your decision. You may want to meet with friends at some point today to get feedback. Another perspective can be helpful.

Thursday, October 6 (Moon in Aquarius)   You're working up to the moon in your sign on Monday. So get a head start and begin tying up your obligations, completing projects at work and at home, and generally making space in your life for everything new. Also, there will be a full moon in your sign on October 11—another reason to finish up what you're doing.

Friday, October 7 (Moon into Pisces, 9:14 p.m.) There are times when a water-sign moon, like this one, stirs up your emotions to such an extent that it seems you're nothing *but* emotion. There isn't much you can do about it except ride the wave. You're feeling these emotions for a reason, and once you take a deeper look at what's going on, you can probably rectify the situation.

Saturday, October 8 (Moon in Pisces)   You may feel as if you're being pulled in many directions. The truth is that you're being pulled in only two—your heart screams to go one way, and your head demands that you go another. So your best way is to delay any decision until Monday, when the moon enters your sign.

Sunday, October 9 (Moon in Pisces)   Venus enters Scorpio, your solar eighth house. This transit lasts until

November 2 and could bring very intense experiences in romance and the arts. Others will be willing to share their resources with you, and your spouse or partner could land a significant raise or promotion.

Monday, October 10 (Moon into Aries, 8:57 a.m.)
The moon enters your sign and is working up to tomorrow's full moon in Aries. You could be feeling some of the effects today. Something in your life is culminating—a project is nearing completion; a payoff is around the corner—and you're feeling intense excitement and anticipation. Carry that feeling through the day.

Tuesday, October 11 (Moon in Aries)   Today's full moon in your sign should be quite beneficial, a bit crazy, and fun. You actually may be the voice of reason in a crowd of frenzied individuals. Apply that description to whatever group you want—family, coworkers, acquaintances, fellow students, or coconspirators. If they think you're the voice of reason, then be it!

Wednesday, October 12 (Moon into Taurus, 9:35 p.m.)
You are handed a project or assignment that pleases you. You may want to keep it quiet at least until the ink is dry on the contract. An unexpected check could arrive—perhaps repayment on a loan, an insurance refund, or a royalty check.

Thursday, October 13 (Moon in Taurus)   Mercury enters Scorpio, joining Venus in your solar eighth house. Any time these two planets travel together, the possibility of great conversation is emphasized. In this instance, since both planets are in Scorpio, the conversations and discussions are likely to be about profound and intriguing topics. Mercury will be in Scorpio until November 2.

Friday, October 14 (Moon in Taurus)   Whatever you can imagine, Aries, you can manifest. In terms of quantum physics, it's all about taking that wave of probability through your desires and intentions, and collapsing the wave into physical reality. The trick is to believe that you can do this, to believe that *you* create your reality and that reality isn't thrust upon you.

Saturday, October 15 (Moon into Gemini, 10:15 a.m.)
The Gemini moon usually fits you pretty well. You're able to communicate well (as long as Mercury is moving direct!). If you're in sales, you can sell anything to just about anyone. Today you may have contact with a sibling or neighbor about a project in which you're involved. Or perhaps a brother, sister, or neighbor needs some help, and you're glad to pitch in.

Sunday, October 16 (Moon in Gemini) Do something that excites you, moves you, or stirs your intellectual passions. The Gemini moon prompts you to express yourself in some way—through writing, dance, photography, or art. Whatever venue you choose, do it well, with passion and joy.

Monday, October 17 (Moon into Cancer, 9:39 p.m.)
If a parent is of concern today, don't make decisions in a vacuum. Consult your relatives or be sure you and the doctors are on the same page. It's also possible that you could be finishing up some home-improvement project or something related to work that you do in your home office. Home is key.

Tuesday, October 18 (Moon in Cancer) This moon forms a harmonious angle to both Mercury and Venus in Scorpio, and is opposed to Jupiter and Pluto in Capricorn. There are several ways these placements could play out. Your emotions could be exaggerated so that a situation really isn't as dire as it appears to be. Or your interest in metaphysics deepens, and you begin to recognize connections that may not make sense rationally.

Wednesday, October 19 (Moon in Cancer)   You're closing in on the new moon in Scorpio on October 26. Start making your list today on the kinds of experiences you would like to manifest in your life with this new moon. If your list is long, narrow it down to one or two areas. Be specific about what you want but not so specific that you limit yourself.

Thursday, October 20 (Moon into Leo, 6:07 a.m.) Finally, a lunar transit that fits you like the proverbial glove. This moon forms a beneficial angle to Uranus in your sign, so you can expect unusual experiences—perhaps psychic or synchronistic. Unusual people may also surface in your life, individuals with unique perspectives, talents, or insights. Emotionally, you may feel edgy, attuned to your environment.

Friday, October 21 (Moon in Leo)   Your creative drive is strong. It's as if some idea you have is struggling to be born, and you may be playing around with different venues for expression. You may want to experiment with various divination systems to explore the direction in which you should go—astrology, tarot, the I Ching. Or, if you know a good psychic, schedule a reading.

Saturday, October 22 (Moon into Virgo, 10:42 a.m.) This moon forms a beneficial angle with both Mercury and Venus in Scorpio. The combination should prompt interesting discussions and conversation with a partner, where you each spell out your expectations, needs, and other details about the relationship. The Virgo moon is about emotional perfection, and the primary challenge is to keep from criticizing yourself or others.

Sunday, October 23 (Moon in Virgo)   If you're more discriminating today than usual, it's the Virgo moon at work. A coworker may suggest an idea that sounds terrific, but once you dissect and analyze it, you realize the idea is flawed. Or a boss or employer requests that you carry out a particular task, and you balk at the request for some reason. This moon doesn't have to create or cause tension, but it often does because fire and earth just don't mix.

Monday, October 24 (Moon into Libra, 11:50 a.m.) The moon joins Saturn in your seventh house. Saturn is a heavy, no matter where it appears. But when linked with the moon, you may feel a kind of emotional weight or heaviness that you can't shake. Often, it's connected to responsibilities and obligations that seem too great to bear alone. You can mitigate the situation by requesting help from family and friends.

Tuesday, October 25 (Moon in Libra) If yesterday's mood was aided by others, then today's mood can be remedied by doing something you enjoy. Whether it's getting off by yourself, spending time with close friends, or hitting the road with your backpack and ATM card, your mood will lift.

Wednesday, October 26 (Moon into Scorpio, 11:09 a.m.) Today's new moon in Scorpio could usher in new financial opportunities for your partner or spouse. It should be easier to obtain a mortgage, loan or insurance that fits your needs and lifestyle. Pluto and Jupiter both form harmonious angles to this new moon, suggesting an expansion of some kind is at work, and the opportunities that surface should be quite lucrative.

Thursday, October 27 (Moon in Scorpio) With the moon joining Mercury and Venus in Scorpio, there's an element of secrecy to events, emotions, experiences. You're looking for the absolute bottom line in a relationship, issue, challenge, or project. You may just find it before the day is over.

Friday, October 28 (Moon into Sagittarius, 10:46 a.m.)
This fire-sign moon is harmonious with your sun sign
and also with Mars in Leo, Saturn in Libra, and Uranus in Aries. With that kind of lineup, it's a great day to
initiate projects, launch a business or website, submit a
manuscript or screenplay, or start anything new. So get
busy, Aries. Figure out where you want to start, then go
for gold!

Saturday, October 29 (Moon in Sagittarius) Your
magnanimous feelings attract more reasons for this
mood to last and last. When you wake up today, spend a
few moments looking around your room—and your life—
and appreciate where you are in the moment. Esther
and Jerry Hicks recommend practicing "rampaging appreciation," where you find something in everything to
appreciate. The universe then responds by offering you
even more to appreciate. And since the Sadge moon is
expansive by nature, it's a perfect day to start making
this part of your routine.

Sunday, October 30 (Moon into Capricorn, 12:39 p.m.)
If you have kids, then you may be preparing for Halloween. The preparations don't have to be elaborate, but
you may want to go the extra mile—carve a pumpkin,
decorate your yard or your front door, and yes, don't
forget the treats!

Monday, October 31 (Moon in Capricorn) Happy
Halloween! Trick or treating aside, today is when the
bridge supposedly opens between the world of the living
and the world of the dead. So if you're the mystical sort,
you might schedule a reading with a medium or psychic.
Also, make a list of what you would like to experience
or achieve by the end of the year. Meditate on it. Then
release the desires.

NOVEMBER 2011

Tuesday, November 1 (Moon into Aquarius, 6:08 p.m.)
You hang with a group today—friends, coworkers, or members of an organization to which you belong. You're either brainstorming about a project or perhaps about the group itself. If the group is only loosely organized, you may be asked to head up a committee of some kind.

Wednesday, November 2 (Moon in Aquarius)   Venus and Mercury enter Sagittarius and your solar ninth house. Mercury will be in this sign through the end of the year and will be retrograde for part of that time. Venus will be in Sadge until November 26. During this period, while the planets are traveling in direct motion together, you are in a perfect position for an overseas trip. So line up your passport now, and figure out where you would like to go.

Thursday, November 3 (Moon in Aquarius)   Work you do within a group or for a community organization could bring in extra money. And if you're planning on that overseas trip, Aries, the money could come in handy. Also, with the holidays coming up . . . You get the idea. Jupiter is still expanding your financial venue. Take advantage of it.

Friday, November 4 (Moon into Pisces, 3:18 a.m.)
Feeling prompted to do some cleaning? Well, the moon is in Pisces again, so it's an excellent time to do it. You can either do physical cleaning—clear out closets, the garage, your attic—or go within and clear up old issues and concerns. Also consider taking stock of where you are and where you're headed throughout the rest of this year.

Saturday, November 5 (Moon in Pisces)   Old issues and concerns could be surfacing today or even tonight, through your dreams. Deal with whatever these issues are so that you'll be ready to move forward tomorrow, when the moon enters your sign. If you don't already keep a dream journal, consider starting one. Once you get into the habit of recording your dreams, the information and insights you receive are sure to come more frequently.

Sunday, November 6—Daylight Saving Time Ends (Moon into Aries, 2:02 p.m.)   Be sure to set your clocks appropriately so you wake in time for work tomorrow. It's another power day, and you're at the top of your game. Be prepared to launch your projects, pitch your ideas, and plan something special with the one you love.

Monday, November 7 (Moon in Aries)   You're on target. In fact, all you have to do to succeed is to pitch your idea or implement your plan. People around you will be receptive. With the moon and Uranus in your sign, your passions are powerful, and your love life should be in a very positive place. If you aren't involved now, that could change after December 10, when Uranus turns direct in your sign.

Tuesday, November 8 (Moon in Aries)   If you're still keeping those secrets that started building up in late October, it may be time to let go of them. It will be difficult to keep all this stuff to yourself with the moon in your sign. If the secrets concern only you, then letting the cat out of the bag is certainly your decision. But if the secrets have been entrusted to you by others, check with them first.

Wednesday, November 9 (Moon into Taurus, 2:46 a.m.)   Neptune has retrograded back into Aquarius, where it will be until early February of next year. Then it will enter Pisces again for 168 years! So while it's in compatible air sign Aquarius, use its energy to get involved with a charity group or volunteer your time for a cause in which you believe. You should also try to implement your ideals in your daily life.

Thursday, November 10 (Moon in Taurus)   Today's full moon in Taurus highlights your finances. Saturn forms a wide but challenging angle to this moon, suggesting that you may have to make an adjustment of some kind in your monetary situation. This moon also prompts you to consider what makes you feel most emotionally secure. Is it a certain amount of money in the bank? A stable home life? A job that you love?

Friday, November 11 (Moon into Gemini, 3:11 p.m.) Mars enters Virgo and your solar sixth house, where it will be for the rest of the year. This transit will trigger a lot of activity in your daily work and may have you scratching your head time and again over some detail or nuance that you hadn't been aware of earlier. You may be putting in longer hours at work or could find a part-time job to help with the holidays.

Saturday, November 12 (Moon in Gemini)   You're gathering information today. It may be related to your work or career, or perhaps you're on a quest of some kind. You try the usual places first—the Internet, books, libraries. If you don't find what you're looking for from these sources, you hit the phones, your e-mail list, and the people you know. Sometimes, the nugget of information you need the most is in plain sight.

Sunday, November 13 (Moon in Gemini)   "Communication" is the day's keyword, and you're at the top of your form. If you need to convince a boss, coworkers, or partner about something, do it when the moon is in Gemini or in a fire sign and definitely do it before Mercury turns retrograde on November 24. The Mercury retrograde will be in Sagittarius and will end just twelve days before Christmas. At least this year, your holiday travel plans won't be disrupted by mischievousness from Mercury!

Monday, November 14 (Moon into Cancer, 2:20 a.m.) For the next two days, it's possible to launch a home business. The Cancer moon forms a great angle to Jupiter in Taurus, so just about anything you do involving home, hearth, and family should be successful. In fact, it would be a good idea to start planning for Thanksgiving before Mercury turns retrograde on Thanksgiving Day!

Tuesday, November 15 (Moon in Cancer) A child or parent is at the forefront of your concerns today. It isn't necessarily that something is wrong, only that your focus is on this person. So give yourself over to this individual until you figure out why you're concerned. It could be that the individual simply needs to be reassured of your affection and love.

Wednesday, November 16 (Moon into Leo, 11:18 a.m.) Your love life should be looking very nice. And if it isn't, it may be due to your lack of concern and focus about it. In other words, you get what you concentrate on. It could be that you're more interested now in exploring your creativity in some way. Or, if travel is your greatest source of enjoyment, you may be caught up in a whirlwind of preparations or already on the road.

Thursday, November 17 (Moon in Leo) Since this moon forms a terrific angle to Uranus in your sign, you're in rare form today. Your reaction to emotional situations is unusual in some way, and the people around you could comment on it, particularly if these individuals know you well. But your response is exactly what the situation needs.

Friday, November 18 (Moon into Virgo, 5:20 p.m.)
Be sure that your Thanksgiving plans are lined up now and that your work is measured out so that you can afford to take a couple days off. You have a solid grasp on what you need to do between now and the holidays to take off with a clear conscience. Your work ethic is sometimes extreme, so go easy on yourself, Aries.

Saturday, November 19 (Moon in Virgo)   If you brought work home with you this weekend, you may not really be in the mood to tackle it. And that's fine. Don't beat yourself up about it, a tendency with this moon—but generally not for an Aries sun. Your competitive spirit is strong, and if it isn't poured into work, there is some other area of your life where that spirit is dominant.

Sunday, November 20 (Moon into Libra, 8:17 p.m.)
The moon joins Saturn in Libra, your opposite sign. If you've learned to shrug off the heaviness of this combination, then you're in an excellent position to manifest your dreams and desires. Lunar transits are fleeting, with the moon remaining just two and a half days in each sign. But at least you're able to lay the groundwork, Aries.

Monday, November 21 (Moon in Libra)   Gearing up for the Thanksgiving holidays should be a joyful event, Aries, not stressful. To some extent, external details make a difference—where the festivities are located, if you're the cook, how many are arriving for dinner. But regardless of the externals, joy is about perception. Remember that if you're complaining!

Tuesday, November 22 (Moon into Scorpio, 8:59 p.m.)
In two days, Mercury turns retrograde. That means today is the day to start backing up computer files, finalizing travel plans, buying your tickets, tying up loose

ends. You're going to be entering a period of revision, rethinking, and revisiting. Be ready.

Wednesday, November 23 (Moon in Scorpio)   Your passions boil over today. The challenge is whether you can keep your feelings to yourself. If you can't, say your piece and be done with it. Otherwise, write down what you're feeling. Give negative emotions and situations a positive spin. Keep reaching for a more upbeat emotion.

Thursday, November 24 (Moon into Sagittarius, 8:58 p.m.)   Happy Thanksgiving! Mercury turns retrograde in your solar ninth house and remains that way until December 13. During this period, it wouldn't behoove you to travel overseas, submit manuscripts, apply to college or graduate schools. The ninth house represents those areas. Read the section in the big-picture chapter on this retrograde. Thanksgiving travel and plans could be a bit dicey. The good news is that the retrograde will be finished before the December holidays.

Friday, November 25 (Moon in Sagittarius)   Today's new moon in Sagittarius is a solar eclipse. Despite Mercury's retrograde, this eclipse should attract new opportunities for higher education, publishing, overseas travel, and the exploration of your own belief system. Uranus forms a tight, beneficial angle to the eclipse degree, indicating an excitement and unpredictability to events.

Saturday, November 26 (Moon into Capricorn, 10:05 p.m.)   Venus enters Capricorn, marking the beginning of one of the best times for you professionally. Despite Mercury's retrograde, you should be able to make significant strides in your career between now and December 20. Other people are receptive to your ideas and recognize your work and achievements. This transit could trigger some sort of flirtation or romance with someone in your work environment.

Sunday, November 27 (Moon in Capricorn)   With Venus, Pluto, and the moon in Capricorn, you're in charge—of your office, division, or department and of your love life. You're able to strategize, set realistic goals, and inspire the people around you with your dedication and focus. Even though it's Sunday, you're in the work groove, Aries, preparing for the week ahead.

Monday, November 28 (Moon in Capricorn)   Jupiter forms a beneficial angle to this moon and to the other planets in Capricorn, so there should be a lot of expansion occurring in your life right now. Financially and professionally, opportunities are surfacing. Take advantage of them. In June 2012, Jupiter will enter Gemini, so you've got less than a year to use this expansive energy to your own benefit.

Tuesday, November 29 (Moon into Aquarius, 2:02 a.m.) The moon enters your eleventh house, heightening contact with friends and groups. This lunar transit also brings your focus to your own wishes and dreams. You may be clarifying your desires now and could be plotting a different course through life.

Wednesday, November 30 (Moon in Aquarius)   Tomorrow the countdown begins to the end of the year. Take stock today. Brainstorm with friends about where all of you would like to be and what you'd like to be doing come the new year. By sharing in this way, each of you gains fresh insight into yourselves.

Thursday, December 1 (Moon into Pisces, 9:46 a.m.)
The countdown to the end of the year begins today. Your dreams should be particularly active and may be imparting insight into events that are taking shape in your future. Depending on how closely you track your dreams, today and tomorrow could bring precognitive ones. Pay close attention.

Friday, December 2 (Moon in Pisces) If possible, delay your holiday shopping, especially for big-ticket items, until after December 13, when Mercury turns direct again. Otherwise, you may be in long lines on December 26, returning items that you bought. With Venus forming a harmonious angle to this moon and Mars opposing it, you and a partner may not see eye to eye on an issue or situation. But if you think before you blurt out your opinion, Aries, tensions ease considerably.

Saturday, December 3 (Moon into Aries, 8:52 p.m.)
For the next two and a half days, the moon is in your sign, joining Uranus in your first house. This results in excitability, triggers your sense of adventure, and should keep your love life moving at a swift clip. Uranus will be in Aries until the spring of 2019, and generally, the first year or two of a Uranus transit through your sun sign tend to be the most intense.

Sunday, December 4 (Moon in Aries) Your energy and enthusiasm carry you far today. But the distance you travel is irrelevant if you're not happy with what you're doing or feeling joyous about the direction in which your life is moving. So if you find yourself feeling gloomy or a bit down, find something to appreciate. Turn your thoughts around. You're actually in a very good place.

Monday, December 5 (Moon in Aries)   You're fired up about something today. You may feel somewhat overwhelmed because of work or a personal issue or maybe just because of the proximity of the holidays. But the stars are lined up in your favor, and with just a little organization, you're able to pull off whatever you're trying to do.

Tuesday, December 6 (Moon into Taurus, 9:36 a.m.) At times you live your life jammed in fast-forward. Then along comes one of these earth-sign moons that asks you to slow down, take your time, smell the proverbial roses. While you're at it, make time today to check over your bank statements.

Wednesday, December 7 (Moon in Taurus)   The moon links up with Jupiter in your money house. One possible result of this combination is an urge to spend, spend, spend. Avoid excess, Aries. You want excess in the other direction: *more* money in your account, not money leaving your account. So if you go shopping, pay cash. It will make you more aware of what you're spending.

Thursday, December 8 (Moon into Gemini, 9:54 p.m.) The family has appointed you the holiday organizer. If your family is small, it shouldn't be a problem. If your family numbers more than four or five, with dozens of relatives living in different areas of the country or world, then you may want to say thanks, but no thanks. If the holiday festivities are going to be at your place, with people arriving from out of town, then you should get busy planning the events.

Friday, December 9 (Moon in Gemini)   Books and information are what keep you going today. Whether you're on a spiritual quest or just looking for a new recipe, you're determined to find what you need. Your energy could feel a little scattered, perhaps because you have so much on your plate. Tomorrow's lunar eclipse will prompt you to connect with friends, neighbors, and relatives. Social contact may soothe your nerves.

Saturday, December 10 (Moon in Gemini)   Today's lunar eclipse in Gemini and the fact that Uranus turns direct in your sign should bring about an exciting, informative day. Mars forms a wide, challenging angle to the eclipse degree, indicating some tension related to work left undone, and Mercury forms a close but challenging angle that suggests you must adjust your attitude in some way.

Sunday, December 11 (Moon into Cancer, 8:27 a.m.) This moon forms a nice angle to Mars in Virgo. Don't be surprised if you stick close to home today, doing whatever needs to be done to either leave town for the holidays or receive guests. You've got a precise to-do list that defies your usual way of doing things. You're ready to move forward, which Mercury's direct motion in two days will enable you to do.

Monday, December 12 (Moon in Cancer)   You're eager to get things moving so that you can take off some time during the holidays. But there could be delays that you don't have any control over. Just bite the bullet, keep your business to yourself, and try to move things forward again on December 14. The stars will be better aligned for you then.

Tuesday, December 13 (Moon into Leo, 4:49 p.m.) Celebrate! Mercury turns direct! And with the moon in fellow fire sign Leo and Uranus still in your sign, you've got plenty of drive and determination. Even though it's early in the week, you may knock off to do something you enjoy. Whether it's a sport, chilling at home, or spending time with your newest romantic interest or a partner, you feel you've earned the chance for some fun.

Wednesday, December 14 (Moon in Leo)   Now that Mercury is moving direct, you're ready to shop for the holidays. If you enjoy shopping on the Internet, you may have to pay express charges, so it might be wiser to hit the closest mall or shopping center and do most of the shopping in one fell swoop. On other fronts, your kids may need some of your time now. If you don't have children, then the "kids" may be born from your creative endeavors. Books, for instance. Screenplays. Music you've written.

Thursday, December 15 (Moon into Virgo, 10:59 p.m.) The moon joins Mars in your solar sixth house late this evening. These two urge you to be very discriminating in everything you do and feel. You may overcompensate in some areas, as with employees or coworkers or with your own work. There's a tendency toward perfectionism with this duo. The challenge is to know when to stop polishing that diamond in the rough.

Friday, December 16 (Moon in Virgo)   You're on a detailed path today. Nothing escapes your attention. It's easy to clutter your mind when you're absorbing everything around you, so as the day goes on, you begin to filter out the details that aren't pertinent to whatever you're doing. You're urged to put a practical spin on all your ideas and projects.

Saturday, December 17 (Moon in Virgo)   Time to set up your personal barriers, perhaps. Whether you're staying home for the holidays or heading out of town, you could get a little nuts being around people 24-7. So all you have to do, Aries, is to begin erecting an invisible barrier around yourself. Use your imagination. Build a wall of light that permits only the positive and upbeat to penetrate.

Sunday, December 18 (Moon into Libra, 3:07 a.m.) Whenever the moon and Saturn travel together in gregarious Libra, you may not feel like partying. You can mitigate this heavy feeling by sticking to what is known and familiar and by meeting your obligations and responsibilities. It sounds simplistic, but it should work beautifully.

Monday, December 19 (Moon in Libra)   Your partner would like some of your time today. Maybe a lot of your time! If that's the case, then you may want to extend your weekend and take the day off. With Saturn in your seventh house until the fall of 2012, both of you may have to make adjustments in your partnership to accommodate delays or restrictions that Saturn may impose.

Tuesday, December 20 (Moon into Scorpio, 5:33 a.m.)
Venus enters Aquarius and your eleventh house, where it will be until mid-January 2012. This transit certainly favors group activities and even a possible romance with someone you meet through friends or through a group to which you belong. Venus forms a beneficial angle to your natal sun, which helps to bolster how others see you.

Wednesday, December 21 (Moon in Scorpio)   Is your shopping done? Are your plans in place? Are you thinking about your New Year's goals? If you're celebrating New Year's, do you know what you're doing yet? In other words, there are a lot of loose ends to tie up before the end of 2011, and you may not know where to start. So just pick a task, Aries. Any task. And dive in.

Thursday, December 22 (Moon into Sagittarius, 7:03 a.m.)   Gnashing your teeth yet? Feeling an almost insurmountable itch to get out and do something different? Given your penchant for impulsiveness, you may decide to do something totally off the wall today and throw the people around you into a tizzy. As long as no one is hurt, don't worry about it. You've added the sort of spice and excitement to events that everyone expects from you!

Friday, December 23 (Moon in Sagittarius)   Early festivities may be going on around your house. You could be welcoming someone back from overseas or could be going overseas yourself or have dealings with foreigners. Whatever is going on, you grasp the larger implications and are prepared to deal with all of it.

Saturday, December 24 (Moon into Capricorn, 8:48 a.m.)   Today's new moon in Capricorn receives a wide conjunction from Pluto, indicating power plays could be a part of Christmas Eve. But you're in a good position to mitigate the possible fallout. It could involve an older person, possibly a male. Jupiter in Taurus forms a beneficial angle to this moon, however, suggesting that things turn out fine and could even expand someone's worldview!

Sunday, December 25 (Moon in Capricorn)   Jupiter turns direct today in Taurus, in your solar second house. And how perfect that it happens on Christmas Day. This movement sets you up nicely for a financial expansion that takes you into the New Year. Maybe you find out you've gotten a significant raise. Or that the job you applied for is now yours. No telling.

Monday, December 26 (Moon into Aquarius, 12:15 p.m.)   Cutting-edge stuff today—that's where your ideas and insights can be filed. There could be some lively post-Christmas discussions today—politics, religion, all the hot-button issues. You may want to think twice before you venture into that area. Peace on earth, remember?

Tuesday, December 27 (Moon in Aquarius)   Hopefully, you avoided the mall yesterday, and if you need to return gifts today, the crush of shoppers won't be as extreme. But you may decide to forgo the mall altogether and meet with friends or a group of acquaintances whose interests are similar to yours. In fact, take your visitors. Make it a party of ideas and conversation.

Wednesday, December 28 (Moon into Pisces, 6:46 p.m.) You may volunteer for an organization or a community project today. You have the free time, and your spirit has been considerably softened this year by some sudden, unexpected changes. Besides, it may be time for you to begin giving back, right? If visitors are still at your place, take them along. Get them involved too.

Thursday, December 29 (Moon in Pisces) It's possible that during the next two days, your dreams prove prescient. If you're the type whose dreams are laden with symbolism, decipher the symbols even if you have to share the dreams with others. A person who is close to you may understand you better than you understand yourself and will be able to interpret the dreams correctly.

Friday, December 30 (Moon in Pisces) It's a day to relax by a fire if you're in a cold area or to meander along a lazy river if you're in a temperate climate. The Pisces moon enjoys opportunities for imagination to flow and drift. What better place to do this than in front of a fire to satisfy your sun sign or on a river or ocean to satisfy the Pisces moon?

Saturday, December 31 (Moon into Aries, 4:49 a.m.) Is this great or what? The year ends on a power day for you, with the moon in your sign, joining Uranus in your first house. The combination of planets, with every planet in direct motion, should make for an enjoyable New Year's Eve.

HAPPY NEW YEAR!

Sunday, January 1 (Moon in Aries) The year begins, Aries, with the moon on your ascendant. You're dealing with your emotional self, the person you are becoming. You also spend time thinking about how the public relates to you and conclude that the way you feel about yourself is the way others see you. Your appearance and personality shine. Your feelings and thoughts are aligned today.

Monday, January 2 (Moon into Taurus, 5:17 p.m.) You're about to shift into a new mode. The old cycle is over; a new one begins. It's time to break away from the New Year and find a new path. You'll probably find that the old ways have outlived their usefulness. Look for a new approach, a new perspective.

Tuesday, January 3 (Moon in Taurus) With the moon in your second house, expect emotional experiences related to money. You have the opportunity now for more stability if you can stay grounded. You identify emotionally with your possessions or whatever you value. Watch your spending.

Wednesday, January 4 (Moon in Taurus) Yesterday's energy flows into your Wednesday. It's a good day to get out into nature, do something physical. Use common sense and take a down-to-earth perspective. You could be dealing with marriage, finances, real estate, or property. Try to avoid stubborn behavior.

Thursday, January 5 (Moon into Gemini, 5:45 a.m.) You're innovative and creative and communicate well. You have a chance to expand whatever you're doing now. Luck is on your side today. Follow your fortunes—including this one. However, avoid scattering your energies.

Friday, January 6 (Moon in Gemini)   The moon is in your third house today. As yesterday, you communicate well, either in writing or speaking. Your mental abilities are strong now, and you have an emotional need to reinvigorate your studies. It's a good day for journaling. You could be influenced by matters from the past.

Saturday, January 7 (Moon into Cancer, 4:06 p.m.) Promote new ideas; follow your curiosity. Look for adventure. Freedom of thought and action is key. But so is moderation; avoid excess in whatever you're doing. It's a good day to work on your own or pursue self-employment. You're courageous and adaptable.

Sunday, January 8 (Moon in Cancer)   With Mercury moving into your tenth house today, the energy of the last few days is enhanced. Your writing and speaking abilities are strong. You have a chance to gain recognition for what you do. You should plan carefully now for a career move. Your goals are within reach. It's also a good time for getting something published.

Monday, January 9 (Moon into Leo, 11:35 p.m.) There's a full moon today in your fourth house. That means you reap what you've sown, especially related to your home. You gain insight and illumination, possibly about a home-remodeling project or real estate. That fresh insight could also relate to your parents or family life.

Tuesday, January 10 (Moon in Leo)   The moon is in your fifth house today. Be yourself; be emotionally honest. In love, there's greater emotional depth to a relationship now. It's a good day to take a chance, experiment. However, be aware that your emotions tend to overpower your intellect.

Wednesday, January 11 (Moon in Leo)   It's a great day for initiating projects, Aries. Drama is highlighted.

You strut your stuff. You're creative and passionate. Focus on publicizing yourself; advertise your skills. Animals and pets figure prominently in your day.

Thursday, January 12 (Moon into Virgo, 4:44 a.m.)
You're at the top of your cycle today. Look for a new project coming your way. You're inventive and make connections that others overlook. You break with the past. Be independent and creative, and don't get discouraged by those who would like you to keep doing the same old thing. Trust your hunches. Stress originality.

Friday, January 13 (Moon in Virgo)   It's a service day. Others rely on you now. You're the one they go to for help. You improve, edit, and refine their work. Alternately, keep your resolutions about exercise, and watch your diet. Attend to details related to your health. Make a doctor or dentist appointment. Your personal health occupies your attention.

Saturday, January 14 (Moon into Libra, 8:29 a.m.)
With Venus moving into your twelfth house today, you have a love of secrecy and working on your own. Solitude feels good. Your emotions are controlled subconsciously, and they are also strong. You could be feeling frustrated regarding a romantic relationship. It's a good day to help others who are less fortunate than you.

Sunday, January 15 (Moon in Libra)   Loved ones and partners are more important than usual today. The focus turns to personal relationships. You get along well with others now. You can fit in just about anywhere. Women play a prominent role in your day, especially Gemini or Aquarius.

Monday, January 16 (Moon into Scorpio, 11:34 a.m.)
Change and variety are highlighted now. Think outside the box. Think freedom, no restrictions. Variety is the

spice of life. Take risks; experiment today. Promote new ideas; follow your curiosity. Look for adventure.

Tuesday, January 17 (Moon in Scorpio)   Your experiences are more intense than usual. Managing shared resources takes on new importance. You have a strong sense of duty and feel obligated to fulfill your promises. It's a good time to get involved in a cause aimed at improving living conditions for large numbers of people.

Wednesday, January 18 (Moon into Sagittarius, 2:30 p.m.)   It's a number 7 day. You're a searcher, a seeker of truth. Secrets, intrigue, confidential information play a role. Be aware of decisions made behind closed doors. You investigate, analyze, or simply observe what's going on. You detect deception and recognize insincerity with ease.

Thursday, January 19 (Moon in Sagittarius)   You may feel a need to get away now, a break from the usual routine. You yearn for a new experience. Sign up for a workshop or seminar, or plan a long trip. A foreign-born person or a foreign country plays a role. A publishing project goes well. Publicity and advertising are highlighted.

Friday, January 20 (Moon into Capricorn, 5:42 p.m.)
Finish what you started. Make room for something new. Visualize the future; set your goals, then make them so. Use the day for reflection, expansion, and concluding projects.

Saturday, January 21 (Moon in Capricorn)   Professional concerns are the focus of the day. You gain an elevation in prestige. Your life is more public today, and business dealings are highlighted. It's a good day for sales and working with the public. You're more responsive to the needs and moods of a group and of the public in general.

Sunday, January 22 (Moon into Aquarius, 9:54 p.m.) The spotlight is on cooperation. Your emotions and sensitivity are highlighted. There could be some soul-searching related to relationships. New relationships could form now. Help comes through friends or loved ones, especially a partner.

Monday, January 23 (Moon in Aquarius)   There's a new moon in Aquarius today. That means new opportunities come your way related to groups and social events. You have a greater sense of freedom now. You're dealing with new ideas, new options, originality. A doorway opens, and you get a fresh start, a new beginning.

Tuesday, January 24 (Moon in Aquarius)   Yesterday's energy flows into your Tuesday. Friends play an important role in your day, especially Leo or Sagittarius. You find strength in numbers and meaning through friends and groups. Work for the common good, but keep an eye on your own wishes and dreams.

Wednesday, January 25 (Moon into Pisces, 4:12 a.m.) Whatever you've been thinking about, the answer is yes. Go ahead. Change, travel, and communication are highlighted. Approach the day with an unconventional mind-set. Release old structures; get a new point of view.

Thursday, January 26 (Moon in Pisces)   Imagination is highlighted. Watch for psychic events, synchronicities. Ideas are ripe. Compassion, sensitivity, and inspiration are highlighted. Your imagination is strong. You respond emotionally to whatever is happening.

Friday, January 27 (Moon into Aries, 1:29 p.m.) Mercury moves into your eleventh house today. You tend to avoid any emotional conflicts. Your mind is sharp, and you work well with others, exchanging ideas with a variety of people. But emotionally you keep your distance.

Saturday, January 28 (Moon in Aries)   The moon is on your ascendant today, Aries. Your appearance and personality shine. The way you see yourself now is the way others see you. You're recharged for the month ahead, and this makes you more appealing to the public. You're physically vital, and relations with the opposite sex go well.

Sunday, January 29 (Moon in Aries)   With the moon in your first house, you could be dealing with your health and emotional self today. You're sensitive to other people's feelings. You may feel moody one moment, happy the next, then withdrawn and sad. Your self-awareness and appearance are important now.

Monday, January 30 (Moon into Taurus, 1:29 a.m.) It's a number 1 day, so you're at the top of your cycle as the week begins. Take the lead, Aries, and don't be afraid to turn in a new direction. Get out and meet new people, have new experiences, do something you've never done before. You're determined and courageous today. In romance, a flirtation turns more serious.

Tuesday, January 31 (Moon in Taurus)   It's a good day to cultivate new ideas, but make sure that they are well grounded. Your senses are highly attuned today, and you tend to be opinionated. Health and physical activity are emphasized. Money matters play a role. Watch your spending.

Wednesday, February 1 (Moon into Gemini, 2:15 p.m.)
The old cycle ends today. Get ready for something new.
Visualize the future; set your goals, then make them
so. Accept what comes your way now. It's all part of a
cycle. Clear up odds and ends. Make room for something new.

Thursday, February 2 (Moon in Gemini) Take
what you know and share it with others. However, keep
conscious control of your emotions when communicating. Your mental abilities are strong now, and you could
be exploring matters from the deep past. Short trips today are likely, but be careful talking on your cell while
driving.

Friday, February 3 (Moon in Gemini) Neptune
moves into your twelfth house today. Your creative efforts are enhanced with a boost in your intuitive abilities. You'll also be feeling more romantic this year. It's a
good time for pursuing any interest in acting or any fan-
tasy and make-believe concepts. You can remake your
image now.

Saturday, February 4 (Moon into Cancer, 1:04 a.m.)
Spread your good news, and take time to listen to others today. Your charm and wit are appreciated, and you
can influence people now with your upbeat attitude.
Take time to relax, enjoy yourself, and recharge your
batteries. In romance you're an ardent lover, and a
loyal one.

Sunday, February 5 (Moon in Cancer) With the
moon in your fourth house, it's a good day to spend
time with your family and loved ones. You feel close to
your roots. You're dealing with the foundations of who
you are and who you are becoming. Retreat to a pri-

vate place for meditation. Try to remember your dreams today.

Monday, February 6 (Moon into Leo, 8:24 a.m.)
Travel and variety are highlighted today. You're also more comfortable than usual in front of an audience. Freedom of thought and action is key. But so is moderation; avoid excess in whatever you're doing. Remain flexible and ready for change.

Tuesday, February 7 (Moon in Leo)   With a full moon in your fifth house today, you reap what you've sown related to your creative efforts. You're also dealing with children. It's a good day for romance, even pregnancy. However, with Saturn turning retrograde in your seventh house, there could be delays or second thoughts in the coming weeks related to marriage or romance. Things clear up by the end of June.

Wednesday, February 8 (Moon into Virgo, 12:33 p.m.)
With Venus moving into your first house today, you're more socially outgoing this month. Your grace and friendly demeanor are appreciated. That Aries aggressiveness is softened. You also could be somewhat vain about your appearance.

Thursday, February 9 (Moon in Virgo)   With the moon in your sixth house today, it's a good day to clarify any health or work issues. Try to follow a regular schedule now. Help others, but don't deny your own needs. Keep your resolutions about exercise, and watch your diet. Attend to details related to your health. Make a doctor or dentist appointment.

Friday, February 10 (Moon into Libra, 2:55 p.m.)
Clear your desk for tomorrow's new cycle. Make room for something new, but don't start anything today. Com-

plete a project now. Clear up odds and ends. Spiritual values arise.

Saturday, February 11 (Moon in Libra) Loved ones and partners are more important than usual. You feel a need to be accepted. Be careful that others don't manipulate your feelings, especially related to any legal matter that comes to your attention.

Sunday, February 12 (Moon into Scorpio, 5:02 p.m.) Yesterday's energy flows into your Sunday. Partnerships are highlighted. Your intuition focuses on relationships. Don't make waves. Don't rush or show resentment; let things develop. Be kind and understanding.

Monday, February 13 (Moon in Scorpio) Mercury moves into your twelfth house today. Hidden communication is the theme of the day. You work behind the scenes at a home office. E-mails play a role. So do private discussions, meditation, or a therapy session.

Tuesday, February 14 (Moon into Sagittarius, 7:57 p.m.) It's a number 4 day. Your organizational skills are highlighted. Fulfill your obligations. You're building foundations for an outlet for your creativity. Emphasize quality. Plan or fantasize about a long journey with your loved one this evening. Happy Valentine's Day!

Wednesday, February 15 (Moon in Sagittarius) The moon is in your ninth house today. You yearn for a new experience. Think more about that trip. Sign up for a workshop or seminar. An interest in mythology, religion, or philosophy could play a role. You're a dreamer and a thinker.

Thursday, February 16 (Moon in Sagittarius) You see the big picture now, not just the details. Don't limit yourself. Spiritual values arise. Worldviews are emphasized. You're restless, impulsive, and inquisitive. Publishing or the law could play a role in your day.

Friday, February 17 (Moon into Capricorn, 12:04 a.m.)   Secrets, intrigue, confidential information play a role today. You might feel best working on your own. You investigate, analyze, or simply observe what's going on now. You quickly come to a conclusion and wonder why others don't see what you see. It's best to hold off on making any final decisions for a couple of days.

Saturday, February 18 (Moon in Capricorn)   The moon is in your tenth house today. Your career or profession is the focus of the day, and now you can see that you're moving steadily ahead. Your life is more public. You're more emotional and warm toward coworkers. Avoid emotional displays in public.

Sunday, February 19 (Moon into Aquarius, 5:29 a.m.)   It's a great day for completing projects and getting ready for something new. Clear up odds and ends. Take an inventory on where things are going in your life. Look beyond the present, but don't start anything new until tomorrow.

Monday, February 20 (Moon in Aquarius)   Friends play an important role in your day, especially Leo and Sagittarius. Focus on your wishes and dreams. Examine your overall goals. Make sure that those goals are an expression of who you really are. Social consciousness plays a role. Your sense of security is tied to your relationships and friends.

Tuesday, February 21 (Moon into Pisces, 12:32 p.m.)
There's a new moon in Pisces, your twelfth house, today. New opportunities arise for working behind the scenes. It's a good time to begin a new project, Aries, but keep it to yourself for now. You could be dealing with a mat-

ter from the past that has returned to haunt you. Follow your intuition.

Wednesday, February 22 (Moon in Pisces)   Yesterday's energy flows into your Wednesday. Take time to reflect and meditate. Think carefully before you act today. Avoid any self-destructive tendencies, especially by revealing too much too soon. Watch for psychic events, synchronicities. Keep track of your dreams, including your daydreams. Ideas are ripe.

Thursday, February 23 (Moon into Aries, 9:48 p.m.) It's a number 4 day, and that means your organizational skills are highlighted. Control your impulses. Persevere to get things done, and don't get sloppy. Tear down the old in order to rebuild. Be methodical and thorough. Revise, rewrite. It's not a good day for romance.

Friday, February 24 (Moon in Aries)   With the moon in your first house today, your feelings and thoughts are aligned. It's all about your health and your emotional self: how you feel and how you feel about yourself. You are sensitive and responsive to the needs of others, so you are easily influenced by those around you.

Saturday, February 25 (Moon in Aries)   The moon is on your ascendant now. You're feeling physically vital and recharged for the month ahead. You get a fresh start. You're assertive and outgoing. Your appearance and personality shine. You get along well with the opposite sex.

Sunday, February 26 (Moon into Taurus, 9:30 a.m.) It's a number 7 day. You investigate, analyze, or simply observe what's going on now. You quickly come to a conclusion and wonder why others don't see what you see. You detect deception and recognize insincerity with ease. Gather information, but don't make any absolute decisions until tomorrow. Go with the flow.

Monday, February 27 (Moon in Taurus)　　The moon is in your second house today. You feel best when surrounded by familiar objects in your home environment. It's not the objects themselves that are important, but the feelings and memories you associate with them. Put off making any major purchases now. You equate your financial assets with emotional security.

Tuesday, February 28 (Moon into Gemini, 10:28 p.m.) Look for a new approach, a new perspective. The old cycle is ending; a new one about to begin. Visualize the future; set your goals, then make them so. Clear up odds and ends. Take an inventory on where things are going in your life.

Wednesday, February 29 (Moon in Gemini)　　You're dealing with siblings, other relatives, or neighbors now. Let them know what you think, but don't get overly emotional. Don't focus so much on the past. Stay in the present moment. A short trip works to your benefit. You write from a deep place today, a good day for journaling.

MARCH 2012

Thursday, March 1 (Moon in Gemini)　　The moon is in your third house today. Take what you know and share it with others. You could be getting involved in a demanding mental activity, such as on-line gaming, a debate, or a game of chess—anything that challenges your mental prowess. A short trip works to your benefit now.

Friday, March 2 (Moon into Cancer, 10:09 a.m.) With Mercury moving into your first house, you communicate well this month. You also adapt quickly to changing circumstances. You're mentally restless, always seeking new and useful ideas and information. It's a good month to express yourself through writing.

Saturday, March 3 (Moon in Cancer)   Spend time with your family and loved ones today. Work on a home-repair project; beautify your home. You're intuitive and nurturing now, sensitive to the moods of others. Snuggle with your loved one.

Sunday, March 4 (Moon into Leo, 6:19 p.m.)   You tend to stay with the tried and true today. It's not a day for experimentation or new approaches. You're building a creative base for your future. Tear down the old in order to rebuild. Be methodical and thorough.

Monday, March 5 (Moon in Leo)   With Venus moving into Taurus today, it's a great day for romance, Aries. You also find material success this month, meaning more income. You enjoy the comforts of life. You're more artistically inclined, and you can make money from your creative efforts.

Tuesday, March 6 (Moon into Virgo, 10:28 p.m.)   Be sympathetic, kind, and compassionate. Diplomacy wins the way, even in a difficult matter. Focus on making people happy, but avoid scattering your energies. A domestic adjustment works out for the best. Dance to your own tune.

Wednesday, March 7 (Moon in Virgo)   The moon is in your sixth house today. It's a service day. Others rely on you now. You're the one they go to for help. You improve, edit, and refine their work. Keep your resolutions about exercise, and watch your diet. Attend to details related to your health. You could be feeling somewhat emotionally repressed.

Thursday, March 8 (Moon into Libra, 11:51 p.m.) With a full moon in your sixth house today, you gain insight and illumination regarding matters in the workplace. Now you understand what's been going on. Alternately, you hear news about a health issue that has been on your mind. You reap what you've sown now, either in the workplace or related to a health matter.

Friday, March 9 (Moon in Libra)   The focus turns to relationships, both business and personal, today. Women play a prominent role. You get along well with others now, but feel a need to be accepted. You're looking for security, but you have a hard time going with the flow.

Saturday, March 10 (Moon in Libra)   You're at the top of your cycle today. Take the lead, Aries. You get a fresh start, a new beginning. Stress originality, and don't be afraid to turn in a new direction. Trust your hunches; intuition is highlighted.

Sunday, March 11—Daylight Saving Time Begins (Moon into Scorpio, 1:25 a.m.)   Your experiences are more intense than usual today. Security is an important issue now. It can affect your feelings about your possessions, as well as things that you share with others, such as a spouse. You could be dealing with shared resources. Avoid any feelings of desire to possess it all for yourself.

Monday, March 12 (Moon in Scorpio)   Mercury goes retrograde in your first house today and stays there until April 4. That means you can expect delays and glitches related to personal matters. Others might misunderstand your intentions, so you tend to ponder excessively about what they think. As a result, you change plans or procrastinate. Take heart, the confusion ends in three weeks.

Tuesday, March 13 (Moon into Sagittarius, 2:54 a.m.) Your organizational skills are highlighted. Stay focused, and take care of your obligations. Control any impulse to wander off task. You're building a creative base. It's a day of hard work that will make the rest of the month go easier.

Wednesday, March 14 (Moon in Sagittarius)   After yesterday's hard work, you might feel a need to get away and break from the usual routine. You're a dreamer and a thinker, and your thoughts tend to rattle the status quo. Worldviews are emphasized. You can create positive change through your ideas, Aries.

Thursday, March 15 (Moon into Capricorn, 6:24 a.m.)   Service to others is the theme of the day. You offer advice and support. Be sympathetic, kind, and compassionate, but avoid scattering your energies. Be understanding and avoid confrontations.

Friday, March 16 (Moon in Capricorn)   The moon is in your tenth house today. Business is highlighted. You're more responsive to the needs and moods of a group and the public in general. You get a boost in prestige and get along well with fellow workers. It's a good day for sales, dealing with the public.

Saturday, March 17 (Moon into Aquarius, 12:12 p.m.) It's a number 8 day. It's your power day, your day to play it your way. You have a chance to expand, to gain recognition—even fame and power. You attract financial success, especially if you open your mind to a new approach.

Sunday, March 18 (Moon in Aquarius)   The moon is in your eleventh house today. Friends play an important role in your day. You find strength in numbers and meaning through friends and groups. Focus on your wishes and dreams. Examine your overall goals. Those goals should be an expression of who you are.

Monday, March 19 (Moon into Pisces, 8:05 p.m.)
You're at the top of your cycle now. Be independent and creative. Stress originality. You're inventive and make connections that others overlook. You're determined and courageous. A flirtation could turn more serious.

Tuesday, March 20 (Moon in Pisces)   With the moon in your twelfth house, it's a good day to work behind the scenes. Unconscious attitudes can be difficult now. So can relations with women. Keep your feelings secret, unless you're confiding in a close friend.

Wednesday, March 21 (Moon in Pisces)   It's a great day for pursuing a mystical or spiritual discipline. Your intuition and imagination are highlighted. Watch for psychic events, synchronicities. Deep healing, compassion, and sensitivity toward others are emphasized.

Thursday, March 22 (Moon into Aries, 5:58 a.m.)
There's a new moon in your first house today. That's good news. You can expect new opportunities to appear. The way you see yourself now is the way others see you. Your face is in front of the public, and you are noticed. You're feeling strong and vital.

Friday, March 23 (Moon in Aries)   Yesterday's energy flows into your Friday. You're appealing to the public. Your appearance and personality shine. Your feelings and thoughts are aligned today, and relations with the opposite sex go well.

Saturday, March 24 (Moon into Taurus, 5:44 p.m.)
It's a service day. You're the one others go to for help. You improve whatever they're doing. It's also a good day to clarify any health or work issues. It's best if you follow a regular schedule now. Help others, but don't deny your own needs.

Sunday, March 25 (Moon in Taurus)   It's time to be practical and down-to-earth. Catch up on any outstanding bills. Money issues are on your mind. Take time to get out into nature as spring arrives. A hike in the woods refreshes and revives. You feel more grounded and peaceful today.

Monday, March 26 (Moon in Taurus)   With the moon in your second house you identify emotionally with your possessions or whatever you value. Money and material goods are important to you now and give you a sense of security. Watch your spending.

Tuesday, March 27 (Moon into Gemini, 6:44 a.m.) Use the day for reflection, expansion, and concluding projects. Don't start anything new today. Visualize the future; set your goals, then make them so. It's a good day to make a donation to a worthy cause.

Wednesday, March 28 (Moon in Gemini)   The moon is in your third house today. Your mental abilities are strong, and you have an emotional need to reinvigorate your studies. You also could be exploring matters from the deep past. Siblings, other relatives, and neighbors could play a role in your day. Make your point, but avoid getting overly emotional.

Thursday, March 29 (Moon into Cancer, 7:08 p.m.) It's a number 2 day. Use your intuition to get a sense of the day. Don't make waves, rush, or show resentment; let things develop. The spotlight is on cooperation. Show your appreciation to others.

Friday, March 30 (Moon in Cancer)   Take time to relax and meditate today. Make plans for the weekend that might include handling a home-repair project or beautifying your home. You're sensitive to other people's moods now. It's best to keep your thoughts to your-self rather than criticize, Aries.

Saturday, March 31 (Moon in Cancer)   Yesterday's energy flows into your Saturday. Spend time with your family and loved ones today. Stick close to home. Parents play a role. You feel a close tie to your roots. You're dealing with the foundations of who you are and who you are becoming.

APRIL 2012

Sunday, April 1 (Moon into Leo, 4:37 a.m.)   Your intuition focuses on relationships. Be kind and under-standing. Show your appreciation. The spotlight is on cooperation and partnerships. If you're married, or con-sidering it, your relationship plays a key role in your day.

Monday, April 2 (Moon in Leo)   With the moon in your fifth house today, Aries, it's a good day to take a chance, experiment. Be aware that your emotions tend to overpower your intellect now. You're sensitive and in touch with your creative side. Alternatively, you are more protective and nurturing toward children.

Tuesday, April 3 (Moon into Virgo, 9:54 a.m.)   With Venus moving into your third house today, you get along with family members. You've got lots to say, but you don't want to argue. You have the ability now to per-suade others to your way of thinking without confront-ing them.

Wednesday, April 4 (Moon in Virgo)   Mercury goes direct in your twelfth house. Confusion, miscommuni-cation, and delays—especially related to any secret or behind-the-scenes activities—are over. You have a bet-ter understanding of matters from the past, possibly your childhood. Everything works better now, including computers and other electronic equipment. Misunderstandings about a health issue are resolved.

Thursday, April 5 (Moon into Libra, 11:33 a.m.)   A domestic adjustment works out for the best. You could face emotional outbursts or someone making unfair demands. Be understanding, and avoid confrontations. Offer advice and support, but do it in a diplomatic way.

Friday, April 6 (Moon in Libra)   There's a full moon today in your seventh house, and that means you gain new insight and understanding related to a partnership. You reap what you've sown, and you're trying to keep everything in balance. A legal matter is resolved now.

Saturday, April 7 (Moon into Scorpio, 11:18 a.m.) It's a number 8 day, a power day, a day for financial and material gain. You move up the ladder now. Think big and act big! You can go far with your plans and attract financial success.

Sunday, April 8 (Moon in Scorpio)   The moon is in your eighth house. In spite of your own success, you could be feeling vulnerable about your partner's finances, or lack of them. Issues about taxes, a mortgage, or insurance arise. It's an excellent time to draw up a living will. It's also a great time to explore the real mysteries of life, such as life after death, past lives, and future lives.

Monday, April 9 (Moon into Sagittarius, 11:13 a.m.) You're at the top of your cycle. You take the lead in something new and get a fresh start, a new beginning. Express your opinions dynamically. Get out and meet new people, have new experiences, and do something you've never done before.

Tuesday, April 10 (Moon in Sagittarius) Pluto goes retrograde in Capricorn until September 17. Professional activities are slowed somewhat, but the effect is marginal, much more subtle than Mercury retrograde. It's not the best time to expect things to get done quickly. So until mid-September, leave some leeway in career plans.

Wednesday, April 11 (Moon into Capricorn, 1:02 p.m.) It's a number 3 day. You're creative and express yourself well today. You communicate clearly. Your artistic talents are highlighted. You're warm and receptive to what others say. Your popularity is on the rise, but your attitude determines everything.

Thursday, April 12 (Moon in Capricorn) Your ambition and drive to succeed are highlighted. Your responsibilities increase. You may feel stressed, overworked, but don't ignore your exercise routine. Get away from your desk. Stretch, relax, walk. Earth signs Taurus and Virgo play a prominent role. Be conservative regarding financial speculation.

Friday, April 13 (Moon into Aquarius, 5:48 p.m.) Promote new ideas, and follow your curiosity, Aries. Approach the day with an unconventional mind-set. Release old structures; get a new point of view. Change and variety are highlighted now. Think freedom, no restrictions.

Saturday, April 14 (Moon in Aquarius) Yesterday's energy flows into your Saturday. You have a greater sense of freedom. You're dealing with new ideas, new options, originality. Take a close look at your goals, and make sure that they're an expression of who you are. You have deeper contact with friends.

Sunday, April 15 (Moon in Aquarius) You get along well with a group today. You find strength in numbers and meaning through friends and groups. Social consciousness plays a role. You work for the common good with like-minded individuals. But keep an eye on your own wishes and dreams.

Monday, April 16 (Moon into Pisces, 1:38 a.m.) Mercury moves into your first house today. You make connections with others easily now. You also adapt to changing circumstances, and you're especially quick and witty. You express yourself well in speech and writing.

Tuesday, April 17 (Moon in Pisces)   The moon is in your twelfth house today. It's a good day to withdraw and spend time in private. Relax and meditate. Keep your feelings to yourself. Finish whatever you've been working on. It's a great day for pursuing a mystical or spiritual discipline.

Wednesday, April 18 (Moon into Aries, 12:00 p.m.) Be independent and creative, and refuse to be discouraged by naysayers, Aries. You're determined and courageous today. Stress originality. Explore, discover, create. In romance, something new is developing.

Thursday, April 19 (Moon in Aries)   The way you see yourself now is the way others see you. You're recharged for the rest of the month, and this makes you more appealing to the public. You're physically vital, and relations with the opposite sex go well. Your feelings and thoughts are aligned today.

Friday, April 20 (Moon in Aries)   It's a great time for initiating projects, launching new ideas, brainstorming. You're passionate but impatient, Aries. Emotions could be volatile. You're also extremely persuasive now, especially if you're passionate about what you're doing, selling, or trying to convey. Imprint your style.

Saturday, April 21 (Moon into Taurus, 12:06 a.m.)
There's a new moon in your second house today. New moneymaking ideas and opportunities come your way. You get a fresh start, a new beginning, Aries. Expect emotional experiences related to money and finances.

Sunday, April 22 (Moon in Taurus)　　Yesterday's energy rolls into your Sunday. You identify emotionally with your possessions, or whatever you value, and feel comfortable surrounded by these objects. It's not the objects themselves that are important, but the feelings and memories you associate with them. Put off making any major purchases now. It's a good day to spend time outdoors, possibly hiking or gardening.

Monday, April 23 (Moon into Gemini, 1:06 p.m.)
Diplomacy wins the way today. Do a good deed for someone. Focus on making people happy. You offer advice and support. At the same time, avoid scattering your energies. Dance to your own tune.

Tuesday, April 24 (Moon in Gemini)　　The moon is in your third house today. You get your ideas across now, especially when you're talking to family members or neighbors. You could be taking one or more short trips and possibly talking on your cell phone. Drive carefully, and take time to check up on your mother.

Wednesday, April 25 (Moon in Gemini)　　You're feeling creative and need to express yourself. You see two sides of an issue, especially when communicating with relatives or people in the neighborhood. It's a good day to visit a bookstore or café to meet with friends.

Thursday, April 26 (Moon into Cancer, 1:43 a.m.)
Take an inventory on where things are going in your life today. Visualize the future; set your goals, then make

them so. Complete a project now. Clear up odds and
ends.

Friday, April 27 (Moon in Cancer)   The moon is in
your fourth house today. Stick close to home, if possible.
Do something to beautify it. You feel best in your home
environment. Spend time with family and loved ones,
but also set aside time for quiet meditation.

Saturday, April 28 (Moon into Leo, 12:11 p.m.)
Use your intuition to get a sense of your day. Be kind
and understanding. Cooperation, especially with partners, is highlighted. Don't make waves. Don't rush or
show resentment; let things develop. Marriage plays a
key role.

Sunday, April 29 (Moon in Leo)   The moon is in
your fifth house today. Be yourself, be emotionally honest. In love, there's greater emotional depth to a relationship now. It's a good day to take a chance, experiment.
You're emotionally in touch with your creative side.

Monday, April 30 (Moon into Virgo, 7:03 p.m.)
Stay focused today. Control any impulse to wander
off task. Fulfill your obligations. Be methodical and
thorough. You're building a strong foundation for an
outlet for creativity. You're at the right place at the
right time.

MAY 2012

Tuesday, May 1 (Moon in Virgo)   With the moon in
your sixth house today, the emphasis turns to your daily
work and service to others. Attend to all the details. Be
careful not to overlook any seemingly minor matters
that could take on importance. Keep up with your exercise plan, and watch your diet.

Wednesday, May 2 (Moon into Libra, 10:04 p.m.)
It's a number 4 day. Persevere to get things done today.
Don't get sloppy. Clean your closet, clear your desk,
straighten up your garage. Tear down the old in order
to rebuild. Be methodical and thorough. You could
be preparing for a long journey or pursuit of higher
education.

Thursday, May 3 (Moon in Libra)   The moon is in
your seventh house today. Loved ones and partners are
more important than usual. You get along well with others now. You can fit in just about anywhere. Be careful
that others don't manipulate your feelings.

Friday, May 4 (Moon into Scorpio, 10:20 p.m.)   Service to others is the theme of the day. Do a good deed
for someone. Visit someone who is ill or in need of help.
Be sympathetic, kind, and compassionate. However, be
aware that you could face emotional outbursts or someone making unfair demands.

Saturday, May 5 (Moon in Scorpio)   You gain insight related to your interest in metaphysical subjects,
such as past lives or life after death. Issues of the day
could include matters of sex, death, rebirth, rituals, and
relationships. Alternatively, it's a good day for dealing
with mortgages, insurance, and investments.

Sunday, May 6 (Moon into Sagittarius, 9:40 p.m.)   It's
your power day, your day to play it your way. You have a
chance to expand, to gain recognition, fame, power. You
attract financial success. Be aware that you're playing
with power, so try not to hurt anyone.

Monday, May 7 (Moon in Sagittarius)   The moon
is in your ninth house of higher education and long-
distance travel today. You could be planning a journey
to a foreign land or simply playing armchair traveler.

It's also a good time to pursue an interest in philosophy, mythology, or comparative religions. A romance might involve a foreign-born person.

Tuesday, May 8 (Moon into Capricorn, 10:01 p.m.) It's a number 1 day, and you're at the top of your cycle. Be independent, creative, and original. Express your opinions dynamically. Ignore those who doubt your abilities. Get out and meet new people, have new experiences, do something you've never done before. A flirtation turns more serious.

Wednesday, May 9 (Moon in Capricorn)   Mercury moves into your second house today. Your mind is sharp now in relation to money issues. Your values are focused on material matters. Your moneymaking ideas can work for you. Be conservative; don't speculate or take any unnecessary risks.

Thursday, May 10 (Moon in Capricorn)   You're feeling financially flush now. Self-discipline and structure are key. Maintain emotional balance. Set your goals, then make them so. Authority figures or elderly people play a role.

Friday, May 11 (Moon into Aquarius, 1:04 a.m.)   You work well with a group today. Focus on your wishes and dreams. Be methodical and thorough. You get along better with friends and associates. Your sense of security is tied to your relationships and friends.

Saturday, May 12 (Moon in Aquarius)   You're dealing with new ideas, new options, originality, Aries. You get a new perspective. Your visionary abilities are heightened, and you have a greater sense of freedom now. Play your hunches. Look beyond the immediate. Bust old paradigms.

Sunday, May 13 (Moon into Pisces, 7:43 a.m.) You're dealing with a domestic situation today. A change in the home, an adjustment or readjustment, is needed now. Don't put off the situation; that will only aggravate the problem. Adjust to the needs of loved ones.

Monday, May 14 (Moon in Pisces) The moon is in your twelfth house today. Think carefully before you act. There's a tendency now to undo all the positive actions you've taken. Avoid any self-destructive tendencies. Be aware of hidden enemies. You might feel a need to withdraw today and work on your own.

Tuesday, May 15 (Moon into Aries, 5:47 p.m.) Venus goes retrograde in your third house today and stays there until June 27. There could be some confusion over the next few weeks related to your love life, and that could cause a lack of harmony. Also, the heating or air conditioning in the building where you work or live could go on the blink.

Wednesday, May 16 (Moon in Aries) The moon is in your first house today. You may feel moody— withdrawn one moment, happy the next, then sad. It's all about your emotional self. You're also sensitive to other people's feelings. You tend to focus on how the public relates to you.

Thursday, May 17 (Moon in Aries) The way you see yourself now is the way others see you. Your feelings and thoughts are aligned. You're recharged for the rest of the month, and this makes you more appealing to the public. You're physically vital, and relations with the opposite sex go well.

Friday, May 18 (Moon into Taurus, 6:04 a.m.) Partnerships are highlighted; so is cooperation. Be kind and understanding. Your intuition focuses on relationships. Don't make waves. Don't rush or show resentment; let things develop. Show your appreciation.

Saturday, May 19 (Moon in Taurus)   The moon is in your second house today. Your money-earning potential increases now. You see what others overlook and find hidden opportunities to make money. A partner plays a positive role. However, expect some ups and downs in your income over the next few months.

Sunday, May 20 (Moon into Gemini, 7:06 p.m.) There's a solar eclipse today in your third house. That means events taking place outside of your control are affecting you. As a result, new opportunities come your way, possibly something that has previously eluded you. But you also might have to give up something. Matters from the past could play a role. So could siblings and other relatives or matters related to your everyday world.

Monday, May 21 (Moon in Gemini)   You're feeling restless today and sending text messages to friends and associates to pass the time. Your mind moves quickly from one thought to another. A change of scenery or an invitation to a social gathering would brighten your day.

Tuesday, May 22 (Moon in Gemini)   It's a good day to spend time with family and siblings, or to get together with neighbors to discuss common concerns. You see two sides of a story now. You communicate well and get your ideas across. A trip to the bookstore would be worthwhile and enlightening.

Wednesday, May 23 (Moon into Cancer, 7:32 a.m.) You launch a journey into the unknown today. You're a searcher, a seeker of truth. Secrets, intrigue, confidential information play a role. Be aware of decisions made behind closed doors. You can detect deception and recognize insincerity with ease.

Thursday, May 24 (Moon in Cancer)   Mercury moves into your third house today. You're alert, adaptable, and versatile. You express your ideas well, but over the next couple of weeks you have trouble staying focused on one matter. You tend to jump from one subject to the next, gathering information, moving on. Others find you particularly witty these days.

Friday, May 25 (Moon into Leo, 6:12 p.m.)   It's a good time to complete a project. Clear up odds and ends. Take an inventory on where things are going in your life. Make room for something new. Accept what comes your way now. It's all part of a cycle.

Saturday, May 26 (Moon in Leo)   Your emotions tend to overpower your intellect today. You might be somewhat possessive of loved ones, particularly children. But eventually you need to let go. Take a chance, experiment. You're also more involved with creative facets of your life now. Sex for pleasure is highlighted.

Sunday, May 27 (Moon in Leo)   Yesterday's energy flows into your Sunday. Drama is highlighted, perhaps involving children. Animals and pets figure prominently. Dress boldly; showmanship is emphasized. Romance and love play a role.

Monday, May 28 (Moon into Virgo, 2:07 a.m.)   You can influence people now with your upbeat attitude. Your charm and wit are appreciated. Spread your good news, and take time to listen to others. In business dealings, diversify now. Insist on all the information, not just bits and pieces.

Tuesday, May 29 (Moon in Virgo)   It's a good day to clarify any health or work issues. Keep your resolutions about exercise, and watch your diet. Attend to details related to your health. Make a doctor or dentist appointment. Your personal health occupies your attention now. Help others, but don't deny your own needs.

Wednesday, May 30 (Moon into Libra, 6:46 a.m.) Change and variety are highlighted today. Think outside the box; take a risk. Approach the day with an unconventional mind-set. Freedom of thought and action is key. But so is moderation; avoid excess in whatever you're doing.

Thursday, May 31 (Moon in Libra)   The focus turns to relationships, both business and personal. You get along well with others. You can fit in just about anywhere. Women play a prominent role. You comprehend the nuances of a situation, but it's difficult to go with the flow.

JUNE 2012

Friday, June 1 (Moon into Scorpio, 8:32 a.m.)   Your organizational skills are highlighted today. Control your impulses. Take care of your obligations. You're building foundations for an outlet for your creativity. Emphasize quality. Be methodical and thorough.

Saturday, June 2 (Moon in Scorpio)   The moon is in your eighth house today. You could be managing another person's money or dealing with an inheritance. Your sense of security or duty is highlighted. Mortgages, taxes, or insurance play a role in your day. Alternatively, you're attracted to the deeper mysteries of life, such as reincarnation or life after death.

Sunday, June 3 (Moon into Sagittarius, 8:33 a.m.) It's a service day. Others rely on you now. You improve, edit, and refine their work. You're particularly good with details. However, don't deny your own needs. It's a good day to clarify any health or work issues.

Monday, June 4 (Moon in Sagittarius)   With Neptune going retrograde in your twelfth house until early November, you could be feeling some difficulties related to the past. Try not to spend too much time dwelling on such matters. Move ahead. There's also a lunar eclipse in your ninth house today, which suggests that you react emotionally to an issue related to your plans for long-distance travel or higher education.

Tuesday, June 5 (Moon into Capricorn, 8:32 a.m.) It's a number 8 day, your power day. Think big, act big! You can go far with your plans and achieve financial success. It's a good day to buy a lotto ticket. You have a chance to expand, to gain recognition, fame, and power.

Wednesday, June 6 (Moon in Capricorn)   The moon is in your tenth house today. Professional concerns are the focus. It's a good day for business dealings. Your life is more public. You're more responsive to the needs and moods of a group and of the public in general.

Thursday, June 7 (Moon into Aquarius, 10:18 a.m.) Mercury moves into your fourth house today. You could be dealing with parents now. You feel a close tie to your roots. Spend time with family and loved ones. You get your ideas across about changes needed in the home. It's a good day to tackle a home-repair project, especially if you need to take bids and deal with service people.

Friday, June 8 (Moon in Aquarius)   The moon is in your eleventh house today. You have deeper contact with friends. Your sense of security is tied to your relationships and friends. You get a new perspective. Play your hunches. Look beyond the immediate. Help others, but dance to your own tune.

Saturday, June 9 (Moon into Pisces, 3:23 p.m.) The moon is in your twelfth house today. It's a good day to stay out of the public eye and work behind the scenes. Avoid confrontations. Keep your feelings to yourself. Matters from the past could arise now. Unconscious attitudes can be difficult, and so can relations with women.

Sunday, June 10 (Moon in Pisces) Imagination is highlighted. Watch for psychic events, synchronicities. Keep track of your dreams, including your daydreams. Your imagination is strong; ideas are ripe. It's a time for deep healing. You respond emotionally to whatever is happening.

Monday, June 11 (Moon in Pisces) Jupiter moves into your second house today and stays there for a year. You're entering a lucky period for finances. It's a good time to expand whatever you're doing related to investments and earnings. However, be careful not to overextend yourself; watch your spending. Your sense of self-worth grows now.

Tuesday, June 12 (Moon into Aries, 12:22 a.m.) It's a service day. You offer advice and support. Be diplomatic, kind, and understanding. Avoid scattering your energies. Change in the home, an adjustment or readjustment, is needed now. You're feeling somewhat moody today and sensitive to other people's feelings. It's difficult to remain detached and objective.

Wednesday, June 13 (Moon in Aries) With the moon on your ascendant today, the way you see yourself is the way others see you. Your appearance and personality shine. Your feelings and thoughts are aligned, and you're recharged for the month ahead.

Thursday, June 14 (Moon into Taurus, 12:22 p.m.) It's another power day, your day to play it your way. Unexpected money arrives. You're playing with power, so be careful not to hurt others. Expect a big bonus, a financial windfall. Business dealings go well.

Friday, June 15 (Moon in Taurus) You identify emotionally with your possessions or whatever you value now. You equate your financial assets with emotional security. You have a tendency to collect things, and those objects make you feel at home and at peace. Look at your priorities in handling your income.

Saturday, June 16 (Moon in Taurus) It's a good day to cultivate new ideas, Aries, but make sure they're down-to-earth. Use your common sense. Try to avoid stubborn behavior when others question your actions. You could be somewhat possessive today. Get out in nature, exercise, cover some ground.

Sunday, June 17 (Moon into Gemini, 1:24 a.m.) A partnership plays an important role in your day. There could be some soul-searching related to a relationship, but don't make waves. Just go with the flow. Be kind and understanding toward family members.

Monday, June 18 (Moon in Gemini) Get in touch with others, especially siblings, other relatives, or neighbors. You'll have some things to talk about, a message to pass on. A matter from the past attracts your attention and influences your thinking now. You're witty, alert, and adaptable today.

Tuesday, June 19 (Moon into Cancer, 1:34 p.m.) Persevere to get things done. Don't get sloppy. Hard work is called for now. You're building foundations for an outlet for your creativity. Tear down the old in order to rebuild. Be methodical and thorough.

Wednesday, June 20 (Moon in Cancer) The moon is in your fourth house today. Spend time with your family and loved ones. Stick close to home, if possible. Take time to retreat to a private place for meditation. It's a good day for dream recall. You feel a close tie to your roots, your home, or the land.

Thursday, June 21 (Moon into Leo, 11:48 p.m.)   Diplomacy wins the way today. An adjustment in your domestic life may be necessary. Be sympathetic, kind, and compassionate, but avoid scattering your energies. Be understanding, and avoid confrontations.

Friday, June 22 (Moon in Leo)   Drama is highlighted, perhaps involving children. You're creative and passionate today. Romance feels majestic. Dress boldly; showmanship is emphasized. It's a good day to take a gamble.

Saturday, June 23 (Moon in Leo)   Be yourself; be emotionally honest. Be aware that your emotions tend to overpower your intellect today. It's a great day for romance. It's also a perfect day for working on a creative project or taking a child or children out for a special event.

Sunday, June 24 (Moon into Virgo, 7:43 a.m.)   It's a number 9 day. That means it's time to complete a project. Clear your desk, and make room for the new, but don't start anything until tomorrow. Spend some time in deep thought. Consider how you can expand your base.

Monday, June 25 (Moon in Virgo)   Mercury moves into your fifth house today. You communicate well over the next three weeks. You write from a deep place. It's a good time to teach others what you know. However, your emotions are tempered by your critical outlook. With Saturn going direct in your seventh house, you take a cautious approach to forming any partnerships until early October.

Tuesday, June 26 (Moon into Libra, 1:16 p.m.)   Use your intuition to get a sense of your day. Cooperation is highlighted. Be kind and understanding; show your appreciation to others. There could be some soul-searching related to relationships.

Wednesday, June 27 (Moon in Libra)   With Venus going direct in your third house today, any artistic projects move ahead smoothly. You get along well with family members because you're not in the mood to argue. Live and let live is your motto, at least for the next couple of weeks.

Thursday, June 28 (Moon into Scorpio, 4:33 p.m.) Your organizational skills are strong now, Aries. Persevere to get things done today, and don't wander off course. You're building a creative base for your future. You can overcome bureaucratic red tape. Missing papers or objects are found.

Friday, June 29 (Moon in Scorpio)   With the moon in your eighth house today, you're an investigator and a problem-solver. You dig deep for information in whatever area interests you or is of greatest importance. Your energy is more intense than usual, and your emotions could affect your feelings about belongings that you share with others.

Saturday, June 30 (Moon into Sagittarius, 6:05 p.m.) It's a service day, so direct your energy toward helping others, Aries. Domestic purchases are highlighted. Focus on making people happy; do a good deed. Be generous and tolerant, even if it goes against your nature.

JULY 2012

Sunday, July 1 (Moon in Sagittarius) The moon is
in your ninth house today. Your mind is active, and you
yearn for new experiences, a break from the routine, a
change from the status quo. You're open to many ideas
and concepts. A publishing project goes well. Publicity
and advertising are emphasized.

Monday, July 2 (Moon into Capricorn, 6:52 p.m.)
Service to others is the theme of the day. You offer advice and support, especially to coworkers. Be sympathetic and kind, generous and tolerant. Focus on making
people happy. Diplomacy wins the way.

Tuesday, July 3 (Moon in Capricorn) There's a full
moon in your tenth house today. You reap what you've
sown related to your career. It's time for a promotion
or commendation. With Mars moving into your seventh
house, you can now actively pursue a business partnership. In romance, you tend to be overly aggressive, and
that can cause difficulties.

Wednesday, July 4 (Moon into Aquarius, 8:26 p.m.)
It's a number 8 day, your power day, and you're in the
power seat. You can go far with your plans and achieve
financial success, especially if you open your mind to a
new approach. You pull off a financial coup. Unexpected
money arrives.

Thursday, July 5 (Moon in Aquarius) The moon
is in your eleventh house today. Friends and associates play an important role in your day and help you
in surprising ways. You work well with a group of like-
minded people. Focus on your wishes and dreams, and
make sure that they are an expression of who you really are.

Friday, July 6 (Moon in Aquarius)   Your individuality is stressed. Your visionary abilities are heightened. You have a greater sense of freedom now. You're dealing with new ideas, new options, originality. You get a new perspective. Play your hunches. Look beyond the immediate.

Saturday, July 7 (Moon into Pisces, 12:29 a.m.)   It's a number 2 day. Your intuition focuses on relationships; new ones form. The spotlight is on cooperation. Show your appreciation to others. Don't make waves.

Sunday, July 8 (Moon in Pisces)   The moon is in your twelfth house today. Unconscious attitudes can be difficult. Keep your feelings secret. You might feel a need to withdraw and work on your own. Take time to reflect and meditate. It's a great time for pursuing a spiritual discipline.

Monday, July 9 (Moon into Aries, 8:14 a.m.)   The moon is on your ascendant. Your batteries are recharged. You're more appealing to the public. You're physically vital, and relations with the opposite sex go well. The way you see yourself is the way others see you. Stay focused. Control your impulses.

Tuesday, July 10 (Moon in Aries)   Your self-awareness and appearance are important now, Aries. You're dealing with your emotional self, the person you are becoming. You might feel moody—happy one moment, sad or withdrawn the next. However, your thoughts and feelings are aligned. You tend to search for ways to improve yourself.

Wednesday, July 11 (Moon into Taurus, 7:30 p.m.) Diplomacy is called for today. Be sympathetic and kind, generous and tolerant. Focus on making people happy, but dance to your own tune. An adjustment in your domestic life may be necessary now. Try not to get overly stubborn this evening.

Thursday, July 12 (Moon in Taurus) With the moon in your second house today, it's a day for dealing with money matters. You identify with your possessions or whatever you value. Look at your priorities in handling your income. Put off making any major purchases.

Friday, July 13 (Moon in Taurus) Uranus goes retrograde in your first house and stays that way until December 13. During this time, try not to start new projects, especially involving something unexpected and startling. It's best to wait until Uranus goes direct again, when your thinking will be sharper and clearer.

Saturday, July 14 (Moon into Gemini, 8:27 a.m.) Mercury goes retrograde in your fifth house today and stays there until August 8. That means you can expect some delays and glitches in communication over the next three weeks, especially related to children or creative and artistic endeavors. There could be some confusion about romance. Others might misinterpret your intentions. It's best to relax and control your emotional reaction to situations now.

Sunday, July 15 (Moon in Gemini) The moon is in your third house today. Take what you know and share it with others. You get your ideas across, but you need to keep your emotions in check. Your thinking is unduly influenced by things of the past. Relatives and neighbors could play a role in your day.

Monday, July 16 (Moon into Cancer, 8:32 p.m.) Co-operation is called for today. You get along well with others, especially a partner. Use your intuition to get a sense of your day. Be kind and understanding. Don't rush or show resentment; let things develop.

Tuesday, July 17 (Moon in Cancer)   The moon is in your fourth house today. Spend time with your family and loved ones; stick close to home. A parent or parents play a role in your day. You're dealing with the foundations of who you are and who you are becoming.

Wednesday, July 18 (Moon in Cancer)   You're feeling somewhat moody today and sensitive to other people's feelings. It's a good day to spend time near a body of water. Tend to loved ones; do something with your children. Let go of any negative thoughts rather than expressing them.

Thursday, July 19 (Moon into Leo, 6:14 a.m.)   New opportunities come your way today related to your home or your family. If you've been considering a move, you might find a new home. The opportunity could also be related to the birth of a child or someone moving into your house—a roommate, a parent, or a child returning from college.

Friday, July 20 (Moon in Leo)   With the moon in your fifth house today, you feel energized regarding a creative project. There's also greater depth to a relationship. Your emotions tend to overpower your intellect. There also could be more involvement with children and pets.

Saturday, July 21 (Moon into Virgo, 1:25 p.m.) You're innovative and creative and communicate well today. Your charm and wit are appreciated. Your attitude determines everything. Spread your good news, and take time to listen to others. Ease up on your routines.

Sunday, July 22 (Moon in Virgo)   It's a service day. Help others, but don't deny your own needs. Visit someone who is ill or in need of assistance. It's a good day to clarify any health or work issues. You could be feeling somewhat emotionally repressed now.

Monday, July 23 (Moon into Libra, 6:39 p.m.) The old cycle is ending; a new one is about to begin. Look for a new approach, a new perspective. Visualize the future; set your goals, then make them so. Clear up odds and ends. Make room for something new.

Tuesday, July 24 (Moon in Libra) The focus turns to relationships, both business and personal ones. You get a fresh start, Aries. You can turn in a new direction now. Loved ones and partners are more important than usual. Be careful that others don't manipulate your feelings.

Wednesday, July 25 (Moon into Scorpio, 10:30 p.m.) Yesterday's energy flows into your Wednesday. Marriage or a partnership plays a key role now. Other people could be nagging you. Your emotions and sensitivity are highlighted. There could be some soul-searching related to a relationship.

Thursday, July 26 (Moon in Scorpio) The moon is in your eighth house today. An interest in metaphysics plays a role in your day. You investigate past lives, life after death, even astrology. Issues of the day could include matters of sex, death, rebirth, rituals, and relationships. Emotions could become intense.

Friday, July 27 (Moon in Scorpio) You have a strong sense of security now. You could be managing resources that you share with someone else. You have a sense of duty, a need to take care of your obligations. You could be dealing with an inheritance, tax, or insurance matters. You might also take an interest in supporting a worthy cause, one that uplifts people.

Saturday, July 28 (Moon into Sagittarius, 1:18 a.m.)
Change and variety are highlighted. Think outside the box. Think freedom, no restrictions. It's a good day to take a risk, especially if you approach the day with an unconventional mind-set. Promote new ideas; follow your curiosity. Look for adventure.

Sunday, July 29 (Moon in Sagittarius) The moon is in your ninth house today. You're a dreamer and a thinker, and you yearn for new experiences. It's a great time to sign up for a workshop or seminar on a subject of interest. You could also follow your wanderlust and plan a long journey. Study and investigate possible destinations and sites along the way. A romance could involve a foreign-born person.

Monday, July 30 (Moon into Capricorn, 3:30 a.m.)
It's a number 7 day. That means you could be launching a journey into the unknown. Secrets, intrigue, confidential information play a role. You investigate, analyze, or simply observe what's going on. You quickly come to a conclusion and wonder why others don't see what you see. You work best on your own today. Knowledge is the key to success.

Tuesday, July 31 (Moon in Capricorn) You communicate your feelings well to coworkers, who are sympathetic. You get along with others in the workplace. You're more open and accessible now, but take care to avoid emotional displays, especially in public.

AUGUST 2012

Wednesday, August 1 (Moon into Aquarius, 5:56 a.m.)
There's a full moon in your eleventh house today. You gain insight related to a friendship. You reap what you've sown. You find strength in numbers and meaning

through friends and groups, especially when you work for the common good.

Thursday, August 2 (Moon in Aquarius)   Yesterday's energy flows into your Thursday. Groups and social events are highlighted. You're dealing with new ideas, new options, and originality, Aries. Help others, but dance to your own tune. Your wishes and dreams come true.

Friday, August 3 (Moon into Pisces, 9:58 a.m.)   It's a number 8 day, your power day, and your day to play it your way. Be courageous. Be yourself; be honest. You have a chance to expand, to gain recognition, even fame. However, be aware that you're playing with power, so try not to hurt anyone.

Saturday, August 4 (Moon in Pisces)   The moon is in your twelfth house today. You feel best staying out of public view. Think carefully before you act. There's a tendency now to undo all the positive actions you've taken. Avoid any self-destructive tendencies. Be aware of hidden enemies.

Sunday, August 5 (Moon into Aries, 4:59 p.m.)   It's a number 1 day, and you're at the top of your cycle, Aries. You're inventive and make connections that others overlook. Be original in whatever you're pursuing. You're determined and courageous today. Avoid people with closed minds. In romance, something new is developing.

Monday, August 6 (Moon in Aries)   Yesterday's energy flows into your Monday. It's a great time for initiating projects, launching new ideas, brainstorming. You're extremely persuasive now, especially if you're passionate about what you're doing, selling, or trying to convey.

275

Tuesday, August 7 (Moon in Aries)   With Venus moving into your fourth house today, you'll be feeling very attached to your home and home life this month. It's a great time to beautify your home. Buy something nice for the house so you can take even greater pride in your abode. You feel particularly close to your parents. Your roots are important to you.

Wednesday, August 8 (Moon into Taurus, 3:28 a.m.) Mercury goes direct in your fifth house today. That means any confusion, miscommunication, and delays you've been experiencing recede into the past, especially those related to a creative project, children, or a love interest. Things move more smoothly now. You get your ideas across.

Thursday, August 9 (Moon in Taurus)   Money and material goods are important to you now and give you a sense of security. You identify emotionally with your possessions or whatever you value. There could be some highly charged discussions related to money. Watch your spending.

Friday, August 10 (Moon into Gemini, 4:12 p.m.)   Do a good deed for someone today. Offer advice and support. Be sympathetic, kind, and compassionate, but avoid scattering your energies. Be understanding, and avoid confrontations. Diplomacy wins the way.

Saturday, August 11 (Moon in Gemini)   The moon is in your third house today. Tell others your ideas as you go about your daily activities. Take what you've learned recently and tell others about it. But avoid getting overly emotional, especially when dealing with neighbors or relatives. You could be looking into matters from the deep past.

Sunday, August 12 (Moon in Gemini)   Visits by relatives or siblings are likely. Also, expect some contact with neighbors. You accept an invitation to a social event. Your mental abilities are strong, and you have an emotional need to reinvigorate your studies, especially regarding matters of the past. You could be attracted to historical or archaeological studies now, such as the Mayan calendar.

Monday, August 13 (Moon into Cancer, 4:29 a.m.)
It's a number 9 day. Finish what you started. Clear up odds and ends. Visualize the future; set your goals, then make them so. Look beyond the immediate. Get ready for something new. Strive for universal appeal.

Tuesday, August 14 (Moon in Cancer)   The moon is in your fourth house today. You're dealing with the foundations of who you are and who you are becoming. Retreat to a private place for meditation. It's a good day for dream recall. Change a bad habit. A parent plays a role.

Wednesday, August 15 (Moon into Leo, 2:06 p.m.)
Use your intuition to get a sense of the day, and go with the flow. A partnership plays an important role. Be kind and understanding. Don't make waves. Cooperation is highlighted.

Thursday, August 16 (Moon in Leo)   There's greater depth in a relationship now. Sex for pleasure is highlighted. It's also a good time for creative or artistic expression. You have the ability to tap deeply into the collective unconscious for inspiration.

Friday, August 17 (Moon into Virgo, 8:34 p.m.)
There's a new moon in your fifth house today. That means doors open for you related to a creative project. Alternatively, you get a new beginning related to romance. You also see new opportunities related to children.

Saturday, August 18 (Moon in Virgo)   It's a service-oriented day. Help others, but be careful not to become a martyr for someone else's cause. Don't let your fears hold you back. Visit someone who is sick or in need of your help. But also tend to your own health concerns. Make a doctor or dentist appointment.

Sunday, August 19 (Moon in Virgo)   Yesterday's energy flows into your Sunday. Take care of details now, especially related to your health. Start exercising, watch your diet. Stop worrying and fretting. Stick close to home. Focus on tidying up the house and attending to details and loose ends. But be sure to take time to relax.

Monday, August 20 (Moon into Libra, 12:46 a.m.) It's a number 7 day. There's mystery in the air. Something hidden or secretive comes to light. Look beneath the surface for the reasons others are shifting their points of view or "changing their tune." But don't make any final decisions on what you uncover until tomorrow.

Tuesday, August 21 (Moon in Libra)   The moon is in your seventh house today. Try not to be overly aggressive now, Aries. There could be some tension with a partner. Be patient and tolerant. You want to move ahead quickly, but a partnership requires cooperation. Take time to listen to your partner's point of view.

Wednesday, August 22 (Moon into Scorpio, 3:54 a.m.) It's a number 9 day, which is about beginnings and endings. Use the day for reflection, expansion, and concluding projects. Take an inventory on where things are going in your life. Make room for something new, but don't start anything until tomorrow.

Thursday, August 23 (Moon in Scorpio)   Mars moves into your eighth house today. Your experiences are more intense than usual. There could be confrontations over the next two to three weeks related to shared possessions or income. Alternatively, you could be very aggressively pursuing a cause aimed at improving living conditions for large numbers of people. Any exploration of psychic or spiritual matters now comes with a strong emotional context.

Friday, August 24 (Moon into Sagittarius, 6:50 a.m.) Use your intuition to get a sense of your day. The spotlight is on cooperation. You could be forming a new relationship now. Help comes through friends, loved ones, especially a partner.

Saturday, August 25 (Moon in Sagittarius) The moon is in your ninth house today. You yearn for new experiences now, Aries. It's a great time to sign up for a workshop or seminar on a subject of interest. You could also follow your wanderlust and plan a long journey. Study and investigate possible destinations and sites along the way.

Sunday, August 26 (Moon into Capricorn, 9:59 a.m.) Take care of your obligations today. You're building foundations for an outlet for your creativity. Control your impulses. Get organized for the week ahead. Revise, rewrite. Straighten up your desk or clean your closet. Tear down the old in order to rebuild. Missing papers or objects are found. Keep your goals in mind; follow your ideas.

Monday, August 27 (Moon in Capricorn) Your ambition and drive to succeed are highlighted. Your responsibilities increase. Earth signs Taurus and Virgo play a prominent role. Self-discipline and structure are key. Maintain emotional balance. Don't ignore your home life now.

Tuesday, August 28 (Moon into Aquarius, 1:39 p.m.)
Service to others is the theme of the day. You offer advice and support. Focus on making people happy. Be sympathetic, kind, and compassionate, but avoid scattering your energies. Be understanding, and avoid confrontations.

Wednesday, August 29 (Moon in Aquarius) With the moon in your eleventh house, you have deeper contact with friends and could join a group of like-minded individuals. Focus on your wishes and dreams. Examine your overall goals. Those goals should be an expression of who you are.

Thursday, August 30 (Moon into Pisces, 6:32 p.m.) It's a number 8 day, your power day and your day to play it your way. You could pull off a financial coup now. You're being watched by people in power. Be aware that fear of failure or fear that you won't measure up will attract tangible experiences that reinforce the feeling.

Friday, August 31 (Moon in Pisces) There's a full moon in your twelfth house today, and Mercury moves into your sixth house. You're very efficient in handling mental tasks, especially over the next couple of weeks. You help others with their work, but you tend to do so today from behind the scenes, possibly through e-mails or text messages. Avoid being overly critical of others.

SEPTEMBER 2012

Saturday, September 1 (Moon in Pisces) You're feeling inspired now. Imagination is highlighted. Watch for psychic events, synchronicities. Keep track of your dreams, including your daydreams. Ideas are ripe, Aries. You feel best working on your own and staying out of the public view today. You're creative and imaginative.

Sunday, September 2 (Moon into Aries, 1:38 a.m.)
It's another power day, and your chance to expand whatever you're doing, especially if you open your mind to a new approach. Be courageous. Be yourself; be honest.

Monday, September 3 (Moon in Aries)   The moon is on your ascendant today. You're ready to step out into the public. You're recharged for the month, and this makes you more appealing to others. The way you see yourself now is the way others see you. Your appearance and personality shine.

Tuesday, September 4 (Moon into Taurus, 11:42 a.m.)
It's a number 1 day, so you're at the top of your cycle. Be independent and creative. Originality is stressed. You can take the lead now. You get a fresh start, a new beginning. Trust your hunches.

Wednesday, September 5 (Moon in Taurus)   It's a great day to cultivate new ideas, Aries, especially if they're well grounded. Use your common sense. Health and physical activity are highlighted. It's a good time for gardening, cultivating ideas, doing practical things.

Thursday, September 6 (Moon in Taurus)   Venus moves into your fifth house today. That means you're feeling romantic, and you're particularly attractive to the opposite sex this month. You get along well with others now. Any dealings with younger people will work to your advantage. Children play a role in your day.

Friday, September 7 (Moon into Gemini, 12:11 a.m.)
You're mentally quick today. Emphasize quality in whatever you're doing. You're building foundations for an outlet for your creativity. Be methodical and thorough. Revise, rewrite. You're at the right place at the right time.

Saturday, September 8 (Moon in Gemini)   It's a good day for expressing yourself through writing and for brainstorming. Take what you know and share it with others. Expect an invitation to a social event. A short trip works to your benefit now.

Sunday, September 9 (Moon into Cancer, 12:50 p.m.) It's another service-oriented day. You offer advice and support to those around you. Do a good deed for someone. Be sympathetic and kind, generous and tolerant. Diplomacy wins the way. An adjustment in your domestic life may be necessary now.

Monday, September 10 (Moon in Cancer)   Yesterday's energy flows into your Monday. Tend to loved ones. Do something with your children, spouse, or partner. You're sensitive to other people's feelings. Be aware that you could be feeling moody today. Water plays a prominent role in your day. Beautify your home; take care of home repairs.

Tuesday, September 11 (Moon into Leo, 11:01 p.m.) The energy shifts today. It's a power day and your day to play it your way. You're ambitious and goal-oriented. You attract financial success. Material gain is within reach, if not already here. Be aware that you're playing with power, so try not to hurt anyone.

Wednesday, September 12 (Moon in Leo)   The moon is in your fifth house today. It's a great day for pursuing romance. There's greater emotional depth in whatever you're pursuing now. Be yourself; be emotionally honest. You're creative now and have the ability to tap deeply into the collective unconscious. Children could play a role.

Thursday, September 13 (Moon in Leo)   Yesterday's energy flows into your Thursday. You're dynamic and imaginative today, creative and passionate. Romance feels majestic. Dress boldly; strut your stuff. Drama is highlighted, perhaps involving children. Animals and pets figure prominently.

Friday, September 14 (Moon into Virgo, 5:31 a.m.)
It's a number 2 day, and that means you're exploring the value of partnership. Your spouse or partner is at your side. Don't make waves or show resentment, but take time again to consider the direction you're headed and your motivation for continuing on this path. Your intuition focuses on relationships.

Saturday, September 15 (Moon in Virgo) With a new moon in your sixth house today, you find new opportunities in your daily work. Others come in search of your services. You have a talent to edit, refine, or improve what they're doing. However, make sure that your role is to guide and advise, not to complete their work.

Sunday, September 16 (Moon into Libra, 8:55 a.m.)
Mercury moves into your seventh house today, suggesting more contact this month with a business or romantic partner. You and your partner might be setting up a Web site or blog or putting together a newsletter. You also could get together with a group of people to discuss a project.

Monday, September 17 (Moon in Libra) Pluto goes direct in your tenth house today. That indicates that things get moving in your career, especially any area that has been stalled. You're in the power seat. However, be aware that there could be power struggles with bosses or others in positions of authority.

Tuesday, September 18 (Moon into Scorpio, 10:46 a.m.)
It's a number 6 day, and that means it's another service day. Adjust to the needs of loved ones. You offer advice

and support. Focus on making people happy. Be sympathetic, kind, and compassionate. Domestic purchases are highlighted.

Wednesday, September 19 (Moon in Scorpio) The moon is in your eighth house today. Your sense of security or duty plays a major role in your day. You help others, especially a partner. You could be managing another person's money or an inheritance. You're dealing with mortgages, taxes, or insurance. Alternatively, you're attracted to the goals of a large social movement.

Thursday, September 20 (Moon into Sagittarius, 12:34 p.m.) It's your power day, and you're in the power seat. You can go far with your plans and achieve financial success. Open your mind to a new approach that could bring in big bucks. It's a good day to buy a lotto ticket.

Friday, September 21 (Moon in Sagittarius) As you go about your everyday life, look at the big picture. Don't limit yourself. Spiritual values arise. Worldviews are emphasized. You're restless, impulsive, and inquisitive. Publishing or long-distance travel could play a role. There's passion in relationships now.

Saturday, September 22 (Moon into Capricorn, 3:21 p.m.) It's a number 1 day. You're at the top of your cycle, Aries. Get out and meet new people, have new experiences, do something you've never done before. Refuse to deal with people who have closed minds.

Sunday, September 23 (Moon in Capricorn) New opportunities come your way in the workplace now, Aries. You're more responsive to the needs and moods of a group and of the public in general. It's a good day for sales, dealing with the public, expanding your base. Aim high; shoot for the moon. No pun intended!

Monday, September 24 (Moon into Aquarius, 7:33 p.m.) You communicate well. You're warm and receptive to what others say. Spread your good news. Ease up on routines. Your charm and wit are appreciated. Play your hunches. Enjoy the harmony, beauty, and pleasures of life.

Tuesday, September 25 (Moon in Aquarius) The moon is in your eleventh house today. You work well with friends and associates. You can bring them together for a common cause. Focus on your wishes and dreams. Examine your overall goals. Make sure those goals are an expression of who you are. Social consciousness plays a role.

Wednesday, September 26 (Moon in Aquarius) Yesterday's energy flows into your Wednesday. Groups and social events are highlighted now. You have a greater sense of freedom. You get a new perspective. Play your hunches. Your visionary abilities are heightened.

Thursday, September 27 (Moon into Pisces, 1:25 a.m.) A domestic adjustment works out for the best. You could face emotional outbursts or someone making unfair demands. Be understanding, and avoid confrontations. Offer advice and support, but do it in a diplomatic way.

Friday, September 28 (Moon in Pisces) You feel best working on your own, remaining behind the scenes. Keep your feelings secret. Avoid any self-destructive tendencies, confrontations, and conflict. Take time to reflect and meditate.

Saturday, September 29 (Moon into Aries, 9:15 a.m.) There's a full moon in your first house today. You gain insights related to your emotional self and health. You're sensitive to other people's feelings. You might feel moody one moment, happy the next, then withdrawn and sad. You are more self-aware, and your appearance is important now. You're dealing with the person you are becoming.

Sunday, September 30 (Moon in Aries)   With the moon on your ascendant, you're physically vital, and relations with the opposite sex go well. The way you see yourself is the way others see you. Your appearance and personality shine. Your feelings and thoughts are aligned today.

OCTOBER 2012

Monday, October 1 (Moon into Taurus, 7:27 p.m.) You start off the month on a number 8 day, your power day, Aries, and your day to play it your way. Expect a windfall. Business dealings go your way. It's all about money, power, success, and responsibility.

Tuesday, October 2 (Moon in Taurus)   The moon is in your second house today. Money and material goods are important to you now and give you a sense of security. You may be dealing with payments and collecting what's owed to you. Look at your priorities in handling your income. Expect emotional experiences related to money.

Wednesday, October 3 (Moon in Taurus)   With Venus moving into your sixth house, you could be getting involved romantically with someone at work. It could be someone who you've been helping. Alternatively, you could be feeling emotionally attached to your workplace, spending long hours at your desk.

Thursday, October 4 (Moon into Gemini, 7:47 a.m.) Use your intuition to get a sense of your day. Be kind and understanding. Cooperation, especially with partners, is highlighted. Don't make waves. Don't rush or show resentment; let things develop. Marriage or a partnership plays a key role.

Friday, October 5 (Moon in Gemini)   Mercury and Saturn move into your eighth house today. If you're interested in metaphysics, you find the proper structure to study it. If you're involved in intuitive development, you find a way of expressing it. You could face some delays related to a mortgage, insurance, or a tax matter. There's a lot of discussion going on, so you can resolve any problems with such matters.

Saturday, October 6 (Moon into Cancer, 8:46 p.m.) Mars moves into your ninth house today. You have an active interest in travel now, possibly related to an athletic activity or event. You're adventurous and aggressive in whatever you pursue. Your philosophy of life guides you, and you have the power to persuade others with your views.

Sunday, October 7 (Moon in Cancer)   The moon is in your fourth house today. Spend time with your family and loved ones. It feels good to stay home. Retreat to a private place for meditation. You're dealing with the foundations of who you are and who you are becoming. It's a good day for dream recall. A parent plays a role in your day.

Monday, October 8 (Moon in Cancer)   It's a good day to deal with any property matters, possibly making an offer on a house, renting one, or selling one. Take time to make any repairs on your home that are needed. You could be feeling somewhat moody. Find the time and space to relax and meditate.

Tuesday, October 9 (Moon into Leo, 7:55 a.m.) There's an air of mystery in your day, Aries. Look beneath the surface, investigate. Confidential information plays a role. Knowledge is essential to success. See things as they are and not how you wish them to be.

Wednesday, October 10 (Moon in Leo)   The moon is in your fifth house today. Your creative assets are emphasized. You bring more emotional depth to any creative project that you're working on. Any involvement with children and animals today goes well. A relationship can reach new levels, but you might be feeling somewhat possessive.

Thursday, October 11 (Moon into Virgo, 3:24 p.m.) Complete what you've been working on, and get ready for something new. Consider ways to expand. Reflect on everything that has happened recently, and follow your intuitive nudges. A new cycle is about to begin.

Friday, October 12 (Moon in Virgo)   It's another service day. Others rely on you for assistance and guidance. So what else is new! Help them, but don't deny your own needs. Visit someone who is ill; do a good deed. But pay attention to any health matters now. Exercise, and watch your diet. Schedule an appointment with a doctor or dentist, if you've been putting it off.

Saturday, October 13 (Moon into Libra, 7:02 p.m.) It's a number 2 day, and that means it's all about partners and getting along. Your intuition focuses on relationships. Don't make waves. Try not to rush about or show resentment. Be kind and understanding. The spotlight is on cooperation.

Sunday, October 14 (Moon in Libra)   With the moon in your seventh house today, yesterday's energy flows into your Sunday. The focus remains on relationships. Loved ones and partners play a role. A legal matter comes to your attention. You comprehend the nuances of a situation, but it's difficult to go with the flow. Be careful that others don't try to persuade you to change your mind.

Monday, October 15 (Moon into Scorpio, 8:07 p.m.)
The week begins with a new moon in your seventh house. That means the energy from the past couple of days continues with new opportunities coming your way related to partnerships, either business or personal ones. It could relate to the resolution of a legal matter in your favor. Women play a prominent role.

Tuesday, October 16 (Moon in Scorpio)   The moon is in your eighth house today. If you are planning on making a major purchase, make sure that you and your partner are in agreement. Otherwise, you could encounter intense emotional resistance. An interest in metaphysics plays a role in your day. You could be dealing with a mystery of the unknown.

Wednesday, October 17 (Moon into Sagittarius, 8:26 p.m.)   Diplomacy wins the way. Adjust to the needs of loved ones. Clear up a situation at home that has lingered too long. Be kind and understanding, but avoid scattering your energies.

Thursday, October 18 (Moon in Sagittarius)   It's a good day to promote or publicize yourself or your activities, Aries. Get away from your usual routines. Find a new perspective. Work with a group to promote your ideas. A publishing project could move forward now. No matter what direction you take, remain grounded and realistic.

Friday, October 19 (Moon into Capricorn, 9:42 p.m.)
It's your power day, Aries. Your day to play it your way. Go for it. Start something new and expect success and financial reward. It's a good day to take a chance, speculate. Business dealings go well.

Saturday, October 20 (Moon in Capricorn)   The moon is in your tenth house today. Your career is about to take a new turn. You could gain a boost in prestige now. You're well regarded by fellow workers, and your warmth toward them is appreciated. Avoid any emotional displays in public, and be careful to keep your private and business lives separate.

Sunday, October 21 (Moon in Capricorn)   Self-discipline and structure are required today. Your domestic scene could need some attention now, Aries. Elderly people could play a role. Maintain emotional balance. Be conservative; don't speculate or take any unnecessary risks.

Monday, October 22 (Moon into Aquarius, 1:03 a.m.) The spotlight is on cooperation. Your emotions and sensitivity are highlighted. Show your appreciation to others. There could be some soul-searching related to relationships. Take time today to consider the direction you're headed in, as well as your motivation for continuing on this path.

Tuesday, October 23 (Moon in Aquarius)   The moon is in your eleventh house today. Friends play an important role in your day, especially Leo and Sagittarius. You get together with a group of like-minded individuals and work toward a common goal. Focus on your wishes and dreams, and make sure that they are still a reflection of who you are.

Wednesday, October 24 (Moon into Pisces, 7:01 a.m.) Stick to practical matters today. You're seen as trustworthy and reliable now. You have a sense of duty. Stick with this energy, Aries, and avoid overly aggressive behavior or responding emotionally to whatever is happening.

Thursday, October 25 (Moon in Pisces)   The moon is in your twelfth house today. You might feel a need to withdraw and work behind the scenes. A troubling matter from the past could rise up now, possibly something related to your childhood. It's a great day for a mystical or spiritual discipline. Your intuition is heightened.

Friday, October 26 (Moon into Aries, 3:32 p.m.) It's another service day. Diplomacy is stressed. Be kind and understanding. Do a good deed. Focus on making people happy, especially those in your home. Offer advice and support, and let others know what needs to be changed now.

Saturday, October 27 (Moon in Aries) It's a great time for initiating projects, launching new ideas, and brainstorming, Aries. You're passionate but impatient. As a result, emotions could get volatile. You're extremely persuasive now, especially if you're passionate about what you're doing, selling, or trying to convey. A sporting event might be the ticket today.

Sunday, October 28 (Moon in Aries) Venus moves into your seventh house today. It's a great time for spending time with that special person. You get along with a partner, spouse, or sweetheart and work well together. Things are running smoothly. You're feeling prosperous now, even if your bank account suggests otherwise.

Monday, October 29 (Moon into Taurus, 2:16 a.m.) With Mercury moving into your ninth house today, you express yourself clearly related to your philosophy or beliefs. A publishing project goes well. You're an excellent teacher now, and you write expertly. You take an interest in foreign travel or studying foreign cultures. You also gain insight into a money matter that has been on your mind.

Tuesday, October 30 (Moon in Taurus) The moon is in your second house today. It's a good day for finances

291

and money matters. Consider your priorities in spending your income. Put off any big purchases for another few days. Your values play an important role in your day.

Wednesday, October 31 (Moon into Gemini, 2:41 p.m.) Use your intuition to get a sense of your day. Be kind and understanding. The spotlight is on cooperation. Marriage plays a key role now. Show your appreciation to others.

NOVEMBER 2012

Thursday, November 1 (Moon in Gemini) You take a thoughtful approach today. You study the details now, especially those concerning the past. Matters related to history or archaeology—possibly the Mayan calendar—could attract your attention. You have a strong emotional need to pursue a subject that will allow you to expand your knowledge.

Friday, November 2 (Moon in Gemini) Yesterday's energy flows into your Friday. You're feeling restless and bored with routine activities. You could be sending text messages to friends and associates or searching the web for new information that supports your ideas. A change of scenery today works well for you. Consider a short trip, maybe meeting friends for lunch or at a bookstore.

Saturday, November 3 (Moon into Cancer, 3:43 a.m.) You're concerned about your home today, your security, or a parent. Flow with the current, accept what comes your way. Take a close look at your finances. Stop worrying; it doesn't do any good. Be diplomatic in dealing with others.

Sunday, November 4—Daylight Saving Time Ends (Moon in Cancer) Yesterday's energy flows into your Sunday. You feel best today sticking close to home. Your personal environment is important now. You're intuitive and nurturing, and sensitive to other people's feelings. Take time to do something with loved ones. Beautify your home.

Monday, November 5 (Moon into Leo, 3:40 p.m.) It's a number 4 day as the work week begins. That means the emphasis today is on your organizational skills. In romance, your persistence pays off. You're building a foundation for the future. Control your impulse to wander off to another task; fulfill your obligations. You can overcome bureaucratic red tape.

Tuesday, November 6 (Moon in Leo) Mercury goes retrograde today in your ninth house and continues to retrograde until November 26. Expect some confusion in your communication with others over the next three weeks, especially related to plans for higher education or long-distance travel. Others might misinterpret your yearnings for new experiences as a personal rejection. You could be feeling frustrated about your inability to communicate effectively. It's best to relax and control your emotional reaction to situations now.

Wednesday, November 7 (Moon in Leo) The moon is in your fifth house today. Your emotions tend to overpower your intellect. You're in touch with your creative side. You're also very security oriented and concerned about children. Think twice about advice you receive regarding a risk-taking adventure. In romance, emotions are powerful, and it's not a good day to upset your partner.

Thursday, November 8 (Moon into Virgo, 12:36 a.m.) Be sure you know what you want. There's a tendency toward self-deception now. A relationship could be wishful thinking. Any difficult events taking place in your life will result in greater inner strength.

Friday, November 9 (Moon in Virgo)   The moon is in your sixth house today. It's a service-oriented day. You improve, edit, and refine the work of others. You could be feeling somewhat burdened and emotionally repressed. Help others, but don't deny your own needs. Your personal health occupies your attention. Watch your diet, and remember to exercise.

Saturday, November 10 (Moon into Libra, 5:36 a.m.) With Neptune going direct in your twelfth house, you're deeply introspective. You could be somewhat obsessive about matters from the past. You're compassionate toward others who are less fortunate than you, especially those who are considered outcasts.

Sunday, November 11 (Moon in Libra)   The moon is in your seventh house today. The focus turns to relationships, both business and personal ones. You get along well with others now. You comprehend the nuances of a situation, but it's difficult to flow with the current. Be careful that others don't try to persuade you to change your mind about what you feel is right.

Monday, November 12 (Moon into Scorpio, 7:11 a.m.) Your intuition focuses on partnerships. Marriage could play a key role. The spotlight is on cooperation. Show your appreciation to others. Help comes through friends.

Tuesday, November 13 (Moon in Scorpio)   There's a solar eclipse in your eighth house today. That means there could be new opportunities related to investments, mortgages, or insurance. It could involve something that has eluded you. It could be the beginning of something new or the end of something. You might have to give up in order to gain.

Wednesday, November 14 (Moon into Sagittarius, 6:53 a.m.)   Mercury continues to retrograde, moving back to your eighth house today. Computer glitches over the next two weeks could affect matters related to shared resources, taxes, insurance, or investments. You can expect some miscommunication related to sex, death, relationships, rituals. If you're involved in a metaphysical pursuit, there could be some delays or miscommunication.

Thursday, November 15 (Moon in Sagittarius) The moon is in your ninth house today. You're a dreamer and a thinker. You feel a need to break from the usual routine. You're looking for something new, something exotic and foreign. Foreigners play a role, or another country plays a role in your day.

Friday, November 16 (Moon into Capricorn, 6:36 a.m.) Mars moves into your tenth house today. Your energy is strongly focused on career matters for the rest of the month and into December. You take the initiative, Aries. You have a need to achieve more, and you aggressively pursue your dreams.

Saturday, November 17 (Moon in Capricorn) Yesterday's energy flows into your weekend. Your ambition and drive to succeed remain strong. Saturday feels like a work day as your responsibilities increase. You might feel stressed, overworked. Self-discipline and structure are key. Maintain your emotional balance, and don't forget your exercise routine.

Sunday, November 18 (Moon into Aquarius, 8:11 a.m.) It's a number 8 day, your power day. Unexpected money or news about money arrives. Open your mind to a new approach, and you can go far. You have a chance to expand, to gain recognition and power. You're playing with power, so be careful not to hurt others.

Monday, November 19 (Moon in Aquarius) The moon is in your eleventh house today. Your thinking is expansive, and you could be exchanging ideas with friends and associates. Your attitude is friendly but impersonal. You contribute to a group, even though others consider your ideas unusual.

Tuesday, November 20 (Moon into Pisces, 12:55 p.m.)
It's a number 1 day, and you're at the top of your cycle, Aries. Be independent and creative, and refuse to be discouraged by doubters. You get a fresh start. You're inventive and make connections that others overlook. Stress originality. In romance, something new is developing.

Wednesday, November 21 (Moon in Pisces)   With Venus moving into your eighth house today, you gain financially through a partnership. Your partner gets a raise, or you could get a break in taxes or insurance. It's also a great time for psychic exploration. You could take an interest in synchronicity.

Thursday, November 22 (Moon into Aries, 9:12 p.m.)
Your attitude determines everything today. You communicate well. You're warm and receptive to what others say. Take time to relax, enjoy yourself, and recharge your batteries. Have fun in preparation for tomorrow's discipline and focus.

Friday, November 23 (Moon in Aries)   With the moon in your first house today, you can take the lead, Aries. You get a new start, and you can turn in new directions and launch new ideas. You're energized now for the month ahead, and this makes you more appealing to the public. Be careful about any reckless behavior.

Saturday, November 24 (Moon in Aries)   With the moon in your first house today, you're dealing with your emotional self, the person you are becoming. You focus on how the public relates to you. It's difficult to remain detached and objective now. Your feelings tend to fluctuate by the moment. You could spend time either procrastinating or changing your plans.

Sunday, November 25 (Moon into Taurus, 8:18 a.m.)
It's a number 6 day, and that means it's all about service. Do a good deed for someone. Visit a sick family member. Focus on making people happy. A domestic adjustment works out for the best.

Monday, November 26 (Moon in Taurus) Mercury goes direct in your eighth house today. Any confusion, miscommunication, and delays that you've been experiencing, especially related to shared resources, recede into the past. Also, any delays related to tax issues, insurance, or investments come to an end. Financial matters affecting your partner are better understood. Everything works better now, including computers and other electronic equipment.

Tuesday, November 27 (Moon into Gemini, 8:59 p.m.)
It's your power day again, a good day to play the lottery . . . and win! Play the number 8. Be courageous. Open your mind to a new approach, and expect a windfall. You attract financial success now. Business dealings go well.

Wednesday, November 28 (Moon in Gemini) There's a lunar eclipse in your third house today. Control your anger when dealing with siblings, other relatives, or neighbors. Otherwise, you could be revisiting an upsetting matter from the past that might haunt your day. It's a good day to get out and get away, at least for a couple of hours.

Thursday, November 29 (Moon in Gemini) Take what you know and share it with others. However, as yesterday, keep conscious control of your emotions when communicating. Your thinking is unduly influenced by things of the past. You take a few short trips handling your everyday chores, and your cell phone is in your hand more than not.

Friday, November 30 (Moon into Cancer, 9:56 a.m.)
The energy of the past two days continues into your Friday. Don't make waves. Don't rush or show resentment. Focus on your direction, your motivation. Where are you going and why? Cooperation is highlighted. Use your intuition to get a sense of the day.

DECEMBER 2012

Saturday, December 1 (Moon in Cancer)   You feel very comfortable at home today, especially if you're working on a home-repair project. Spend time with your family and loved ones. You feel close to your roots now. A parent plays a role. It's a good day to beautify your home.

Sunday, December 2 (Moon into Leo, 9:58 p.m.)
Your intuition focuses on relationships today. There could be some soul-searching regarding a current one. Alternatively, a new relationship is on your mind. Flow with the current; accept what comes your way. Show your appreciation to others.

Monday, December 3 (Moon in Leo)   The moon is in your fifth house today. There could be more involvement with kids. You feel strongly attached to loved ones. You're more protective and nurturing, but eventually you need to let go. You're emotionally in touch with your creative side now. Pets or animals play a role in your day.

Tuesday, December 4 (Moon in Leo)   The energy from yesterday flows into your Tuesday. You're creative and passionate today, impulsive and honest. Dress boldly; strut your stuff. Drama is highlighted, especially involving children or a creative project.

Wednesday, December 5 (Moon into Virgo, 7:53 a.m.) Change and variety are highlighted now. Think outside the box. Take risks; experiment. Release old structures; get a new point of view. You're versatile and changeable today, but be careful not to spread out and diversify too much.

Thursday, December 6 (Moon in Virgo) The moon is in your sixth house today. You work well with others who come to you for help. You improve, edit, and refine their work. Help others, but don't deny your own needs, and don't let your fears hold you back. Remember to exercise and watch your diet.

Friday, December 7 (Moon into Libra, 2:37 p.m.) It's a number 7 day, a mystery day. Secrets, intrigue, confidential information play a role. You work best on your own today. Gather information, but don't make any absolute decisions until tomorrow. Go with the flow.

Saturday, December 8 (Moon in Libra) With the moon in your seventh house today, you turn your focus to partnerships, both business and personal. A legal matter could come to your attention. It's difficult to remain detached and objective. Women play a prominent role. Be careful that others don't manipulate your feelings.

Sunday, December 9 (Moon into Scorpio, 5:52 p.m.) Finish what you started. Visualize the future; set your goals, then make them so. You'll probably find that certain old habits have outlived their usefulness. Use the day for reflection, expansion, and concluding projects.

Monday, December 10 (Moon in Scorpio)   Mercury moves into your ninth house today. Your mind is active, and you could be focusing on matters of higher education, especially philosophy, religion, law, or publishing. You could be studying or teaching these subjects. It's a great month to improve your skills with a foreign language. You have a strong curiosity now about foreign cultures.

Tuesday, December 11 (Moon into Sagittarius, 6:22 p.m.)   It's a number 2 day. That means it's all about cooperation and partnerships. You're diplomatic and capable of fixing whatever has gone wrong. As usual, you're determined to succeed, Aries. You're ambitious in pursuing a partnership. You excel in working with others now. You're playing the role of the visionary today. Be honest and open.

Wednesday, December 12 (Moon in Sagittarius) The moon is in your ninth house today. You're feeling as if you need to break out of your usual routine, or it could turn into a rut. Travel or higher education plays a role. Plan a trip or sign up for a seminar or workshop. A foreign country or person of foreign birth could play a role.

Thursday, December 13 (Moon into Capricorn, 5:43 p.m.)   With Uranus going direct in your first house today, your individuality gets a boost of energy. You're seeking more freedom now, and that's a trend that will stay with you for several years! In fact, people might think you're a bit eccentric. You're also very inventive and bring together ideas that others wouldn't realize were related. With a new moon in your ninth house today, you also get new opportunities related to higher education or travel.

Friday, December 14 (Moon in Capricorn)   You're concerned about professional matters, either regarding your career or education. You could be dealing with a matter related to your reputation. You get a boost in prestige, or you're seeking one. You're received well by others, but avoid making emotional displays in public.

Saturday, December 15 (Moon into Aquarius, 5:53 p.m.) Venus moves into your ninth house today. It's a great day to visit an art galley or study a philosophy that interests you. You might be learning about creating your own reality. Alternatively, you could be falling in love with someone from a foreign country or enamored with a foreign land.

Sunday, December 16 (Moon in Aquarius) Friends play an important role in your day, especially Leo and Sagittarius. You find strength in numbers. You get along better with friends and associates. Focus on your wishes and dreams. Examine your overall goals.

Monday, December 17 (Moon into Pisces, 8:48 p.m.) It's another power day, and you're in the power seat. Think big and act big! You attract financial success. Open your mind to a new approach that could bring in big bucks. You're playing with power, so be careful not to hurt others. Avoid becoming caught up in the collective muck related to fears of the upcoming end of the Mayan Calendar this Friday.

Tuesday, December 18 (Moon in Pisces) Your imagination is highlighted. You respond emotionally to whatever is happening now. Watch for psychic events, synchronicities. Turn inward for inspiration, universal knowledge, eternal truths. It's a day for deep healing.

Wednesday, December 19 (Moon in Pisces) Unconscious attitudes can be difficult. Keep your feelings secret. It's best to work behind the scenes now and follow your intuition. You communicate your deepest feelings to another person. It's a great day for a mystical or spiritual discipline.

Thursday, December 20 (Moon into Aries, 3:44 a.m.)
It's a number 2 day. That means cooperation and partnership are highlighted again. There's a new beginning or a new opportunity coming your way, Aries. Your intuition focuses on relationships. Don't make waves. Don't rush or show resentment; let things develop.

Friday, December 21 (Moon in Aries) The Mayan Calendar ends today! The old world ends; the new one begins. Look for transformation on a large scale as the old paradigm fades. The moon is on your ascendant today, Aries. You're feeling physically vital and recharged for the holidays. You're assertive and outgoing. Your appearance and personality shine. You get along well with the opposite sex.

Saturday, December 22 (Moon into Taurus, 2:26 p.m.)
Your organizational skills are highlighted. Control your impulse to wander off task. Stay focused; fulfill your obligations. You're building a creative base.

Sunday, December 23 (Moon in Taurus) The moon is in your second house today. You identify emotionally with your possessions now, or whatever you value. You tend to equate your assets with emotional security. You feel best when surrounded by familiar objects, especially in your home. It's not the objects themselves that are important, but the feelings and memories you associate with them.

Monday, December 24 (Moon in Taurus) Cultivate new ideas, but keep them down-to-earth. Go for a walk; get out in nature. Try to avoid stubborn behavior when others question your actions. You could be somewhat possessive now. Enjoy your material blessings.

Tuesday, December 25 (Moon into Gemini, 3:14 a.m.)
Mars moves into your eleventh house today, Aries. It's a good day to gather people together. You're the organizer and initiator. Others are willing to take orders from you! It could be family and relatives now for the holidays. Merry Christmas!

Wednesday, December 26 (Moon in Gemini) The moon is in your third house today. Yesterday's energy flows into your Wednesday. You're busy interacting with neighbors, relatives, or siblings in a social gathering. You get your ideas across, but try not to get too emotional. A female relative plays an important role.

Thursday, December 27 (Moon into Cancer, 4:08 p.m.)
Make room for something new. Clear your desk for tomorrow's new cycle. Visualize the future; set your goals, then make them so. Look beyond the immediate. Strive for universal appeal. Spiritual values surface.

Friday, December 28 (Moon in Cancer) There's a full moon in your fourth house today. That means new opportunities come your way related to your home. You could be planning to renovate, make repairs, or beautify your personal environment. A parent could play a role in what's going on.

Saturday, December 29 (Moon in Cancer) Yesterday's energy flows into your Saturday with the focus remaining on the home scene. Tend to loved ones; do something with your children or that special person. You could be somewhat moody today and sensitive to other people's comments.

Sunday, December 30 (Moon into Leo, 3:47 a.m.)
Enjoy the harmony, beauty, and pleasures of life now. Remain flexible. You communicate well; you're warm and receptive to what others say. Your attitude deter-

mines everything. Spread your good news, and take time to listen to others. Your charm and wit are appreciated.

Monday, December 31 (Moon in Leo)   With Mercury moving into your tenth house today, you're thinking about your career and your goals for the coming year. You exchange ideas with friends, even ones who know very little about what you do. They offer interesting points of view.

HAPPY NEW YEAR!

Locate your date of birth, find the sign of your North Node, then read the description in chapter 11.

07-04-1930 NN Taurus
12-29-1931 NN Aries
06-25-1933 NN Pisces
03-09-1935 NN Aquarius
09-14-1936 NN Capricorn
03-04-1938 NN Sagittarius
09-11-1939 NN Scorpio
05-23-1941 NN Libra
11-19-1942 NN Virgo
05-13-1944 NN Leo
12-01-1945 NN Cancer
12-10-1945 NN Cancer
12-14-1945 NN Cancer
07-31-1947 NN Gemini
01-22-1949 NN Taurus
07-26-1950 NN Aries
03-29-1952 NN Pisces
10-10-1953 NN Aquarius
04-02-1955 NN Capricorn
10-04-1956 NN Sagittarius
06-16-1958 NN Scorpio
12-15-1959 NN Libra
06-08-1961 NN Virgo
12-21-1962 NN Leo
08-25-1964 NN Cancer

02-18-1966 NN Gemini
08-20-1967 NN Taurus
04-20-1969 NN Aries
11-04-1970 NN Pisces
04-27-1972 NN Aquarius
10-27-1973 NN Capricorn
07-11-1975 NN Sagittarius
01-08-1977 NN Scorpio
07-04-1978 NN Libra
01-11-1980 NN Virgo
09-23-1981 NN Leo
03-16-1983 NN Cancer
09-13-1984 NN Gemini
04-01-1986 NN Taurus
04-14-1986 NN Taurus
04-22-1986 NN Taurus
11-30-1987 NN Aries
05-24-1989 NN Pisces
11-19-1990 NN Aquarius
08-03-1992 NN Capricorn
02-01-1994 NN Sagittarius
08-01-1995 NN Scorpio
01-25-1997 NN Libra
10-19-1998 NN Virgo
04-12-2000 NN Leo
10-11-2001 NN Cancer
04-11-2003 NN Gemini
12-24-2004 NN Taurus
06-19-2006 NN Aries
12-15-2007 NN Pisces
08-22-2009 NN Aquarius
02-28-2011 NN Capricorn

SYDNEY OMARR

Born on August 5, 1926, in Philadelphia, Pennsylvania, **Sydney Omarr** was the only person ever given full-time duty in the U.S. Army as an astrologer. He is regarded as the most erudite astrologer of the twentieth century and the best known, through his syndicated column and his radio and television programs (he was Merv Griffin's "resident astrologer"). Omarr has been called the most "knowledgeable astrologer since Evangeline Adams." His forecasts of Nixon's downfall, the end of World War II in mid-August of 1945, the assassination of John F. Kennedy, Roosevelt's election to a fourth term and his death in office ... these and many others are on the record and quoted enough to be considered "legendary."

ABOUT THE SERIES

This is one of a series of twelve *Sydney Omarr®
Day-by-Day Astrological Guides* for the signs of
2012. For questions and comments about the book,
go to www.tjmacgregor.com.